I0794959

ARCANA II

ARCANA II
MUSICIANS ON MUSIC

EDITED BY
JOHN ZORN

HIPS ROAD 2007

Copyright ©2007 by John Zorn/Hips Road

All rights reserved. No part of this book may be reproduced by any means
without express written permission of the authors or publisher.

Book design by Heung-Heung Chin.
Special thanks to Steve Clay.

Library of Congress Control Number: 2007928273

First published in 2007
ISBN 978-0-9788337-6-3
ISBN 0-9788337-6-7
Printed on acid-free paper
Printed and bound in the United States of America

Hips Road
200 East 10th Street #126
New York, NY 10003
http://www.tzadik.com

Distributed to the trade by D.A.P / Distributed Art Publishers
155 Avenue of the Americas, Second Floor
New York, NY 10013

Orders: (800) 338-2665 Tel: (212) 627-1999
Fax: (212) 627-9484

CONTENTS

PREFACE

JOHN ZORN

> "This will be our response to violence: to make music more intensely, more beautifully, and more devotedly than ever before."
>
> —Leonard Bernstein

In the ten years since the first *Arcana* volume came into being the Dark Ages have gotten darker. Age-old tactics of fear and oppression are used to divide us. Career building is taught in music schools, integrity is replaced by compromise, news has become advertising, and our popular culture—more and more bereft of intellectual properties—numbs us, impeding creative thought. People are listening with their eyes, not with their ears. To survive in this world of distractions and adversity, good music has gone underground, becoming more invisible than ever. It is always there, but to find it one has to make an effort.

Preserving the Art of the Underground is the responsibility of the Underground and here, in this second volume of *Arcana*, thirty distinguished voices speak out on the subject of art, music, and culture. They write about it eloquently and passionately. Courageous musical adventurers one and all, these are artists who believe in a vision and are realizing it with craft, honesty, and integrity. Although they live in this world and suffer its rules in various ways and to different degrees, they are for the most part outsiders. But they are not outsiders looking in. They are outsiders looking *out*—toward a beautiful new world of truth and beauty. This world is essential to their existence, and they do what they do because they are compelled to—out of necessity—because the truth must be told at all costs. They ask questions and take risks; they continue to work in the face of extreme personal and conceptual obstacles; they transcend boundaries and through intense thought and sacrifice they have learned to synthesize disparate ideas and approaches to create a body of work that is the true music of our time. A music of community, spirituality, and love.

Our present culture is in chaos, riddled with corruption, greed, and materialism. A rite of passage is necessary to break from this maelstrom, to gain contact and remain in accord with the ancient continuum of creativity that gives true meaning and order to the universe. Art is one form of such a discipline. It is a sacred trust, and to honor it one must endure hardship and make personal sacrifices. The Dark Ages is a time for coming together, and often Art and Music can function as a call to arms. It is my hope that this volume will be just that. This second installment of what will be a continuing series of books presenting radical, cutting-edge ideas about music is made, like the initial volume, out of necessity. In times of oppression we must all work together—harder than ever—to preserve the beliefs and values we hold dear. Beliefs that unite us. Values that make the world a better place.

—John Zorn, *NYC 2007*

ARCANA II

CHAPTER 1

REFLECTIONS ON CROSS-CULTURAL COMPOSITION

CHRISTOPHER ADLER

I first heard traditional musics from Thailand at the Smithsonian Institution's 1994 Festival of American Folklife in Washington, D.C., on my way to graduate school from having just graduated from the Massachusetts Institute of Technology.[1] Having performed as a pipe organist for nearly a decade prior, I was drawn in particular to the *khaen*, the bamboo free-reed mouth organ of the Lao, who live in Laos and northeast Thailand. I was also impressed by the classical ensemble music of central Thailand, a tradition nurtured by the royal courts but practiced also among commoners in Thai society. The music is structured in a manner similar to Balinese *gamelan*, an ensemble music I had studied and performed while an undergraduate. However, while Balinese *gamelan* is a strictly communal activity, involving all musicians equally and indispensably in realizing the musical totality, Thai classical music is a collaboration of virtuoso soloists. These two musics, Lao *khaen* playing and Thai classical music, at the time gripping yet impossibly foreign, became my principal research areas as I entered graduate school to study composition. This research has evolved into what I expect will be a lifelong engagement with the cultures and musical traditions of Thailand. I have formulated my voice as a composer and musician through my parallel experiences performing in Thai, Lao, and Western traditions and through the creation of explicitly cross-cultural compositions for Thai, Lao, Western, and Chinese instruments individually and in combination.

My research into the musics of Thailand and Laos began with an intent to understand (primarily from a musical/structural/analytical perspective) what I was hearing in the performances and recordings which fascinated me, and from a desire to be able to play and perform the music which I was coming to love. There was, nonetheless, an inexorable pressure

1. I would like to acknowledge my friend and colleague Sidney Marquez Boquiren for reviewing this paper and providing thoughtful discussion over many years.

to exercise my creative energies as much through those distant traditions, made decreasingly foreign through experience, as through those in which I had grown up. So, while still and always learning musical traditions both distant and familiar, I sought to compose explicitly cross-cultural music, to engage with those multiple musical languages through which I was learning to speak. To think and write about, with, and through traditions not equally my own was an idealistic project begun at a time when the problematics of cross-cultural politics were a current subject in academia and in popular discourse. I sought to compose, then, in response to and in light of post-colonial discourse in the wake of Edward Said's *Orientalism* (1978), a legacy of Western musical creation fueled by inspiration and appropriation acquired in a colonial context,[2] troubling cross-cultural appropriations in popular music,[3] and the scholarly critique of other contemporary composers who have sought to work cross-culturally.[4] With each explicitly cross-cultural composition that I write, I endeavor to further develop a methodology through which I can treat my musical Other with respect and not inadvertently reproduce colonial (or in the case of Thailand, which remained independent during the colonial era, neo-colonial) relationships.

2. For example, Born and Hesmondhalgh (2000).

3. For example, Meintjes (1990) on Paul Simon's *Graceland*, Feld (1996) on the imitation of Mbuti pygmy singing, Zemp (1996) on *Deep Forest*, and Guy (2002) on Enigma's *Return to Innocence*.

4. For example, Taylor (1995) on Kevin Volans.

In this paper I will articulate a philosophical approach to cross-cultural composition, less through direct explication than through the contextualized analysis of the compositions which are a product of that approach. I will survey a number of works, composed between 1996 and 2006, in order to exemplify general principles of my compositional approach, and delve into analytical details only to the extent necessary. In choosing to emphasize compositions, convenient to an extent because of their tangible notated form and because they are recorded and partly available, I shall leave out a more personal narrative of my ongoing fieldwork and research, discussion of my traditional performances, and my cross-culturally informed approach to improvisation, even though these also would help to elucidate a broader philosophy of musical practice.

I regard each individual composition as a frozen moment from an ongoing cross-cultural encounter, one in which my knowledge of the Other is always in a process of formation and reformation, always incomplete. I could spend a lifetime involved with the musical traditions of Thailand, just as I could spend a lifetime dedicated to any one of the musical traditions closer to home, and yet never acquire complete knowledge, complete authority. The questions of when one becomes qualified to create and expand a tradition, as opposed to just reproducing it, or when one acquires "artistic license," and the extent to which it may be applied, are culturally situated ones.

The two foreign traditions with which I have been most closely involved address the matter of qualifications quite differently, and differently in turn from the Western concert tradition in which youthful and naive creation is a step to becoming a creative contributor to a growing tradition. Prior to the latter half of the twentieth century, composition (held as distinct from the mere improvisation of variations) in the Thai classical tradition was considered the domain of only the most experienced performing musicians. Knowledge of the tradition was obtained through, and situated in, the embodied action of performance.[5] Those musicians who had attained an advanced level of ability and experience, and who, by matter of traditional obligation, were also the most respected senior teachers of the musical tradition, were considered to be uniquely qualified to compose new melodies and thoroughly new variations on older melodies. In the latter half of the twentieth century, public education has largely resituated Thai classical music into educational institutions alongside the Western classical and jazz traditions, in which creation (composition and improvisation) is understood to be part of the pedagogy and a legitimate vehicle for youthful musical expression. The traditional reluctance to create has a given way to a great deal of cross-genre and cross-cultural creation among younger generations of musicians. Nonetheless, there is a persistent awareness among serious musicians of a distinction to be made between such youthful and "undisciplined" musical explorations and the creations of senior teachers. Thai musicians have expressed to me that my motivation as a composer is understood as existing somewhere between these two positions, exploratory and unusual and therefore nonsensical from the standpoint of conventional stylistic expectations and of little relevance to the tradition as it progresses, but at the same time qualified by the Western authority of my being a composer, and one with academic qualifications in particular. In highly status-conscious Thai society, this latter point is not to be underestimated. A Western academic qualification,

5. Wong (2001) treats the Thai epistemology of music and performance in detail.

in my case as a professor with a Ph.D. from a reputable American university, is generally understood, by default, to be analogous to and affording a nearly equivalent status to that obtained through musical experience (though certainly not affording an equivalent embodied musical ability). More important, from my point of view, was the permission to create that was granted to me, while still a graduate student, from my Thai classical music teacher, Khruu Panya Roongruang. Having already entered into his tutelage formally through a *wai khruu* ("honoring the teacher") ceremony, and thereby accepting what is in effect the "rights and responsibilities" of participating in the tradition, he explained that there is no indigenous principle of copyright limiting the use of Thai traditional musical material, and that I was free to make use of that material as a composer and performer. What remained unsaid, as it was already well-understood in having come to that point as a student, that his permission was not a carte blanche to do as I saw fit with all of Thai music, but pertained only to certain non-sacred bodies of repertoire and was constrained by an ethics of musical practice that is coextensive with the tradition.[6]

The tradition of *khaen* playing in Northeast Thailand, by contrast, maintains neither a formal system of education nor a notion of qualification. Young *khaen* players traditionally learned by imitation, experimentation, and occasional informal tutoring, although this methodology has been somewhat replaced by formalized public education recently. Traditional *khaen* music is improvised, and players gradually acquire the skills to improvise through experience. Composition, or the creation of new genres, is limited to popular musics (such as those using Western rock instruments like *lam sing* and *phleng lukthuung*) and has no relevance to traditional playing. Being taken seriously as a *khaen* player comes simply from a demonstrated ability to play and to accompany a singer effectively. By playing *khaen* competently in a traditional context, my authority to create with the instrument is (thus far and to my best knowledge) unquestioned, although the foreignness of my nontraditional compositions for *khaen* also renders them little more than curiosities and of no relevance to the tradition for musicians in Northeast Thailand.

6. The deep significance of the *wai khruu* ceremony in reproducing an ethics of traditional musical practice is beyond the scope of this paper, but has been admirably explicated by Wong (2001).

Structure and Instrumental Function

Many traditional ensemble musics throughout Asia are statically structured according to a principle of instrumental function, in which individual instruments or classes of instruments contribute one component of static musical texture, and without which the texture would be considered incomplete. I have attempted to express this notion in the most general way possible, in order to illustrate an underlying commonality of musical structures across multiple musical cultures in many countries, particular instances of which have been given diverse names by ethnomusicologists (such as stratified polyphony or idiomatic heterophony). In such structures, instruments are divided into functional classes, each contributing a distinct and noninterchangeable component to a sonic totality which is generically consistent across repertoires and performance contexts. The sonic result, especially from the perspective of an outsider, is a highly consistent and distinctive textural identity, which I propose may be understood as a *normative sound*: a sonic identity characteristic of a type of ensemble, a body of repertoire, or an entire musical tradition. Javanese *gamelan*, for example, despite multiple tuning systems, variation in instrumentation and tuning between different ensembles, and a large and varied musical repertoire, is instantly recognizable as such to anyone who has become familiar with its normative sound. In any given composition, each melodic instrument realizes a single, shared, and abstract melody in a way idiomatic to that particular instrument and characteristic of that instrument's contribution to the sonic totality. The role of the composer (if one exists) in such music may be to create the abstract melody which guides improvised or conventionally rendered variations, to create distinctive melodic variations for particular instruments, or to sculpt the normative sound through the selection of particular instruments, while the role of the performer is to realize their particular contribution strictly, formulaically, or with stylistically appropriate improvisation.

I have described in as much generality as possible this musical structure, which I clumsily term *normative idiomatic instrumental function*, to stress the extent to which it is already a cross-cultural musical characteristic. It is a structure that I came to understand through playing Balinese *gamelan*, through hearing many different Asian ensemble musics, and through studying and playing Thai classical music, and that has informed nearly every composition that I have written, even those for Western instruments. In fact, my fascination with this conception of musical structure resonates with two of my loves in Western music, both of which preceded my study of Asian music: Baroque music and minimalism. The continuo group within Baroque ensemble music may be understood as structured according to idiomatic instrumental function, in that its ubiquitous and consistent presence creates a normative sound and its realization is done to an extent formulaically and through stylistically-appropriate improvisation. The Western principle of orchestration gradually emerged during the Baroque era in distinct contrast to the principle of normative instrumental function. Johann Sebastian Bach's striking ability to evoke the sound of one instrument through another by imitating its idiom both affirmed the reality of conventional instrumental idioms and marked their imminent decline by rendering them as material to be manipulated rather than conventions to be adopted *a priori*. Orchestration evolved to become a coloring of abstract musical material through the selection of instruments thus entirely freed from their normative roles, and then further a palette for color-based music entirely liberated from structural melody (of which spectralism may be considered the most recent incarnation). Heretofore, I will use the term "orchestration" to refer to this principle of instrumental coloration in general, whether it applies to chamber or orchestral forces.

Many American minimalist compositions are based upon an invented notion of structural function. The functions are invented in the sense that there are no conventional instrumental roles, although certain composers elevated invented functions to a personal style through the formation of their own ensembles with very characteristic normative and easily recognized sounds, such as the Philip Glass Ensemble's combination of Farfisa organs, voices, flute, and saxophone. Of course, it is well known that these composers were inspired to adopt such structures by hearing Asian and other non-Western musics, as well as jazz and rock for which the principle of normative idiomatic instrumental function is also quite relevant, and in distinct reaction to the hierarchical social structures that result from the rise of orchestration as an organizing principle.[7]

The structure of Thai classical music is based upon normative idiomatic instrumental function. These functions are in two classes: melodic instruments, each of which perform a variation on the basic melody of the composition in a manner idiomatic to

7. Christopher Small (1998) critiques the social structures that rise with the orchestra in Western society, and which stand in contrast to those created within traditional Asian, jazz, rock, and minimalist ensembles.

that particular instrument, and colotomic percussion instruments that articulate a cyclical rhythmic pattern corresponding to the rhythmic structure of the melody. Colotomic rhythmic structuring is found throughout South Asian and Southeast Asian musics, with a tremendous variety of forms and realizations, from simple two- or four-beat patterns to extended cycles embellished with elaborate patterns or improvisations. The rhythmic cycles which are used in Thai classical music are comparatively simple, although they may be performed with a wide variety of percussion instruments which are selected in accordance with the genre and *samnieng* ("foreign accent," discussed further below).

The basic melody of a Thai classical composition is not played by any of the melodic instruments. Instead, each of the instruments performs a more elaborate variation on the melody in the idiom of that particular instrument. Depending on the repertoire, these variations may be composed in advance or improvised within appropriate stylistic conventions, and in some cases are highly elaborate and demanding of exceptional technique. Although such virtuoso variations are sometimes featured as solos within a performance, the normative sound of the ensemble consists of all of these instrumental variations played simultaneously, in very nearly the same melodic register, accompanied by colotomic percussion. The result is a dense, heterophonic texture. In the Thai tradition it is considered an admirable skill of the aficionado to be able to listen to and recognize the contributions of individual musicians while experiencing the dense, sonic totality.

In the discussion of my compositions which follows, I will fill in some details of this very cursory description of the structure of Thai classical music, which is otherwise beyond the scope of this paper.

Pan-lom, Iris, and Ecstatic Volutions in a Neon Haze

With the composition of *Pan-lom* (1998),[8] I sought to develop a thoroughly cross-cultural approach to composition involving Thai classical music and Western contemporary concert music. To this end, I attempted to hybridize as many of the aspects of the composition as possible, including the instrumentation, structural organization of the ensemble, tunings and pitch materials, rhythmic organization, form, and compositional method. I will refer to this work frequently through the course of this paper, as it

8. *Pan-lom* is included in Adler (2004), and the timings indicated refer to this recording.

exemplifies many of the different compositional strategies which I have employed since. My commentary from the score, reproduced in part below, explains the metaphorical association of the title with this aspiration for a cross-cultural aesthetic.

> "Pan-lom" is the term for the bargeboard of a traditional Thai house. The bargeboard is the board which terminates each angled end of the roof. In Thai architecture it is often elaborately carved, one of the only sites on the traditional house to feature non-functional decoration. The Thai house is elevated above the ground and topped with a steeply angled roof to allow heat to escape and breeze to pass through the house. The name "pan-lom" means "to sculpt the wind", a literal reference to the motion of wind through the house and an allusion to the position of the bargeboard at the boundary between the stability of architectural structure and the transience of the natural environment. The elaboration of the pan-lom is an expression of balance between structure and nature, between stability and impermanence. This expression of the place of architecture in the natural world seems to me an apt metaphor for the balance between structure and intuition, and between the stability of compositional text and the ephemerality of performance. This attention to the aesthetic of the boundary parallels my composing on the boundary between Thai and Western classical musics.

The ensemble of *Pan-lom* consists of eight Western instruments and five Thai instruments, and is organized according to the Thai *mohori* ensemble, the largest Thai classical ensemble and one which incorporates all types of instruments according to Thai organology (struck, plucked, bowed, and blown instruments). One possible constitution of a *mohori* ensemble and the analogy to the ensemble of *Pan-lom* is shown below.

Thai *mohori* ensemble	***Pan-lom* ensemble**
blown instruments	
khlui (flutes)	soprano saxophone, oboe
bowed instruments	
saw duang (snakeskin fiddle)	violin
saw uu (coconut-body fiddle)	viola, cello (arco)
plucked instruments	
jakay (3-string zither)	cello (pizz.), contrabass

<u>struck instruments (melodic)</u>
ranaat ek (principal xylophone) .... *ranaat ek*
ranaat thum (tenor xylophone)............... marimba/glockenspiel
khaung wong yai (large gong circle)........... *khaung wong yai*
khaung wong lek (small gong circle) .... hammer dulcimer

<u>struck instruments (colotomic)</u>
thon rammana (paired drums) .... *thon rammana*
ching (handbell)........................... *ching*
mong (button gong) .... *mong*

A number of different musical structures and instrumental realizations occur through the course of the twenty-three-minute composition. The following three instances, discussed in the order of increasing structural complexity, correspond to the two "first-level" and two "third-level" variations from an original composition in a Thai style, *Phleng Pan Lom Thao*, on which *Pan-lom* is based, and each demonstrates an adaptation of Thai classical musical structure. In these and other sections of the piece which are based on normative idiomatic instrumental function, the idiom of each instrument, Thai or Western, is an invented hybrid between the Thai idiom of the corresponding *mohori* instrument and the more flexible, stylistically diverse approach of contemporary Western chamber music. The normative sound of the music, within any one particular section, is therefore evocative of neither Thai nor Western music but something in between.

Leading to the climax of *Pan-lom* are the first-level variations of *Phleng Pan Lom Thao* which are played by a subgroup of the ensemble consisting of soprano saxophone, *ranaat ek*, marimba, hammer dulcimer, *khaung wong yai*, and contrabass, and later joined by oboe and cello (17:56–18:33). Each of these melodic instruments performs the melody in quasi-unison, with individual instrumental parts adapted according to their respective invented idiom, accompanied by the colotomic percussion instruments, which perform a traditional rhythmic cycle.

The two third-level variations of *Phleng Pan Lom Thao* exemplify the combination of this normative Thai structuring with a Western-inspired approach. In the first variation (7:00–8:20), the melody of *Phleng Pan Lom Thao* is first performed with a Thai structure by a subgroup of the ensemble (oboe, viola, *ranaat ek*) accompanied by colotomic percussion performing a simple, nontraditional rhythmic cycle. This melodic setting is simultaneously accompanied by an orchestrated harmonic progression played by all of the remaining instruments (except saxophone). Halfway through the first variation, the rhythmic cycle changes to a traditional one and the dulcimer and *khaung wong yai* join the subgroup performing with a Thai structure. In the second variation (8:20–10:29), this dual structure is expanded to include a third layer, a second melody in counterpoint to the main one. Now the main melody is performed by the viola, *ranaat ek*, *khaung wong yai*, and colotomic percussion, the countermelody by oboe and cello (themselves in simultaneous heterophonic variations), and the accompanying harmonies by the violin and contrabass. This section concludes with most of the ensemble joining the subgroup, which performs with a Thai structure, as in the first-level variations discussed earlier.

The fluid constitution of instrumental subgroupings allied to particular structures of organization, and the diversity of structures which appear in *Pan-lom* further contribute to the sense of cultural dislocation created by the combination of instruments and the disruption of their customary idioms.

With regard to *Pan-lom* and other compositions in which Thai and Western instruments perform together, I am frequently asked how the tunings of the instruments are reconciled or made compatible. In the case of ensembles involving *khaen*, tuning is not an issue as the tuning of the *khaen* very closely approximates Western tuning. Thai classical instruments, such as those included in *Pan-lom*, however, are tuned in a seven-tone equal temperament (in contrast to the Western twelve-tone equal temperament). The result is that the Thai tonic, generally standardized as a Western B-flat, and the fourth and fifth above the tonic are very close to their Western counterparts, while the other pitches hover in between pitches of the Western equal-tempered scale. I am entirely indebted to my first composition teacher, Evan Ziporyn, for my view that such tuning discrepancies are not a problem to be reconciled but an opportunity to be explored. The simultaneous sounding of two tuning systems results in a hybrid pitch universe that, like the musical structures of my compositions, occupies a space between musical categories. It sounds strange at first, but over time one's ear becomes accustomed to the combined tunings by virtue of their mutual consistency and the consistent harmonic structures which bind them together through the course of any one composition. The ending of *Pan-lom* is played by a trio of soprano saxophone, *ranaat ek*, and contrabass, each performing in distinct registers, placing the tuning systems in starkest contrast. It sounds quite out of tune when heard alone; however, coming at the end of the twenty-three-minute composition during which the ear becomes accustomed to the coexistence of multiple tunings, the sound of the passage acquires a "rightness." Furthermore, the pattern-recognition mechanism of the brain seeks familiar order even among unfamiliar sounds, and will cooperate in making Thai pitches appear to bend and fit into Western tuning according to the harmonic context in which they are situated. The Thai third, which is nearly equidistant between a Western major and minor third, can be perceptually nudged into either position by harmonic context.[9] Likewise, Thai musicians are accustomed to hearing foreign instruments in the context of their seven-tone system, as such instruments have been incorporated, without tuning changes, into Thai ensembles for the performance of compositions in a *samnieng* ("foreign accent"). Many compositions in the Thai repertory are variations on or imitations of music from other countries and ethnic groups. Such compositions are performed with percussion instruments that are thought to aurally signify those nationalities or ethnicities, and sometimes with melodic instruments as well, including *khaen* for the performance of repertoire in a Lao "accent," and organ or violin for the performance of repertoire in a *farang* (Western) "accent." In these cases, no effort is made to reconcile the tunings of the instruments.

9. I have taken advantage of this perceptual effect in my composition *Lineamenta* (2000), for chamber orchestra with Thai classical instruments, with a harmonic cycle involving all twelve Western pitches which is transposed to various scale degrees. This harmonic cycle is embellished by the Thai instruments in an idiomatic Thai style using all seven Thai pitches. Through the course of the cycle and its transpositions, the Thai pitches seem to move up or down to "accommodate" the shifting harmonic context.

In two of my recent compositions, *Iris* (2003) and *Ecstatic Volutions in a Neon Haze* (2005), I have musically acknowledged my indebtedness to American minimalism while attempting to evoke its structural similarities to Southeast Asian ensemble musics. *Iris* was inspired by the instrumentation of the ensemble NOISE, which commissioned it, and which at the time was flute, guitar, cello, and percussion, and developed in particular from the overlapped and interconnected pitches of the open strings of the acoustic guitar and cello. The piece begins with the instruments in pairs, flute and cello, guitar and marimba, playing only the pitches of the lowest two open strings of the cello and guitar, respectively. They play in hocket and with intervening hammer-ons and pull-offs in the guitar and cello, and dampened strokes in the marimba. Here is an invented normative instrumental function, each instrument contributing an idiomatic layer to a static texture. The resulting sonic totality is evocative of an imaginary plucked instrument because each instrument is played in a way not allied to expressive lyricism but oriented toward a delicate and quieter side in which the timbres are barely distinguishable. The result, coupled with the static structuring, is akin to that of a large central Javanese *gamelan*, in which so many instruments of similar timbre play simultaneously that the contribution of any single instrument is no longer discernable. The static structuring and relentless sixteenth-note texture, grouped in irregular and constantly shifting meter, is an homage to the early works of Philip Glass. The number of open strings used is gradually increased as the work progresses, expanding the pitch register, an aural analogue to the opening of an optical iris.

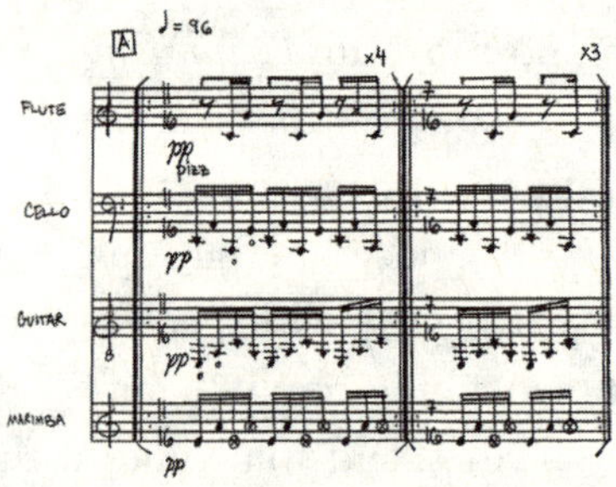

Iris, opening measures

Similarly, the beginning of *Ecstatic Volutions in a Neon Haze* is an homage to Terry Riley's *In C*, with a high C in the piano, here on a rhythmic ostinato (3 + 3 + 3 +3 + 4), and with an open form based on ordered, cellular repetition in each instrument. Here, too, individual instruments contribute idiomatic and normative layers to a static sonic totality, from which individual instrumental solos emerge and a through-composed, groove-based structure gradually precipitates out. The funk-inspired groove which emerges, one by one accumulating cooperating instruments, is also an homage to the normative structuring of so many forms of popular music.

Forms and Methods

My first consideration in composing a new work is the instrumentation, the sonic and technical characteristics of individual instruments, and the coincidences of their combination, as well as their cultural and traditional associations. From these considerations emerges a concept for the work that in turn motivates a compositional method and the particular "set of tools," familiar or newly created, from which the work will be built. These compositional tools have included, for example, consistent modal harmonic frameworks, non-octave scales in two or three octaves, original algorithms for pitch permutation, original algorithms for generating self-similar pitch series,[10] and the variety of culturally situated concerns discussed in this paper. I have made no effort to apply the same approach to different pieces or to ensure that instruments are used to their fullest capabilities in any one piece, but sought instead to apply tools fundamentally related to the motivating concept. *Iris* is an example of a work motivated by a single, instrumentally-derived concept, and in which the instrumental palettes are severely limited in close adherence to that motivating concept. My works, as a result, are stylistically diverse, though sharing in this underlying methodology of conception and interwoven by the application of related tools to different pieces. This general methodology has allowed me to integrate cross-cultural concerns into certain works without fundamentally changing my approach to composition.

10. These are the basis of both versions of *Signals Intelligence* (2002), which was motivated by a request for a solo composition for six brake drums. The ensemble version is an arrangement and expansion of the virtuoso solo piece.

Viewed in retrospect, the central concept for a composition likewise motivates a strategy for the act of composition itself. In practice, at least in some cases, the process of composing and the evolution of the motivating concept are convergent concurrent processes rather than separate steps. This is especially the case for compositions which grew from improvisations, as did most of the works for solo *khaen*. By the "act of composition" I am referring to the process through which musical ideas are organized and eventually expressed in conventional notation. Musical form, for example, may be preconceived, as in the case of the expanded *thao* form of *Pan-lom*, discussed below, or emergent as in the case of works distilled from improvisations, resulting in very different processes of writing. I have composed a number of pieces for Western instruments based on algorithms[11] which predetermine aspects of organization but only to a limited extent. The act of writing such pieces thus involves a constant back-and-forth between intuitive, at-the-piano composition, musically or conceptually motivated adjustments to the parameters of the algorithm, and the algorithmic generation

11. These include, among others, *things that flow* (1996), *Signals Intelligence* (2002), *Liber Pulveris* (2005), and *Petit Hommage à Jehan Alain* (2007).

of musical material (by hand or by computer).

For works with explicitly cross-cultural motivation, the act of composition thus becomes a cross-cultural one. Once again, I seek through this methodology to arrive at an ethical, respectful, and nonappropriative approach to cross-cultural composition. Each of the compositions discussed below exemplifies this aspiration, and yet remains the product of an instance in an evolving and deepening understanding, a relic of thinking that in retrospect may evince naiveté or misunderstanding, and which is always subject to ethical reconsideration.

Pan-lom and *Phleng Pan Lom Thao*

When I composed *Pan-lom*, I was interested in composing with Thai-style normative idiomatic instrumental functions, but reticent to use a traditional melody as the basis of the composition. Although the structure of Thai music is based on the principle of variation, and new compositions often begin as variations of old ones, existing compositions are not merely raw musical materials to be exploited but living musical works with specific histories, meanings, well-known variations, and often associated texts and relationships with other pieces in the repertory. At that stage of my research, I was not confident that I would be aware of all the attendant associations brought with any given piece from the repertoire. I felt that basing a new, hybrid composition on an existing piece would result in too clear an orientation of cultural borrowing, a *taking from* rather than a balanced meeting between musical traditions. I therefore composed an original melody, ostensibly for Thai ensemble (although I composed only the main melody and not particular instrumental variations), using a Thai classical form, Thai rhythmic structures, and Thai musical notation. This composition, *Phleng Pan Lom Thao* ("composition entitled Pan-lom in the *thao* form"), is then arranged as part of the overall composition, *Pan-lom*. I incorporated into *Phleng Pan Lom Thao* some nontraditional characteristics, including a very free use of shifting modality, closer canon than is typical in Thai music, and a substantially larger coda than is customary. Set within *Pan-lom*, it then becomes a Thai-style composition incorporating Western ideas embedded within a Western composition incorporating Thai ideas.

In the excerpt of *Phleng Pan Lom*

12. The complete score of *Phleng Pan Lom Thao*, in cipher notation, is printed in the liner notes to Adler (2004).

13. The Thai classical tradition is an oral/aural one, but notation has become common in the twentieth century as a result of the institutionalization of music education in public schools and the adoption of a variety of Western historiographic and archival practices.

Thao[12] shown below, a modified form of Thai notation[13] is used, in which numbers replace the Thai alphabetic characters used to signify the seven different pitches (1 = Thai "do" = B-flat). Dots above or below a cipher indicate an octave above or below, respectively. The ciphers are simply read from left to right, with each cipher or dash (rest) corresponding to one unit of rhythmic subdivision (customarily rendered as sixteenth notes in Western notation). The first row shows the open (○) and closed (+) strokes of the *ching* (handbell), analogous to weak and strong structural beats, respectively, and a circled closed stroke indicates the completion of one rhythmic cycle, a point of arrival and the strongest structural beat, musically articulated by the *mong* (button gong).

	○		+		○		⊕		○		+		○		⊕
							$\dot{2}$	–	$\dot{2}$	$\dot{3}$	$\dot{2}$	–	$\dot{2}$	$\dot{1}$	7
$\dot{1}$	6	7	5	6	4	5	2	4	2	1	2	4	5	6	7
$\dot{1}$	6	7	5	6	4	5	2	$\underset{\cdot}{7}$	1	2	1	2	4	5	6

Phleng Pan Lom Thao, first-level variation, excerpt

Composing *Phleng Pan Lom Thao* at the *ranaat ek* (the Thai principal xylophone) and in Thai notation was a strategy to resituate my thinking as a composer into a Thai frame of mind. Although this is impossibly idealistic, the attempt facilitated the process of trying to write coherently using Thai musical conventions. I could avoid being distracted by the incorrect tuning of the Western piano, the temptation to use more than the seven notes of the Thai scale, and, most important, I could be constantly aware of rhythmic orientation of every melodic phrase to its concluding structural downbeat, a characteristic of many Southeast Asian musics and a crucial one for the proper organization of the traditional form I was using.

The Thai *thao* form is based on three variations of the same melody in which the durations between the structural tones of the melody are compressed or expanded by a factor of two while the rate of musical subdivision remains constant. The three levels of melodic variation, the third being the longest and slowest and the first shorter and faster by a factor of four, are accompanied by rhythmic cycles of corresponding length. The number of regular rhythmic subdivisions per closed stroke of the *ching* aurally identifies the level of the rhythmic cycle. These periodic closed strokes of the *ching* align with the most important structural tones of the melody, which are generally preserved in the process of compression or expansion. In the example below, a short second-level excerpt consisting of half of one second-level rhythmic cycle[14] is compressed to yield the corresponding first-level melody. Note that, in this case, both weak and strong structural tones are strictly preserved. An elegant composition in *thao* form will frequently deviate from such strictness in order that each level have a distinctive melodic character.

14. The rhythmic cycle of *Phleng Pan Lom Thao* is *naathap probkai*, a common cycle of four closed *ching* strokes per cycle.

			○				+				○				⊕
–	6	5	6	–	5	4	5	–	4	3	4	6	4	3	2
									○		+		○		⊕
								$\dot{1}$	6	7	5	6	4	5	2

Phleng Pan Lom Thao, corresponding excerpts of second- and first-level variation.

The Thai *thao* form became popular in the nineteenth century as a vehicle for the creative expansion of older melodies (customarily rendered in the second level) and the incorporation of virtuoso variations therein. The temporal orientation of the *thao* form is that of a gradual and inexorable acceleration and crescendo, analogous to the tapered conical spires of traditional Thai architecture and Theravada Buddhist iconography.[15]

15. Symbolic of a focusing towards the point of extinction of the self, *nibbana* (nirvana).

3rd level (slow)—2nd level (medium)—1st level (fast)—coda

The form of *Phleng Pan Lom Thao* adheres to the conventional parameters, with a climactic, albeit larger than customary, coda. While the order of formal sections is preserved in the setting of *Phleng Pan Lom Thao* within *Pan-lom*, the surrounding musical material undergoes a transformation of a different nature through the course of the piece. The ending of *Pan-lom* becomes a juxtaposition of opposites: the climactic coda of the *thao* form dissolves amongst serene drones and leads to a reflective and melancholy coda, the aforementioned trio for soprano saxophone, *ranaat ek*, and contrabass. This coda, coming after so much music built from layers upon layers of cross-culturally hybrid compositional strategies, is a hazy vision of a new hybrid music. It is an intuitive music made possible by, but no longer evincing the formalism and self-reflexivity of, those intentionally cross-cultural compositional strategies.

Khaen Solos

It is this premonition of an intuitively cross-cultural music that has motivated many of my subsequent compositions. And it is in my compositions for *khaen*, an instrument with which I am as comfortable as I am with the piano and pipe organ, that I have come closest to achieving an intuitive cross-cultural music.

The *khaen* is the free-reed bamboo mouth organ of the Lao people, who predominantly live in lowland Laos and northeast Thailand.[16] It consists of sixteen bamboo pipes mounted vertically in two rows into a wooden windchest. Inside the windchest, each pipe contains a small bronze reed. By covering a small hole in each pipe, located above the windchest, with a finger, air directed through the instrument sets the reed into vibration. The *khaen* is thus a polyphonic instrument, capable of sounding up to ten pipes simultaneously, or even more if some finger holes are blocked mechanically. In addition, the pipes will sound regardless of the direction of airflow, so the sound produced is continuous when all breathing is done through the instrument.

16. Terry Miller (1985, 1988) has written extensively about *khaen* construction, *khaen* music, and the musical and cultural practices with which it is associated. The *khaen* is closely related to ancestors of other, more modern free-reed mouth organs in Asia, such as the Chinese *sheng* and the Japanese *sho*.

Traditional Lao and Northeast Thai music for the *khaen* is improvised and provides accompaniment to solo singers. Solo *khaen* playing is traditionally based upon these accompaniments, while being unconstrained by the melodic and rhythmic implications of poetic form and the improvisation of the singer. The music is based on the combination of drone and embellished melody. Within a given melodic mode, certain pipes provide a continuous drone while a subset of the other pipes, yielding a pentatonic scale, is used to perform a very rhythmic and elaborate melody. The melody is improvised, based upon the variation and combination of short cells of music, conventional melodic patterns, imitations of singing, or sometimes the variation of a cyclically repeated melody. One of my earliest explicitly cross-cultural compositions, *Three Lai* (1996),[17] for *khaen*, violin, and viola, deals most directly with this traditional style of *khaen* playing. Two of the three sections of this work are, in effect, transcriptions of my own improvisations in two different traditional genres, augmented in differing ways by the stringed instruments.

17. *Three Lai* is included in Adler (2004).

As improvisation is fundamental to traditional *khaen* playing, and therefore to the way I learned to play the instrument, it has been a method through which I compose for the instrument. In contrast to the premeditated and highly structured compositions discussed elsewhere in this paper, most of my compositions for solo *khaen* were born from improvisations in which I was working with and through traditional playing and experimenting with nontraditional playing. As traditional music is improvised, it cannot be theoretically generalized by dissociation from the individual musicians who play it. Every *khaen* player plays differently and there is no correct model or ideal form, just a shared sense of conventions and aesthetics to which every individual has a contingent, and possibly only tenuous, relationship. As a student of the tradition, I have learned to improvise in a style my own, and although I can switch between improvising in a manner I consider to be entirely within traditional conventions (which are regionally and historically specific) and improvising in a manner augmented by nontraditional approaches, my playing retains the stamp of my individuality. Thus, the deliberate cross-cultural structuring of a work such as *Pan-lom* has less place here. To play *khaen* is to improvise, which is to synthesize experiences that cannot be separated from their cultural origins. So, in a sense, to exercise intuitive music making through improvisation is to achieve an un-self-reflexive cross-cultural music. The philosophical challenge that remains from such a conclusion is to retain a place for the ethical concerns discussed at the outset. I will return to this issue at the close of the paper.

Most of my compositions for solo *khaen, the wind blows inside* (1997), *Tashi Delek* (1998), *Telemetry Lock* (1999), and *Epilogue for a Dark Day* (2001),[18] began as improvisations and then coalesced into notated form. All but *the wind blows inside* retain at least a residue of this process in sections that call for structured improvisation or flexible realization. *Telemetry Lock*, for example, consists of a rapid improvised line, the pitch domain of which is specified in the score, along with various other chords, cells, and melodic fragments which are to be superimposed against it through improvisation. It is a guided and highly constrained improvisation, the details of which may vary from performance to performance but the identity of which as a composition is unmistakable. There are likewise sections in *Epilogue for a Dark Day* which call for improvisation on a certain theme, or the repetition and juxtaposition of given patterns.

18. *The wind blows inside* and *Epilogue for a Dark Day* may be heard on Adler (2004), and *Telemetry Lock* may be heard on Art of the States (http://www.artofthestates.org).

In all of the pieces, I have been concerned, perhaps to a decreasing degree over time, with using the drone-and-melody structure, the modality, and the characteristic harmonic and melodic embellishments of traditional *khaen* playing. These cannot be considered independently from the structure of the instrument and fingering, that is, the constraints placed on pitch choice forced by the layout of the pipes and the holding of particular notes as drones. I will refrain from discussing this here, as I have written about it elsewhere in detail.[19] The general principle of interest here is that the physical constraints of the instrument are not unrelated to the music played with it. All instruments afford such constraints, but traditions sometimes evolve instrumental technique to a point remote from what might seem most natural given the physics of the instrument itself. Modern Western notions of orchestration, as discussed above, have contributed to such a divergence, as instruments are understood to be able to transcend their identities and peculiarities in service of more-abstract musical demands.[20] The principle of normative idiomatic instrumental function, on the other hand, is based upon the notion that an instrument retains a specific idiom, and that idiom is often (though not necessarily) closely related to the physics of the instrument itself. *Khaen* playing is traditionally informed by stylistic conventions more restrictive than the physical constraints of the instrument itself, so many of the pieces I have written for *khaen*, as well the improvisations that I continue to play with the instrument, are based upon my attempts to identify fingering patterns that are both idiomatic *and* nontraditional while yielding musically interesting results.

19. Adler (2001). The final untitled example in this paper is from an early version of *Epilogue for a Dark Day*.

20. It is ironic that some of the so-called extended techniques developed during the twentieth century in an attempt to expand the vocabulary of instrumental possibilities are, in fact, quite natural and easily played techniques closely allied to the physical functioning and design of instruments.

Music for a Royal Palace

Eight years after writing *Pan-lom*, I was more confident in my knowledge of the meanings and expectations of at least some Thai classical repertoire and I could consider composing my own variations on a Thai melody and thereby participate in the creation of new repertoire in the Thai manner rather than just in the Western one. The occasion for doing so came with a commission from the Weill Music Institute at Carnegie Hall and the Silk

Road Project, calling for a work for the Chinese free-reed mouth organ *sheng*, viola, marimba, and percussion, to be performed by the Silk Road Ensemble. In contrast to the overtly bicultural and idealistic conception of *Pan-lom*, *Music for a Royal Palace* (2006) enacts a more complex interaction between multiple musical cultures, each with relevance to my personal musical experience, and in a manner evocative of the complexity of real life.

My commentary, reproduced from the score, analogizes this cultural complexity to that of Thai royal architecture and discusses the history of the traditional Thai composition on which *Music for a Royal Palace* is based.

The Bang Pa-In Palace in Ayuthaya Province, Thailand

The royal palace at Bang Pa-In, also known as the "summer palace," was established during the Ayuthaya period, in the mid-17th Century, but abandoned when Ayuthaya fell and the kingdom re-established near Bangkok. The fourth king of the present Chakri dynasty, King Mongkut (Rama IV, reigning 1851–1868), rediscovered the site in the mid-19th Century, restored existing buildings and expanded the palace. Between 1872 and 1889, King Chulalongkorn (Rama V, reigning 1868–1910) added extensive new construction in European styles and Thai-European hybrid styles and used the palace for the reception of foreign dignitaries and as a suburban retreat.

The Phra Thinang Isawan Thippha-art ("The Divine Seat of Personal Freedom Royal Residence") Pavilion, which stands in the middle of an artificial lake, exemplifies classical Thai architecture, with a multi-layered and multi-colored tile roof, a central spire and elaborate gold decoration. Nearby, among mansions in a European Classic Revival style stands the Ho Withun Thasana ("Sage's Lookout"), an observatory tower in a European-inspired style, built by King Rama IV for surveying the countryside and for astronomical observations. Such a building represents an architectural innovation in Thailand and King Rama IV's dedication to modern Western principles of science and geography, marking an early moment in the dramatic shift from traditional cosmography to European rationalism and nationhood. Immediately adjacent to the Ho Withun Thasana stands the Phra Thinang Wehart Chamrun ("Heavenly Light Royal Residence"), a large and extremely ornate throne hall in an entirely Chinese style, built in China and given to King Rama V by an association of Chinese merchants living in Thailand.

The jarring stylistic juxtapositions now preserved at Bang Pa-In reflect a kingdom and monarchy in transition and are a physical manifestation of the relations of power and ethnic and national identities at play in the late 19th Century. In the mid-19th Century, the tributary relationship with China waned as royal relationships with European counterparts rose. King Rama IV began a project of modernization intended to establish an international reputation for the Thai monarchy, to reconceptualize Thailand as a nation in the modern European sense, and to preserve the kingdom's independence from colonial occupation. Although the tributary relationship to China waned, ethnic Chinese living in Thailand comprised a substantial economic class and provided much of the funding and labor required for the construction of royal architecture and other modernization projects for much of the 19th Century. Donations such as the Phra Thinang Wehart Chamrun were meant to express loyalty, preserve economic relationships and secure social status as Thai ethnic identity became the basis for the modern concept of nationhood. The inclusion of traditional Thai architecture in royal palaces affirmed the Thai ethnic identity as central even as dramatic cultural changes were unfolding. European architecture in Thai royal palaces, as well as in public works, embodied the royal desires to be regarded as equals among European royalty and marked a shift in the symbolism by which authority as a national leader was asserted, away from decreasingly relevant Brahminic rituals and towards conspicuous consumption of European goods and styles.

Music for a Royal Palace is both for and about the Bang Pa-In Palace, a musical reflection of the multiethnic stylistic juxtaposition, and an imaginary tribute to a moment in time now frozen as a museum. The ensemble of Chinese and Western instruments performs a traditional Thai composition in Chinese style, arranged from my contemporary Western perspective and framed by original music which is informed by my music for Western instruments and the Lao mouth organ, *khaen*. The hidden presence of the *khaen*, which has contributed to my style of writing for the *sheng*, is fitting as the ethnic Lao provide labor for the Thai nation but are traditionally marginalized and their influence is conspicuously absent from palace architecture.

Jin Khim Lek

Jin Khim Lek was composed by one of the most important teachers and composers known in Thai history, Mi Duriyangkul, also known as Khruu Mii Khaek. He composed it during the reign of King Phranangklao (Rama III, reigning 1824–1851), based on a melody he heard performed by a Chinese musician playing the *khim* (dulcimer). As there was already a composition in the Thai repertory entitled *Jin Khim*

("Chinese-style *khim* composition") dating from the Ayuthaya period, this new composition became known as *Jin Khim Lek* and the older piece as *Jin Khim Yai* (*lek* and *yai* meaning "small" and "large", respectively, here in the sense of lesser and greater in terms of historical age).

This composition is the basis for the second half of *Music for a Royal Palace*, in which it serves as a theme presented in variations in a conventional Thai classical form. Thai ensemble music consists of variations of a single melody performed simultaneously with percussion accompaniment. Each melodic instrument in the ensemble performs a variation idiomatic to that particular instrument as understood within the Thai tradition. In *Music for a Royal Palace*, newly-conceived instrumental idioms for the *sheng*, viola and marimba are based upon the combination of instrumental idioms in the Western, Chinese (in the case of the *sheng*) and Thai traditions. In the manner of virtuoso arrangements in the Thai classical tradition, all the variations are newly-composed including ensemble and solo variations.

In addition, the original "second-level" composition is followed by a "first-level" variation, in which the structure of the melody is rendered in double-time while the rate of rhythmic subdivision remains constant. Although first- and third-level variations of *Jin Khim Lek* exist within the Thai tradition, the first-level variation in *Music for a Royal Palace* is newly-composed.[21] Here, a modified repetition structure is used for the first-level variation, in which the third section is not repeated, making the twenty-four-measure original into a nine-bar version, which is then varied and extended.

21. The syncopated rhythmic character of the newly-composed first-level variations was inspired by the composition *Hang Khreuang Kaliya Yiam Haung*, by Khruu Boonyong Ketkhong, which often follows *Jin Khim Lek* in suites of Chinese-style compositions.

Music for a Royal Palace is the first composition in which I implemented a Thai-style musical structure with individual instrumental parts of a level of virtuosity equivalent to that of virtuoso Thai classical music. The structure of the composition is a quite straightforward series of variations of the second-level *Jin Khim Lek* and then of the new first-level variation, followed by a climactic coda. The simple structure places the focus on the dense and intricate heterophony of the three melodic instruments each playing in their respective invented idioms, and very demanding solos by each of the performers.

The featuring of each musician in turn with solos, as in a small jazz ensemble, is customary for professional-level Thai ensembles. In traditional performances, these solos may be composed, improvised, or something in between. In *Music for a Royal Palace*, the colotomic percussion improvises (as a group) over the traditional rhythmic cycle used to accompany compositions in a Chinese style. The rest of the composition, including the solos, is notated. Although I could imagine improvised solo variations as done by the best Thai musicians, the musicians playing *Music for a Royal Palace* came to the piece without prior knowledge or experience with the idiosyncratic and cross-cultural idioms which I invented for each of the instruments. Nonetheless, through intensive rehearsal and a welcome dedication and openness to the unfamiliar on their part, the musicians acquired an intuitive understanding of their respective instrumental idioms and began to adapt these to their own personalities through selective improvisation. The premiere performance,[22] as a result, was very much akin to the experientially informed combination of composition and improvisation with which the best Thai ensembles perform traditional music. As such, with the cross-cultural nature of the music manifest both in the materials of the composition as well as in the experiences of the musicians themselves, I consider this to be my most successful cross-cultural work to date.

22. The premiere performance was given by Wu Tong, *sheng*, Andrea Hemmenway, viola, Joseph Gramley, marimba, Rod Thomas Squance and John Hadfield, percussion.

Foregrounding

> Foreignness does not start at the water's edge but at the skin's. (Geertz 1985: 261)

I have characterized my motivation for *Pan-lom*, to create a pervasively cross-cultural composition with overtly hybrid features of construction and intellectual design, as idealistic. It is so because neither the thoroughly designed hybridity of its structure nor the concluding vision of an intuitively cross-cultural music transcends the particularity of the piece as a product of one person's cross-cultural experiences. These cannot immunize the composer or composition against potential implications in politics, nor can the work become an actual crossing of cultures. I, like many other composers who work cross-culturally, am at pains to point out that neither an individual composition nor the entire body of work of but one person can constitute a merging of traditions or cultures, which by definition transcend individual experience. To write cross-cultural music is to write music, to negotiate the sum of one's experiences, musical and otherwise, the burdens of tradition, and the even greater burdens of innovation. And yet, it is not *merely* to write music. I have come to regard cross-cultural music as distinctive in that it brings to the foreground the subjectivity of musical meaning and the ethical dimensions of authorship which are relevant to all artistic creation.

By explicitly seeking an artistic expression that reaches beyond the bounds projected onto the artist by their cultural or stylistic location, the artist obviates the contingency of their knowledge and experience. And cross-cultural artistic expression once released into the world is subject to the divergent interpretive apparatuses of the musical cultures implicated in the work (as well as those of any others who care to listen). The cross-cultural work, heard from the standpoint of any one of the implicated musical traditions, will be both sensical and nonsensical. For every aspect that is familiar, there will be another that is unfamiliar; for every rightness about the work, a wrongness along with it.[23] The full meaning of the work cannot be had within the interpretive frameworks of only one musical culture—this music has no home. For any music which seeks to be more than the lowest common denominator between musical cultures, there will be a persistent cultural distance articulated by the work and reinforced by the cultural specificity of the interpretations brought upon it. It is for this reason that cross-cultural music should not be naively understood as utopian, as cultural reconciliation or "global harmony." On the contrary, this music, by its nature, is encumbered by the potential for implication in the pervasive inequities of power and in the complexities of identity politics.[24]

I take it as axiomatic that the formation of musical meaning is a dialogic process, always subject to negotiation between the "text" of work, the contexts surrounding its creation and performance, and the subjective interpretive frameworks brought to bear upon it. There is, therefore, no apolitical music, no music above the fray of what human beings will choose to think about it and do with it, no

23. One of the most challenging but necessary aspects of the analysis of cross-cultural music is in cross-cultural reception studies, to understand the degree to which an individual piece of music can be rendered coherent by listeners from the respective musical traditions. My earlier remarks, to the effect that my music is of no traditional use "over there," should be qualified. While the idea of contemporary composition in the Western sense may not have relevance to traditional practitioners in general, it would take an ethnomusicological reception study to fully investigate the uses to which my and other modern music is heard as meaningful or actually put to use by individuals.

24. I have written elsewhere, but without conclusion, about the politics of representation in cross-cultural composition (Adler 1998). It is a persistent challenge to theorize the capacity of music to simultaneously constitute individual expression and the representation of culturally situated categories (such as "Thai music" or "jazz") and thus become implicated in unresolvable discourses of appropriation, authenticity and cultural change. Born and Hesmondhalgh, in their introduction to *Western Music and Its Others* (2000), survey the problem as it pertains to cross-cultural music in the West.

matter the intentions of the composer or the prevailing ideology associated with the tradition in which they work.[25] It is this dialogic nature of musical meaning which is brought into the foreground by the cross-cultural work, for which there can be no single, depoliticized interpretation that can claim truth over all others. Carolyn Abbate theorizes music's ability to be politically relevant, especially in the context of the modern Western ideological assertion of music's autonomy, by invoking the useful notion of *aura*:

25. Taylor (1995), for example, critiques the modern Western ideology of the opposition of art and politics, which I will refer to as a claim to music's autonomy.

> Again, the point is not that musical works are being explained as reflecting cultural values or biographical facts. It is not even that musical works are said to reveal something inaccessible, some social truth not conveyed by any other medium, though this is an idea well worth scrutinizing in greater detail. The point is that these ideas and truths are being made monumental and given aura by music. (Abbate 2004: 520)

The bringing into contact of multiple interpretive frameworks is the domain of ethics. In the case of Thai classical music, the ethical dimension is conveniently explicit: the ceremonial process of becoming part of the tradition instills a deeply felt sense of ethical responsibility that is inseparable from the act of making music. In writing music which crosses between the Western classical and Thai classical traditions, musical ethics are brought into contact and compromise, but again from the idiosyncratic standpoint of my own subjective experience. Kofi Agawu, in his critique of scholarship about African music, calls for "an ethical attitude, a disposition towards frameworks and styles of reasoning that finally seek—actively, rather than passively—to promote the common good" (2003: 220). In understanding music as politically relevant, as a site for the negotiation of meaning and the articulation of representations, the demands of authorship are no less than those of the scholarship Agawu critiques. With the ineffability of its meaning, music is even more dangerous than scholarship. Misinterpretation and politicization are re-readings as much part of the landscape of musical interpretation as any other which the composer seeks to anticipate. Yet no degree of introspection immunizes the composer from criticism. An intuitivization of cross-cultural composition through improvisation as in the case of my works for solo *khaen*, like a recourse to "poetic license" or claim of music's autonomy, cannot provide an alibi for the individual artist to eschew an ethical attitude. The ethical attitude cannot be monological.

Nor can there be an unassailable methodology which ensures the ethical attitude will be attained, neither in the idealist, structural concerns of a work such as *Pan-lom* nor in the subjectivities of improvisation. The process of discoursing set in motion by a work is one in which the composer can only participate or listen, not dictate, confine, or predetermine. The ethical attitude demands a never-ending process of re-research, reconsideration, and re-evaluation in pursuit of a music moving forward toward the unknown and as-yet-unachieved. A music encumbered by the inequities of power can nonetheless evince the aspiration to transcend them. An ethical cross-cultural music gives aura to the notion that cultural distances can be mediated, that ethical systems can be brought into contact without destructive conflict.

> Our music foretells our future. Let us lend it an ear. (Attali 1985: 11)

Bibliography

Carolyn Abbate, "Music—Drastic or Gnostic?" (*Critical Inquiry* 30: 505–536: 2004.)

Christopher Adler, *Cross-Cultural Hybridity in Music Composition: Southeast Asia in Three Works from America.* (Unpublished manuscript: 1998.)
"Drone Placement and Fingering in Traditional and Contemporary Music for *Khaen.*" (*The Free-Reed Journal* 3: 47–54: 2001.)
Epilogue for a Dark Day. (Tzadik, TZ 8004; 2004.)

Kofi Agawu, *Representing African Music: Postcolonial Notes, Queries, Positions.* (New York: Routledge, 2003.)

Jacques Attali, *Noise: The Political Economy of Music.* Translation by Brian Massumi. (Minneapolis: University of Minnesota Press, 1985.)

Georgina Born and David Hesmondhalgh, eds. *Western Music and Its Others: Difference, Representation, and Appropriation in Music.* (Berkeley: University of California Press, 2000.)

Steven Feld, "Pygmy POP. A Genealogy of Schizophonic Mimesis." (*Yearbook for Traditional Music* 28: 1–35, 1996.)

Clifford Geertz, "The Uses of Diversity." (The Tanner Lectures on Human Values, University of Utah, 1985; http://www.tannerlectures.utah.edu/lectures/geertz86.pdf.)

Nancy Guy, "Trafficking in Taiwan Aboriginal Voices." In *Handle with Care: Ownership and Control of Ethnographic Materials*, ed. Sjoerd R. Jaarsma (Pittsburgh: University of Pittsburgh Press, 2002, pp. 195–209.)

Louise Meintjes, "Paul Simon's *Graceland*, South Africa, and the Mediation of Musical Meaning." (*Ethnomusicology* 34, no. 1, 1990, pp. 37–73.)

Terry E. Miller, "Laos." In *The Garland Encyclopedia of World Music, Volume 4: Southeast Asia*, ed. Terry E. Miller and Sean Williams. (New York: Garland Publishing, Inc., 1998, pp. 335–362.)
Traditional Music of the Lao: Kaen Playing and Mawlum Singing in Northeast Thailand. (Westport: Greenwood Press, 1985.)

Edward W. Said, *Orientalism.* (New York: Vintage, 1978.)

Christopher Small, *Musicking: the Meanings of Performing and Listening.* (Hanover: University Press of New England, 1998.)

Timothy D. Taylor, "When We Think About Music and Politics: The Case of Kevin Volans." (*Perspectives of New Music* 33, no. 2, 1995, pp. 504–536.)

Deborah Wong, *Sounding the Center: History and Aesthetics in Thai Buddhist Performance.* (Chicago: University of Chicago Press, 2001.)

Hugo Zemp, "The/An Ethnomusicologist and the Record Business." (*Yearbook for Traditional Music* 28, 1996, pp. 36–56.)

CHAPTER
2

DRAWING DENSITIES FOR GUITAR

MICK BARR

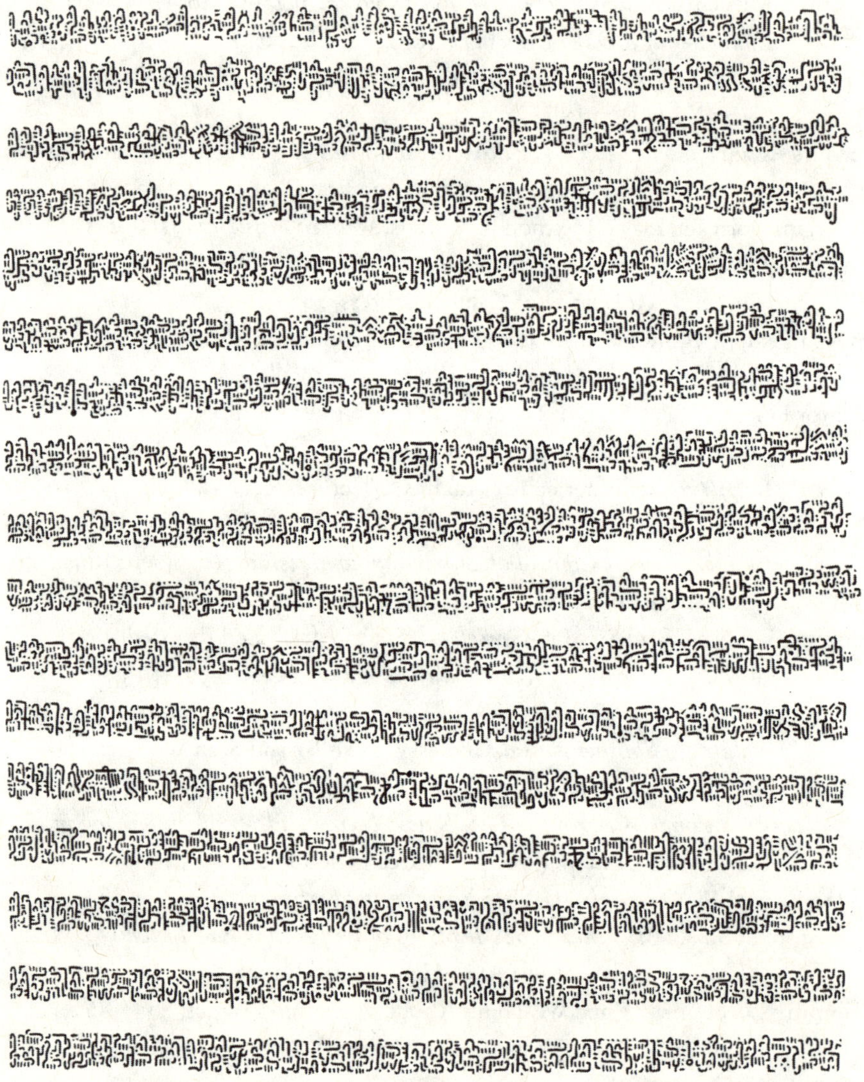

I see the above text to be somewhat of a form of improvised music. Or maybe it is a form of improvised notating. As I am drawing these lines, every mark has a note value in my head, and I just sort of let it take its own shape.

Sometimes I add my own rules, like how the above lines are presented in a roughly uniform shape and density. But that's because I was trying to make it look like text. While I am drawing, my mind is usually blank except for the rhythms of the marks I am making. I have pages and pages of drawings like this, in various shapes and densities. And everytime I read back over these lines, the music in my head sounds different to me. I may have started reading it at a different angle, or just see it differently. I haven't ever tried to play these drawings on guitar, but I have a loose system of how every mark or shape could be played.

Dotted lines are single note descensions/ascensions on the high E string.

Single dots are single note punches on any string.

Short lines are diminished tri-tones played anywhere on the neck. Usually all lines in a grouping are played on the same chord.

Small circle is a quick hammer on.

Filled in circle is a quick hammer on followed by scratching the strings with a pick.

Any *curved line* is an arpeggiated run following the direction of the line from either starting point.

Strike notes are a quick slide (glissando?) up or down the neck, depending on which direction the line is pointing.

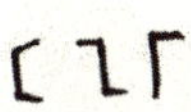

Any *sharp angle shapes* indicate a single note for each line and a great jump in tone for each line.

I'm sure I left out some shapes, but that's how I think I'd play it.

CHAPTER
3

CROSSED HANDS

BORAH BERGMAN

I **once saw the one-handed** (left hand) Paul Wittgenstein perform. It really inspired me to develop my left hand, to make it the complete equal of my right hand in both strength and independence. It took years but now I am completely ambidextrous. I can improvise hornlike phrases with both hands, sometimes crossed, in a contrapuntal and polyphonic, multi-layered dialogue that allows pieces to be turned upside down without loss of rhythmic intensity or aesthetic shape. I call my style "ambi-ideation."

Crossed Hands Structures. R = Right Hand L = Left Hand

The rest of the article will deal with *crossed hands*—the left hand plays in the treble and the right hand plays in the bass.

The left hand no matter how skillful and powerful it is made to be will never sound like the right hand, not because the muscles and tendons are any less in strength and dexterity—that all can be developed.

There is something else involved—it is this, aside from the respective sounds which the different registers produce.

The hands are mirror images of each other.

The wide stretch of the right hand—the thumb and second finger—are on the bottom or left side of the hand. However, the wide stretch of the left hand—its thumb and second finger—are on the top or right side of the hand.

The close fingers—two, three, four, and five are on the right side of the right hand and conversely—two, three, four, and five are on the left side of the left hand.

Wide means the structures or notes are farther away from each other.

Close means the structures or notes are nearer to each other.

As a result *wide* sounds different from *close* and *close* different from *wide*.

And what does all the above mean? We have a product that lends itself to originality.

CHAPTER
4

WHERE ARE WE?—ON LOCATION

LISA BIELAWA

Aimlessness Song

Where are we?
Is this the right way?
Where's the guy with the directions?
Maybe we should all relocate.
Do you know how many blocks it is from here?
Ten blocks seems like a fucking journey to me now.

Where are we?
Is this the right way?
Where's the guy with the directions?

I already waited in this line.
I think I should take a day off.
Maybe we should all relocate.

So then I was back in line and now I've been rerouted.
Do you need an appointment or can you just walk in?
I thought of 500 ways not to make this trip.

Where are we?
Is this the right way?
Where's the guy with the directions?

We both headed for the same guy.
He thought we were talking German.
No one had any idea what I was talking about.
I can't remember where this conversation was going.
We gotta move around a lot—that's how it is in the resistance.
We need to find out where the party is.

I'm trying to catch my breath.
I hope they know what they're doing.
I found a place where we can sit together.

When I see people on the train listening to iPods, they seem hermetically sealed off from others and from their surroundings. Similarly, the composer who is exploring new sounds through new technologies is often making music at a sad little qwerty station, alone in a studio somewhere with headphones on. I know that some listeners feel less lonely with their earbuds on. They do feel connected—not to their own physical surroundings, but to the creator of the music, or to the community that defines itself by the music, that they are listening to. Similarly, any act of creative music-making conducted in solitude, whether at a computer or at a piano or other instrument, can feel like an act of communication and connection, just not in real time and space. When I write an orchestra piece, I sustain myself on the vivid knowledge that, eventually, people will come together and make the music happen, in some location, with the real-time participation of musicians and listeners. Sounds created on and emitted by computers, on the other hand, do not require real space, even eventually. Spatial relevance can be added back in, of course, but this act, even when it is beautifully successful aesthetically, seems inorganic to me. I've figured it out: to me, these technology-mediated musical acts feel lonely because they have no location. Do we no longer require location in our musical experiences? I feel an urgent desire not to let go of location. Does this make me nostalgic?

It's true that location has its own bugaboos. The design of the concert hall grew organically out of aristocratic social structures, and so it is famously fraught with class issues. But it is worth remembering that in spite of these issues, music was at one time, before music-capturing devices were invented, an activity that required a location. And not just a location—a complex system of human interactions. Later in cultural history, the music club emerged from a similar set of social needs, although amplification was already introducing some location slippage: "The instruments are up there, but I am hearing them from over here." Amplification = the genesis of Location opaqueness. The introduction of new technologies continues to create such fissures. Technology changes the way people relate to each other, and to location, and not just within musical contexts. Again, am I expressing a Luddite nostalgia? A yearning for a time when, if you wanted to hear the clarinet more, you had to get closer, or the clarinet had to play louder? Perhaps a little, but then I also see new values emerging from recent technological developments that I find very exciting, in the realm of communication. Computer-assisted interactivity is creating new wrinkles on the surface of this erstwhile lonely virtual landscape.

After the virtual drought come the virtual rains. A computer music researcher I met recently commented (nostalgically!) that he remembers the day when he used to have to wait forty-eight hours for his work to be realized at the big computer across campus, only to discover that he had generated fifteen minutes of silence because he forgot a comma. This is perhaps the loneliest story ever told, an artifact from a time in which computers still obfuscated human-scale communication, rendering its users socially isolated. Now we are enjoying the flowering of a whole new dimension in technological advancement that is putting us more and more in touch with one another through computers, after years of requisite solitude. International real-time collaborations, YouTube micro-stars, the rich architecture of the blogosphere—the picture is no longer such a lonely one.

Does this architecture imply a location? Do we "need" location anymore, now that technology has given us human company back? Is a virtual location a musical location?

I remember writing my piece for piano and chamber orchestra, *The Right Weather*, for the first season of Zankel Hall in New York. Originally I wanted to use technology somehow in the piece, in a particular way. I was interested in finding a way to heighten listeners' awareness that they were in an actual location. And not just a concert hall, but an actual unique location in the universe—seat K103 in the parterre, for example. I wanted every person in the hall to feel that he or she was having a unique, ephemeral, unrepeatable experience, dependent on the space delimited by his or her body, and on the "now-line" of the present moment. This is a kind of musical experience that the iPod listener is not getting, because of the capturedness (repeatability) of the sound and the elimination of location. The difference is both sonic and phenomenological. The two experiences have underlying values that are directly at odds with one another. My desire was not to refute the values of the one, which include this capturedness and a transcendence of the physical, but simply to heighten awareness of the other, which celebrates the ephemeral and awareness of the physical.

I wanted to use the many speakers around the hall, in combination with actual spatialization of the orchestra, to make every listener's experience a unique one. But when I began discussions with their technical staff, I learned that this brand-new hall had been designed, according to the latest innovations, to ensure that every seat would sound the same. This decision reflects certain values that could be deemed democratic and even progressive, since by making the cheap seats sound as good as the expensive seats, it collapses the hierarchical social order inherent in concert hall design. But I wanted to heighten the differences of experience inherent in location. I wanted every person's listening experience to be different. Unfortunately, in order to do what I had in mind, we would have needed to circumvent their spanking-new sound system and rent monitors instead. Needless to say, I eschewed all technology and used only acoustic means in this piece. The players migrated, during the piece (but never while playing), from the stage to the lobby to various spots in the house and back to the stage again. While in the lobby they played a group drone that embraced the entire house, leaking through the entrance doors, which were cracked open on cue by a handful of super-qualified ushers.

After this experience I took stock of the experiment, and decided that the values underlying the design of concert halls work counter to my particular aims, at least in this line of inquiry. I decided that, in my exploration of the phenomenon of location, I would have to go outside of that system. At about that time, soprano Susan Narucki and I began speaking about the social limitations of the concert hall, and our shared desire to find new interfaces with audiences. What if we were to do a piece for soprano and acoustic instruments in a place where people would not be already spatially and socially situated: no rows of chairs, no unidirectional listening, no cost of tickets, even possibly no expectation of a musical experience. In short, we wanted to go outside into public spaces and pursue the experiment anew. This conversation was the beginning of *Chance Encounter,* which at this writing is in full progress, several months away from its first performance.

Both Susan and I travel so much that it became a difficulty to have meetings and to do research on possible texts to set for this piece. I remember sitting in yet another airport, trying to concentrate on reading in one of the three heavy books I had lugged along in my carry-on. I realized that, as usual, I was trying to shut out the public environment I was in, in order to concentrate on my inner picture of the public environment of my piece. All at once these efforts revealed their absurdity to me—I was spending all of my time trying to shut out public transient environments in order to concentrate on a piece that was ostensibly going to celebrate and articulate public transient environments. There was location in my piece, and I was right there in it. The split consciousness we all internalize as a result of the locationlessness of modern life had prevented me from seeing the nose on my face. I decided to leave the books at home and turn my attention outwards.

I bought a little notebook and began to carry it with me everywhere, writing things down that I overheard people say in public spaces—airports, bus stations, out on the street, on line for hot dogs. I asked Susan to do the same. I noticed that people say certain kinds of things while in transit—things that help them locate themselves in space and time ("Last time I ate here by myself;" "Remember—it was snowing horribly? And she was holding the dog?"), or provide a summary understanding of 'the way things are' ("They used to give you a paper bag with a sandwich and an apple, and that was the beginning of the end;" "It's tough when you know what's out there, and all you can do is look"). By writing, as opposed to using a recording device, I was able to be at the ready all the time to capture any utterance from any direction in any context. I was also acting as a filter, separating utterances from their sonic features and contexts right away and selecting utterances intuitively for their plasticity, singability, and unwitting poetic beauty. I found I was also able to use my sense of sight to help me understand spoken words through lip-reading. So, analog from the very beginning, our process of articulating transient public space back into itself was underway.

Thus unaided by technology in the Collection process, I felt that we were, from the very beginning, immersing ourselves in location-ness. Nevertheless, I wanted to find a way to participate in the strand of technological progress that arguably enhances human-to-human interaction: the blogosphere. I started a *Chance Encounter* blog, where I post photographs of the public spaces in which I overhear things, share the phrases themselves, muse on the issues that I encounter while composing, and generally conduct my conceptual work on the piece in a totally transparent way. Others post comments—including their own overheard fragments—and thoughts about the process. In this way, a virtual community has sprung up around the piece, one that makes my own creative process feel less lonely, and gives others a sense of shared ownership in the piece. These little phrases are there for anyone to use, since of course they never belonged to me in the first place. Perhaps there are other pieces being written using them too.

These utterances number in the hundreds now, and I have organized it into a libretto of sorts, through an entirely personal method. This second process of Categorization necessarily follows Collection, but the two feed each other and spur each other forward, and so I have been engaged in both simultaneously.

Categorization is glorified sorting. Of course, in sorting activities the desired result is systematic efficiency. My desired result is maximum poetic beauty.

I remembered a friend of mine who, having no sorting skills, had meticulously labeled his file folders with totally non-analogous categories—October; Telephone; 1996. Where, I ask you, in this system would one find the phone bill from October 1996? I wouldn't want him running my home office, but as an expression of the whimsical and very personal workings of the human mind, his system had poetic beauty. I knew I wanted non-analogous, non-exclusive categories like these. It looks like a system! But it's really just a person—me—organizing my experiences of location. I remember a panel discussion among computer music researchers and composers that centered around the categorization of sound data. Are researchers (who are usually not composers, but often partner with composers in the creation of new works) fooling themselves if they think that they can exhaustively categorize sound data according to discretely definable parameters? I say yes, but joyfully. The act of categorization is necessarily and wonderfully creative. Why apologetically gloss, or agonize, over the most human element in the process—the inability to objectivize the categorization of data?

So I began to parse out every possible kind of category that might be suggested in these quotes. Thus "They used to give you a paper bag with a sandwich and an apple, and that was the beginning of the end" would end up both in the *Food* category and in the *Drama–Self-Pity* category; "Remember—it was snowing horribly? And she was holding the dog?" would end up in the *Animals* category and the *Nostalgia* category; and "I hope they know what they're doing" would end up in the *Aimlessness* category and the *Mistrust of Others* category.

My criterion for the creation of a category is whether or not it seems to want to be a song. Does this category (*Nostalgia*, *Drama–Self-Pity*,

Animals) help me hear a sound-world that might be able to be a song? Can I imagine that song articulating a transient public space?

And speaking of articulating space, how can I arrange my players so as to open up the maximum amount of awareness of the listener's self in space? Now I am out of the concert hall, and my listeners might be happening upon the piece on their way home from work, or on their daily walk around a familiar neighborhood. Or maybe they are there expressly to see the piece, having followed its development in virtual space for months, even contributing their own overheard phrases.

Listeners will find themselves around and between two groups of players. Issues of balance, and to some degree texture, are largely determined by where the listener chooses to stand. If you want to hear more clarinet, move closer to the clarinet. If you want the textures to shift, move around the space while listening. There is no correct way to listen to the piece, and no two people will experience the same piece. Democratic? Not by the standards of concert hall design. But this kind of music environment encourages maximum participation from the listener, in real time and in real space. One of the values inherent in the piece is the multiplicity of experiences it invites. I hear things that are said in public spaces and they filter through my mind, find their siblings among other collected phrases, organize themselves into categories which become songs. By the grace of the musicians I am able to offer these impressions, projecting them back into the kinds of shared public spaces which gave rise to the phrases in the first place. Through whatever means I can devise, I empower the listener to be aware of his or her own act of listening, and encourage a maximum variety of experiences of the piece.

Conceiving and scoring this piece begged many logistical questions. I decided to put the twelve players in two locations, at a remove from one another that would be determined by sound, not absolute distance. Because the piece has no conductor, players from Group 1 need to hear cues from Group 2, and vice versa. A sound check for this piece consists of trying the section with the most delicate cue, and selecting the distance accordingly. Each song has slightly different groupings, so any given player might be in Group 1 for *Nostalgia* but Group 2 for *Animals*. Time to make these moves is built into the score, so that the different songs can be performed without pause, taking into account that wind players cannot be out of breath while playing, and cellists need to move their instruments slowly.

Group 1 always includes Susan, who is fixed in her location. She is the only one who will emerge from private space, making her entrance from within a building on the site, onto a balcony, fire escape, or picture window (as will be the case at the Seward Park Library in Lower Manhattan, where the piece will be premiered). Other players will arrive on the site just as the transient listeners do, from within a deli perhaps, or the subway or bus. Having coordinated their watches earlier in the day via conference call, the entrances can be made using absolute time, with the help of aleatoric processes in the first section that can absorb some time uncertainty.

Each section/song is an opportunity for me to explore a different way for the groups to interact with and depend on one another in the space. Simple alternating antiphony is one model. Others are built around shifting leadership roles as foreground and background trade off between the two groups. There is only ever one event, in one of the groups, that drives the piece forward in time. Followers may maintain a texture while listening for cues, or they may interject distinct utterances at cues. The two groups may start at the same time, both playing fully-realized material, until the material is exhausted, at which point another event can begin, or may have already begun. Absolute time can govern realignments, and a broad range of possible sonic outcomes must be anticipated and accommodated.

* * *

In these ways I enhance and encourage variability within the experience of my piece. What is my private hope, my artistic intent, in doing so? I admit: I hope that by having a musical experience in which this variability is celebrated and highlighted, a listener may come to the realization that, in fact, even when the source itself is not variable, experience is always so. Human consciousness is located within the thinking, creative listener, whose inner world is always unique, and whose listening experiences are always necessarily ephemeral. No matter how much we think we can have a reliable experience by listening to captured sound on an iPod, no matter how much we composers think we can, through craft and mastery, create music that delivers a reliable, preferred, durable experience to a listener, the private experience of the present moment always reigns. Technology may offer the semblance of an even greater and more variegated control of artistic products, but its breakthrough in human interconnectivity has also abetted a breakdown of the myth of centralized experience. The result is a widespread empowerment of the listener-as-participant, no longer confined to seat K103. The sacrifice, often, is location.

Listeners are everywhere, making ephemeral experiences for themselves every day. *Chance Encounter* is my own chaotic act of listening. It is also my nostalgic articulation of location.

Nostalgia

Do you ever go to your old apartment?
Where are all the things that I remember?
Remember? It was snowing horribly—and she was holding the dog?

Your old neighborhood, right? You always go back.
It's all houses with big yards, and there's snow there.
They used to plant trees on this street, but if they do they're dead within a week.
I used to live on this street, but everything is gone.

What kind of place are you looking for?
I used to live on this street.
We used to have a house there, but my father lost his job.
I never go there now.

What kind of place are you looking for?
Do you have friends here from home?
Remember them?
Remember these?

Animals

The beetles came and chewed it to bits.
Now I know how a sardine feels.
What's with the rain? What are we, ducks?
Remember—it was snowing horribly? And she was holding the dog?
That guy has a fake snake around his neck—did you see that?
All right, kiss my man for me—and kiss my little bird.
Bulls don't want to be around cows all the time.
I don't want to know about fish that came out of the Suez Canal.
Like road kill.

Existential Commonplaces

What kind of place are you looking for?
It doesn't matter.
You don't know me.
I've never been here before.
I'm about to go back underground.
I won't be staying long.

Are you by yourself?
You're sitting there looking at people like you cannot understand.
Where you want to get has to be more desirable than where you are.
I have done nothing, nothing has happened, nothing will happen.
I think that it signifies that there's nothing there.

What do I keep on saying? What do I keep on saying?

CHAPTER
5

THEME AND VARIATION

URI CAINE

As a young jazz musician growing up in Philadelphia I was taught to learn the "changes"—these of course were the chords and harmonies of countless jazz standards that many jazz musicians used as the basis for their improvisations. These "standards" were often songs from Broadway shows and movies of yesteryear, well-known folk and pop songs that became part of the common repertoire of jazz. One of the skills that we were trying to learn was how to improvise over fixed harmonic structures. Around this time I heard Glenn Gould's recording of the *Goldberg Variations* and was thrilled by his playing. When I began to study the piece with its thirty variations, I realized that what I was studying could be seen as thirty very different "choruses" on the changes of the opening aria. It was like studying a transcription of a jazz solo over a thirty-two-bar structure from a Tin Pan Alley song. I was intrigued by the connection between playing over the changes and how composers composed over the changes—by comparing how Beethoven, Bach, Charlie Parker, Wayne Shorter, Rachmaninoff, and many other composers and improvisers treated playing over a specific chord sequence, or what substitutions Tchaikovsky used in the *Rococo Variations* that were similar to those substitutions that Coltrane derived when playing the standard *But Not for Me*. The thirty-two-bar aria that is the basis for Bach's *Goldberg Variations* and Gershwin's thirty-two-bar song *I've Got Rhythm*, that is the basis for countless solos by Charlie Parker, Miles Davis, and many others, both set up a similar musical game. How within the closed structure of a repeating harmonic pattern does a musician create the most varied, intricate, and imaginative solos and pieces? How does one create musical interest when the harmony has a static aspect?

Classical composers often sought out themes that were malleable—the simpler the harmony of the theme, the better to embroider it later in the variations. Sometimes popular songs or arias that were familiar were used as themes so that the art and sophistication of the composers' variations could be better appreciated.

Because theme and variation was primarily concerned with using a fixed harmonic structure to generate other pieces of music, composers often enriched the basic harmony by adding chords and harmonies that are only implied in the theme. Often chords were substituted to create surprise. These substitutions were often subtle changes in the harmonic rhythm, or could be quite radical. If the original chord in the theme went to the dominant at the end of a phrase, in the variation the composer might go to the submediant or even a more distant chord. The character of each variation usually was defined by a compelling detail—a certain texture that was maintained throughout the variation, a melodic or rhythmic motive that was reiterated, or a quotation of a preexisting musical work that was embedded in the variation. Sometimes the variation was a homage written in the style of another composer. Sometimes themes in a major key yielded variations in minor: The structure and drama of the piece depended on the art of quick contrasts and building energy and intensity through a kaleidoscopic and always-changing musical landscape. Sometimes variations were grouped together or were connected to each other over the larger form. The form was another metaphor for the coexistence of structure and freedom in music, and was a creative challenge for the composer. In the Theme and Variations form, the variety of pieces was unified by the structure of the underlying harmonic grid.

Theme and Variations functioned differently than other classical forms such as the sonata or rondo forms, which depended on the repetition of previously heard musical material. In a stereotypical Classical sonata form, two themes (one in the tonic and one in the dominant) were presented in the first "exposition" section. These themes were then developed in a middle section in many ways—by the use of melodic motives, harmonic movement that ventured far away from the tonic, sharp shifts in dynamics, and transformation of musical material heard in the exposition. This central section often had a sense of improvisatory freedom. The final recapitulation section repeated the exposition section (except that both themes were usually in the tonic key) and through repetition created a satisfying arch form where the instability of the development section was balanced by the return to normalcy that the recapitulation to the tonic key represented. The drama of the sonata form was in the going out in the development section and the satisfaction when the tension was resolved by a return to the opening material—the themes journeyed but returned home at the end of the piece.

Theme and Variations is a different thing altogether from sonata form. It is not about development per se—it is about brilliance, variety, and contrast. An opening theme is proposed. Then the harmony of that theme becomes the basis for a series of short contrasting pieces that are often dissimilar in character. These pieces emerge one after the other, seemingly unrelated and disconnected. What binds these pieces together is their adherence to the same harmonic progression of the theme. Instead of the more goal-oriented sonata form, what we hear are short pieces of often very different styles. Sometimes to create a sense of finality the opening theme is played again to remind the listeners what all the music that they have just heard is based on, like a jazz group that plays the "head " out after all the solos are finished. Sometimes, a summing-up gesture such as an additional coda that either restates or refers to the opening theme or a fugal treatment of the theme that leads to a climax ends the piece, like an extended "tag" at the end of a jazz piece. But the structural design of the piece has less to do with developing themes than creating distinct musical moments that bounce off each other in contrasting ways. It is a form made for eclecticism, humorous contrast, contradiction, reference to a variety of styles, and, of course, harmonic imagination.

Two of the most compelling theme and variations are the *Goldberg Variations* and the *Diabelli Variations*. The *Goldberg Variations* were composed by J.S. Bach in 1741 at the request of J.G. Goldberg, a talented pupil of Bach. Goldberg's job was to entertain Count Keyserlink, the Russian Ambassador to the Saxon Court and a notorious insomniac, who desired music in the night. Goldberg presented Bach with a thirty-two-bar *Aria* consisting of four eight-bar phrases. From this simple theme, Bach fashioned thirty diverse variations, all based on the same harmonic structure. Some of the variations refer to the various dance forms of the time, including a gigue and the formal French overture with its strict, dotted rhythms. Some of the variations are among the most technically complex, recalling the keyboard writing of Scarlatti. Variations of the most diatonic nature are juxtaposed with the most chromatic. Every third variation is a canon in which the two upper voices imitate each other at every interval from the second to the ninth over the bass line. Sometimes these canons are quite complex and represent Bach's extreme contrapuntal virtuosity. The *25th*

Variation is full of bizarre chromatic harmonies and extreme substitutions. The final variation combines two drinking songs which would have been sung at the end of a party and signify the end of the piece, a comic touch the listeners of the time would have well appreciated. Throughout the *Goldberg Variations*, Bach exemplifies the compositional freedom of the theme and variation form—that is, generating pieces of extreme diversity from one basic idea. He can invoke contrapuntal and dance forms and refer to French, Italian, as well as German national styles. He presents a comprehensive view of his musical world through the narrow focus of a single set of chord changes.

According to William Kinderman's book *Beethoven's Diabelli Variations*, Beethoven broke off work on the *Variations* for several years. Beethoven's *Diabelli Variations* were composed late in his career, Diabelli was a composer and publisher in Vienna who asked fifty of the leading composers of the day to each write one variation on his original waltz. This piece also was thirty-two bars long, with four distinct eight-bar phrases. Various composers, including Schubert and the very young Liszt, contributed to Diabelli's project, but Beethoven refused to participate. In response he began composing variations that parodied the banalities of Diabelli's waltz—the repeated chords in the right hand, the opening grace note figures D-C-B-C, the falling fourths and fifths in the melody. The first variation is a pompous march and sets the satiric tone of the opening variations. The humorous aspects of the piece are brought out by Beethoven's extreme contrasts between various dynamics, textures, and moods. There are variations that feature a lot of repeated notes. *Variation 25* sounds like a village band playing a waltz and leaving out a bar by accident. *Variation 13* features repeated notes with long pauses. One variation quotes Mozart; another recalls a famous piano pedagogy excercise book. Some variations feature manic left-hand boogie-woogie–like bass lines; others, like the twentieth variation, feature strange, glacierlike harmonic movement with extreme chord substitutions.

Apparently, Beethoven broke off work on the *Diabelli* for several years. When he returned to it, the character of his variations changed. Instead of sarcasm, he seemed to be recalling Bach and the contrapuntal glories of the *Goldberg Variations*. Some of the later variations are archaic, not in the sense of being old-fashioned but in the sense that they show a veneration for the past glories of musical history. We have variations in the form of short fughettas or baroque arias, and a massive fugue before the finale. *Variation 30* features extreme rhythmic intensification in the right hand and some daring harmonic substitutions. The piece moves from a parody and mockery of the Diabelli theme to the transcendental world of baroque counterpoint. The piece ends somewhat quixotically with a finale that recalls a classical minuet but soon develops into a rhythmically intense world of thirty-second and sixty-fourth notes for the final climax. The *Diabelli Variations* exemplify the idea of theme and variations—that of deriving the greatest variety of music from a single chord progression.

The history of jazz in much of the 20th century is also a study in the progression and development of ways to improvise over a recurring set of harmonic "changes." Jazz musicians used the form of theme and variations to structure their solos—the themes were the songs that they used as the basis for their improvisations. Many of the innovations in jazz were rhythmic, and many had to do with the new sounds and textures introduced by each generation of jazz musicians. But it also had to do with the development of new harmonic languages that developed over time as many generations of musicians worked out idiosyncratic ways to play and improvise over harmonic progressions. This harmonic knowledge was also influenced by the blues, by the development of harmony in Tin Pan Alley, and by the influence of classical music and contemporary classical music and newer harmonic developments in pop music.

The great masters of the music each invented their own original harmonic styles, from Louis Armstrong's melodic genius and astounding technical exuberance to Coleman Hawkins' reharmonization and brilliant soloing on *Body and Soul*, from Duke Ellington's harmonic and compositional genius to Art Tatum's stunning chromatic reharmonizations of standards. During the 1940s, Charlie Parker and Dizzy Gillespie devised tricky substitutions and often reharmonized Tin Pan Alley songs to create new compositions with challenging harmonies. Thelonious Monk pioneered the use of space, dissonance, and quirky percussive textures contrasted with brilliant runs. He also reharmonized standards in a unique way. During the 1950s and 1960s, John Coltrane enriched the harmonic language of jazz. During his *Giants Steps* period he found an alternative to the ii-v-i chord progressions by substituting third derived harmony. During his later, more-modal period he took standards like *My Favorite Things* and simplified the chord sequences to get a different sound for his music. Sonny Rollins was also a master of thematic improvisation, building his solos with quotations, repetition of melodic cells, and a tremendous rhythmic virtuosity, harmonic imagination, and humor. During the 1960s, Bill Evans and Herbie Hancock introduced new harmonies in jazz that ushered in more-complex chords and sophisticated substitutions. The structure of the music was still often based on standards, but groups such as the 60s Miles Davis quintet introduced a degree of abstraction to playing these standards that was very free for the time and continues to be emulated today.

Jazz has moved in many directions since then, and playing closed harmonic forms is only one of the ways in which musicians improvise today. The innovations of many of the masters of the 60s and 70s sought a wider variety of structures for improvisation than the closed harmonic form of playing over the changes. But to this day, soloing over repeating changes still exerts a powerful hold on the imaginations of many musicians young and old. For many musicians it is still the primary form of improvisation.

Of course, one crucial difference is that while in classical music each variation usually had a different and distinct character, most traditional jazz solos stay in the same tempo and general character throughout each chorus or repetition of the harmonic pattern. It would be interesting to imagine playing a jazz solo where each chorus changed tempo, texture, and style abruptly—this would be a challenging exercise in group playing and a challenge for the individual soloist. But what is perhaps more interesting is what students of jazz and classical music can learn from each other when contemplating playing over the "changes." Bach and Beethoven and Charlie Parker and John Coltrane each in their own way grappled with the challenges and opportunities of using the repeating harmonic grid as a springboard for inspired composition and improvisation.

CHAPTER
6

THE LUNATION CYCLE AS A POINT OF DEPARTURE FOR MUSICAL IDEAS

STEVE COLEMAN

Introduction

Recently John Zorn asked me to curate his club that he opened in New York City called *The Stone*. This basically involved my doing whatever I wanted to do there for one month in terms of booking bands and arranging the schedule. I decided to plan a musical ritual in which I would participate and ask others to participate.

The word ritual comes from the Latin *ritualis* or *rituale*, from *ritus*, meaning rite. A rite is a ceremony, and in ancient times most of the ceremonies were performed using various cycles of nature for structural, timing, and energy purposes. Many of the common rituals of today still follow this form. For example, the definition of Easter is *an annual Christian festival in commemoration of the resurrection of Jesus Christ, observed on the first Sunday after the first full moon after the vernal equinox, as calculated according to tables based in Western churches on the Gregorian calendar and in Orthodox churches on the Julian calendar* (ref: Dictionary.com).

Most of the calendar systems come from the various cycles of Nature, usually having to do with the Sun, the Moon, or both; these are referred to as Soli-Lunar calendars. The Vernal Equinox (always associated with the direction East) having great significance in all ancient and modern cultures, is itself a cycle of Nature that has been used by humankind since time immemorial to structure various rituals. However, this does not stop with humans. The Vernal Equinox (as with all equinoxes and solstices) is nothing but man's quantizing of Nature's cyclic seasons, and all of Earth, animate and inanimate, responds to the forms of the seasons. I study precisely this kind of thing to trace the origin of ideas and customs. I've found that almost all can be traced back to the cycles of Nature, including music itself. These cycles in combination with other customs created by man sometimes create complicated rules for the observance of rituals.

Lunar Cycles

For the January 2007 musical rituals, the natural cycle that I worked with was the Soli-Lunar Cycle. I timed the concerts and created musical forms using information from the Lunation Cycle, as well as an extension of another, more complex cycle discovered by Dietrech Pessin called the Lunar Gestation Cycle (these extensions are called here Lunar Gestation Families, after Pessin's name). For more information on Dietrech's work see http://Lunar-Shadows.com and click on *Lunar Gestation Cycle.*

One of the more complex cycles of Nature that I have done some research on is the pattern of Saros Cycles (eclipse patterns). It is a beautiful cycle that I see as being very musical.

For example, the following New Moons initiated the Lunar Gestation Families that correspond to the Lunation Cycles of the ritualized lunar month of January 2007. The following Full Moons are the fifth phase of these same Lunar Gestation Families respectively (Solar Eclipses occur at New Moons, Lunar Eclipses occur at Full Moons):

New Moon	Lunar Phase in January 2007	
06/17/04	Gibbous Moon	
10/13/04	Third Quarter Moon	Solar Eclipse (Saros 124 - 6 South)
03/10/05	Crescent Moon	
07/06/05	Full Moon	
12/01/05	Balsamic Moon	
04/27/06	First Quarter Moon	
08/23/06	Disseminating Moon	
01/18/07	New Moon	

Full Moon	Lunar Phase in January 2007	
12/15/05	Gibbous Moon	
04/13/06	Third Quarter Moon	
09/07/06	Crescent Moon	Lunar Eclipse (Saros 118)
01/03/07	Full Moon	
05/31/07	Balsamic Moon	
10/26/07	First Quarter Moon	
02/20/08	Disseminating Moon	Lunar Eclipse (Saros 133)
07/18/08	New Moon	

Although I did not have time to incorporate this concept in this

January 2007 Ritual, I do plan on connecting the Lunation Cycles, Lunar Gestation Cycles, and Saros Cycles. You can find information on Saros Cycles on the Internet. For the sake of simplicity, I will discuss the Lunation Cycle in relation to another cycle called the Lunar Gestation Family, an adjusted eight-phase version of the four-phase Lunar Gestation Cycle.

A Lunar Gestation Cycle is a series of Lunar Phases, separated by about 9.25 months (272 or 273 days), each of which occupies approximately the same location within the zodiac. These Four Major Lunar Phases always begin with a New Moon followed by, in 9.25-month intervals, a First Quarter Moon, Full Moon, and Third Quarter Moon. However, I wanted to use symbolism associated with not only the Four Major Lunar Phases but also the Four Minor Lunar Phases of the Moon, for a total of Eight Lunar Phases. These eight phases are called New Moon, Crescent Moon, First Quarter Moon, Gibbous Moon, Full Moon, Disseminating Moon, Third Quarter Moon, Balsamic Moon. While doing research on how to go about this I discovered that the order of appearance of these eight phases within the Gestation Cycle did not match their appearance in the month within the Lunation Cycle. Let me give an example:

The Lunar Gestation Cycle that includes as a member the Full Moon of January 3 is as follows:

07/06/05	**New Moon**	**14° 31 min Cancer**
04/05/06	**First Quarter Moon**	**15° 34 min Cancer**
01/03/07	**Full Moon**	**12° 48 min Cancer**
10/03/07	**Third Quarter Moon**	**09° 49 min Cancer**

All of these phases occur near the same degree of the zodiac in Cancer, 14°, 15°, 12°, 9° respectively. When I checked the midpoints (273 divided by 2 = 136.5 days) between these phases to see if any of the Minor Phases occurred near these same degrees I found that the eight phases occurred in the following order, called a Lunar Gestation Family:

07/06/05	**New Moon**	**14° 31 min Cancer**
11/19/05	Disseminating Moon	12° 35 min Cancer
04/05/06	**First Quarter Moon**	**15° 34 min Cancer**
08/19/06	Balsamic Moon	11° 40 min Cancer
01/03/07	**Full Moon**	**12° 48 min Cancer**
05/19/07	Crescent Moon	13° 46 min Cancer
10/03/07	**Third Quarter Moon**	**09° 49 min Cancer**
02/17/08	Gibbous Moon	13° 17 min Cancer

So this is the order that these eight phases appear within the Lunar Gestation Family and, as you can see, all of these Moons appear close to the same location within the zodiac. I repeated this method for each of the eight phases of the Lunation Cycle in January 2007 to arrive at a cycle of dates related to that particular Lunar Phase. I then used information gleaned from various sources as well as intuition and logic to correlate the Eight Trigrams of the I Ching to the Eight Lunar Phase as follows:

07/06/05	☷	(K'un)	**New Moon**
11/19/05	☴	(Sun)	Disseminating Moon
04/05/06	☲	(Li)	**First Quarter Moon**
08/19/06	☶	(Ken)	Balsamic Moon
01/03/07	☰	(Ch'ien)	**Full Moon**
05/19/07	☳	(Chen)	Crescent Moon
10/03/07	☵	(K'an)	**Third Quarter Moon**
02/17/08	☱	(Tui)	Gibbous Moon

The correlation of the Trigrams to the phases of the Moon follows the natural order of increasing yang (light) and increasing yin (dark):

☷	(K'un)	●	**New Moon**
☳	(Chen)	◕	Crescent Moon
☲	(Li)	◐	**First Quarter Moon**
☱	(Tui)	◔	Gibbous Moon
☰	(Ch'ien)	○	**Full Moon**
☴	(Sun)	◔	Disseminating Moon
☵	(K'an)	◑	**Third Quarter Moon**
☶	(Ken)	◕	Balsamic Moon

Finally, together with poet and writer Patrícia Magalhães, I created a symbol for each Lunar Gestation Family, identifying the families as A through H. Here is the symbol for Lunar Gestation Family A, which includes the Full Moon of January 3, 2007 (the dates listed on the bottom right are the dates of the lunar phases within this particular family):

Gestation Family A

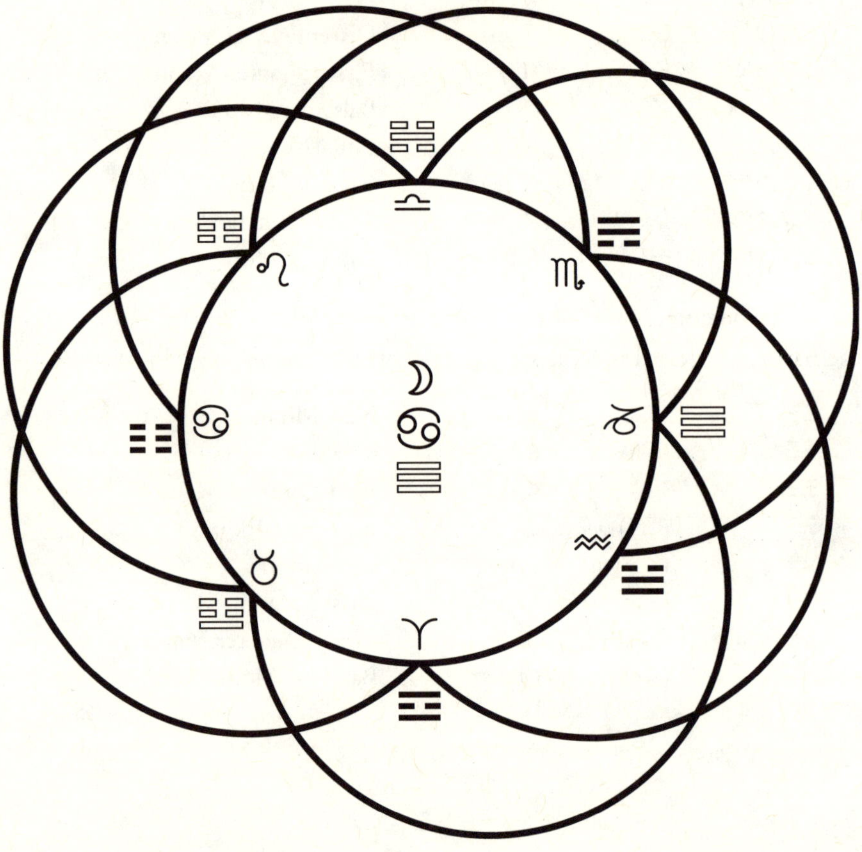

RITUAL DATE	07/06/05
Full Moon	11/19/05
Wednesday, January 03, 2007	04/05/06
08:57 EST	08/19/06
	01/03/07
	05/19/07
CYCLE INITIATION	10/03/07
July 06, 2005	02/17/08

Rhythmic Cycles Example

I will only give one simple example of how this idea could be expressed musically. I plan on writing much more about this at a later time. The basic idea here is to form rhythmic modes that correspond to the various formations of Yin and Yang where:

⚋ is the symbol for Yin and is assigned a value of 2
⚊ is the symbol for Yang and is assigned a value of 3

Therefore the Trigram ☴ is the symbol for Yin-Yang-Yang and corresponds to 233 numerically. These I Ching symbols are normally read from the bottom up. This can be translated into a rhythmic mode in two basic ways, as duplum or triplum (duple time or triple time). When it is duplum time, Yin is the basic pulse or beat; when in triplum, Yang is the basic pulse. What I am describing here are rhythmic modes and not the actual rhythms. A mode is a form that acts as a mental image which the musician uses to visualize arrangements of sounds as a gestalt. The actual rhythm that is thought of as residing within this form is something else entirely. Therefore strings of these Trigrams could represent groups of rhythmic modes. This is a very flexible way of organizing the temporal elements of a spontaneous or preconceived composition. Each of these strings of Trigrams is like a road, and there can be several roads taken simultaneously. Once internalized, this organizational method precludes any need for something like time signatures or the need to count.

It is these kinds of ideas that have allowed the translation of various cycles of Nature. Of course it does not stop with rhythm, melody, harmony, or form; any other aspect that you can imagine can be symbolized and expressed in this same manner. I find this approach very exciting as I have always been fascinated by the cycles of Nature. This kind of correlative thinking is very old and was at one point common in ancient times.

—January 2007

CHAPTER
7

THE EXTENDED PIANO

SYLVIE COURVOISIER

As a composer/improviser it is essential for me to find a distinctive language, a personal sound. For many years I've been developing my personal vocabulary by expanding and combining the possibilities of the piano, using both conventional and unconventional techniques.

Unconventional Techniques

My first experience with a prepared piano was hearing John Cage's *Sonatas and Interludes* as a teenage girl. Since then I've been intuitively exploring the inside of the piano.

In Cage's hands, piano preparations are typically nuts, screws, bolts, and pieces of rubber to be lodged between and entwined around the strings. His preparations had to be done in advance and were fixed for each performance. My interest lies in more-instant manipulations, preparations which do not require objects to be placed inside the piano in advance, and preparations which can be done and undone in an instant. In a way, this is closer to George Crumb's and Henry Cowell's conceptions of inside-the-piano techniques.

> *Crumb has referred to string and prepared piano techniques collectively as "the extended piano": the piano is prepared by placing objects on and between the strings. "String piano" is a term coined by Henry Cowell to describe techniques in which sound is produced by direct manipulation of the strings, rather than the striking of the piano's keys.*

I use a large variety of sounds, timbres, articulations, dynamics, preparations and effects produced by the fingers in contact with the strings (pizzicato, mute) to create my pianistic language, combining moments at the keyboard with inside-the-piano techniques, prepared and unprepared sections to make the piano sound as an orchestra unto itself. My way of preparing the piano is very spontaneous and intuitive and I try to use objects that won't put the piano out of tune. I prefer simple objects (wood, gaffer tape, mallets, etc.) so these preparations can happen very fast. I also like to surprise myself with new preparations and techniques, allowing me to escape the normal piano sonorities and taking me to unknown places.

My inside-the-piano techniques include:

Exploitation of the three pedals

Pizzicato with either fingernail or fingertip (with or without pedal)

—at the tip of the tuning pegs
—between the tuning pegs and the felt
—between the felt strip and the damper
—between the damper and the fret

Glissandi, sweeping, strumming ... (with or without pedal)

—sweeping chromatically across the strings with the finger(s)
—scraping along low strings with the fingernail(s)
—low strings
—glissandi over the strings with either fingernail or fingertip
—strumming along one or more strings with the flesh of the finger(s)

Muting and harmonics (with or without pedal)

—muting a section of the strings with the palm of the hand
—muting one note with the finger while striking the corresponding key with the other hand
—lightly touching string nodes while striking the corresponding key to produce harmonics

Gaffer tape (with or without pedal)

—attaching gaffer tape to the strings of the highest octaves of the piano (the resultant sound is reminiscent of wood blocks)

Drum sticks (without pedal)

—drum stick struck between the low strings and the middle strings section of the instrument (the resultant sound is reminiscent of a gamelan)

Chinese balls (metal balls) (with or without pedal)

—rolling or bouncing them on the strings
—rolling them on the tuning pegs and/or frets
—glissandi on the strings (produces harmonics)
—striking the metal structural beams of the piano with the balls (and mallets)

Conventional Keyboard Techniques

For several years I've been working with Nicolas Slominsky's *Thesaurus of Scales and Melodic Patterns* and it has deeply influenced my work. I've been developing a system of intervallic sequences, expanding them by using a method I call the "pivot system." See Figure 1 below.

Figure 1.

I choose one note (the pivot) of a sequence, and from that note, using different methods of permutations—inversion, retrograde inversion, mirror, retrograde mirror—I extract chords (Figure 2) and proceed through all the possible combinations of superpositions of these extracted chords.

Figure 2.

This method is used for every interval … (The example above uses the interval of major 7th).

Ideas are written in my music notebook and a scrapbook is used to collect these ideas for later use. I often practice phrases from my scrapbook. This has been an important tool for both my compositional and improvisational work, and I often combine this system with my extended piano techniques, trying to integrate them organically. Permutations, combinations, inversions, mirrors, and retrogrades have been always the backbone of my work, but in the end, it's the ears that decide.

CHAPTER 8

HYPERREALISM, HYPERDRAMA, SUPERPERFORMERS, AND OPEN PALETTE

NOAH CRESHEVSKY

Hyperrealism is an electroacoustic musical language constructed from sounds that are found in our shared environment ("realism"), handled in ways that are somehow exaggerated or excessive ("hyper"). Contemporary reality is so densely layered and information-rich and so far removed from a hypothetical state of "naturalness" that hyperrealism is an accurate term for identifying the fabric of daily life. We live in a hyperrealist world.

Hyperrealist music exists in two basic genres. The first uses the sounds of traditional instruments that are pushed beyond the capacities of human performers in order to create superperformers—hypothetical virtuosos who transcend the limitations of individual performance capabilities. These are the "supermen" who appeared in a number of my compositions, beginning with *Circuit* (1971) for harpsichord on tape. The compact disc *Man & Superman* (Centaur CRC 2126) is largely connected to my interest in the ambiguous borders between live performers and their impossibly expanded electronic counterparts.

The idea of superperformers has numerous precursors, including the violin music of Paganini, the piano music of Liszt, conventional music for player piano, and the fully realized player-piano music of Conlon Nancarrow.

Fundamental to the second genre of hyperrealism is the expansion of the sound palettes from which music is made. Developments in technology and transformations in social and economic realities have made it possible for composers to incorporate the sounds of the entire world into their music. Hyperrealism of this second genre aims to integrate vast and diverse sonic elements to produce an expressive and versatile musical language. Its vocabulary is an inclusive, limitless sonic compendium, free of ethnic and national particularity. The compact discs *Auxesis* (Centaur 2194), *Who* (Centaur 2476), and *Hyperrealism* (Mutable 17516-2) present compositions that are representative of my conviction that expanded sound palettes will become a routine characteristic of music in our time.

Essential to the concept of hyperrealism is that its sounds are generally of natural origin, and that they remain sufficiently unprocessed so that their origin is perceived by the listener as being "natural." Since the sounds of our environment vary from year to year, generation to generation, and culture to culture, it is impossible to isolate a definitive encyclopedia of "natural" sounds, but there are a great many sounds that are familiar to nearly all of us. These are the most basic building blocks in the formation of a shared (if temporary) collective sonic reality.

The development and incorporation of expanded palettes consisting of natural sounds also has precursors, most notably the tradition of *musique concrete*.

Hyperrealism celebrates bounty, either by the extravagant treatment of limited sound palettes or by assembling and manipulating substantially extended palettes.

Of my compositions, *Coup d'etat*, *Gone Now*, *Who*, *Ossi di morte*, *et puis*, and *Novella* (among others) share aspects of a particular style. I call that style "hyperdrama." In addition to other qualities, hyperdrama is characterized by a steady level of heightened sensations. Hyperdramas attempt to consolidate and compress intensified states.

> **Hyperrealism** is a language because various composers, using identical sounds (i.e., parts of speech), can produce significantly different kinds of compositions, based on their tastes, intentions, and technical resources. Tonality and atonality speak differently in the voices of legions of composers. Hyperrealism is the work of many, not of one.
>
> **Hyperdrama** is a musical style in which hyperrealistically extended palettes and/or restricted palettes in conjunction with superhuman performance capabilities express a larger-than-life level of emotional intensity.

A guest on a television talk show once described his surprise and disappointment that there was no music to accompany his first romantic kiss. He had seen so many films abounding with the music that generally accompanies such momentous moments. A silent kiss is a slice of real life, but a kiss with music and the crashing waves of an incoming tide is a slice of hyperdrama. Movies are filled with moments that are "beyond" life. We need only focus to notice them. Hyperrealism is an inevitability. Indeed, it already exists in many moments of our lives, but the term has not yet been accepted as a legitimate definition for a great deal of what we already experience on television, in films, and on countless improbably perfect sound recordings.

Open Palette

Every movie soundtrack differs from every other movie soundtrack because it is possible and practical to create new soundtracks for every movie that is made. Audiences would not be pleased to hear identical soundtracks in two different movies. Why are today's audiences—brought up in a varied and information-packed world—asked to respond enthusiastically to another piano sonata?

The term "open palette" implies that our circumstances permit and encourage us to harness all the sounds of the world, and to use these sounds in any ways we like in order to create musical compositions.

Raised as we are in a visual age of film and television, our ears and minds have come to expect a fresh sonic environment for each new show. Every film begins by presenting a unique visual and sonic landscape. No two films use the same materials. Part of our thrill in seeing a new film is the knowledge that we are about to enter into a new world of sight and sound. Why then is it considered reasonable to hear mere variations on the same timbral formats over and over again, through the fixed palettes of pianos, string quartets, wind ensembles, and symphony orchestras? We don't wear someone else's socks; why do we compose new music with someone else's secondhand sonic palette?

Many films have soundtracks with moments in which music (acoustic and synthetic), "sound effects," verbal utterances (words, but also sighs, moans, screams, laughter, etc.) are blended to form an indivisible fabric of sound. Just as viewers expect to see a different movie each and every time they watch a new film, listeners are legitimately entitled to hear a fresh palette whenever they hear a new piece of music. "Open palette"—the idea that music can be made from an ever-changing medley of diverse sounds—is fully accepted by sound editors as a routine state of affairs for the construction of soundtracks, yet it remains a fundamental heresy within much of the professional musical community.

Visual art embraces an ever-broadening palette that has moved outward from paint to include plastic, metal, newspaper, fabric, etc. At the same time, music departments have quarreled over tenor saxophones, electric guitars, and accordions. The inclusion of a bit of noise makes some pieces "concrete" or "electronic," and a kalimba requires an "ethnic" modifying prefix to apologize for its intrusion into a club that is reserved for a select few.

While nearly everyone in any other medium than music rejoices at expanded technological resources, many musicians openly (or secretly) follow a credo devoted to the endless propagation of something quite ridiculous: the deeply held (and deeply foolish) belief that "real" music is only made by traditional instruments—traditional Western instruments (and not all of those either)—and is made with twelve notes. Those twelve notes—probably no fewer, and certainly no more.

Such squabbles are particularly foolish in an age in which any sound that can be heard can also be recorded, manipulated, and shaped into viable, natural, expressive musical compositions. The inclusion of "extra-musical" materials into a piece of non-pop music is generally regarded as something "exceptional," but what is truly exceptional—and exceptionally odd as well—is the tendency to continue writing music for the same few instruments and ensembles.

How did these exclusionary absurdities come to pass for truth? More astonishing than the proposed inclusion of many sounds is the fact that so many sounds have been excluded for so long, and with such blind confidence in a pointlessly discriminatory system that has long since ceased to nurture anyone—composers, performers, or audience.

Concerts

What is it that induces musicians to endlessly compose string quartet after string quartet, or an infinite number of pieces for solo piano? These prefabricated musical formats are generally chosen because composers imagine their music being played by live players in concert halls. In fact, most music is heard through speakers or headphones, at home. The home theater has replaced the concert hall. If it has not yet done so quite completely, it has very nearly done so, especially in the area of contemporary non-pop music.

Concerts of new music are often attended by audiences so sparse that participants are frequently embarrassed to count. The number of players on stage may equal or exceed the number of people in the audience, and if one subtracts the complimentary tickets that have been disbursed, the number of paying customers is generally down to something approaching single digits.

Many composers voluntarily compose unsolicited string quartets for players who will have to be found. If four capable players are somehow acquired, the ensemble will likely confront funding and venue challenges, and therefore have little time or incentive to practice the new composition. With luck, there will eventually be a performance before an audience of fewer than fifty people.

It is both a virtue and a necessity to write for four strings when one has an opportunity to have a decent live performance of a string quartet. It isn't quite playing the game to sneak in extra notes during the mixing of a master tape for a compact disc, but pitch corrections and massive edits are routine parts of modern musical life. It is only a small step from that to rewriting the definition of a string quartet.

The future of music and the future of concerts are not the same issue. If nothing else, those of us who sit together with our students, colleagues, and friends at poorly attended concerts of new music have to wonder what is wrong with this picture. At no time in human history have so many people heard so much music. At the same time, attendance at most non-pop concerts is in critical decline. Perhaps music has lost some of its power through overexposure, but I think that much of the overexposure is related to the steady reiteration of the same twelve notes played on a handful of familiar instruments.

Recordings

Irrelevant economic and social considerations continue to limit our conception of what music can be. When a soprano is hired for a concert performance, it is economically and dramatically appropriate that she be called on to perform enough notes to justify a paycheck and her presence on the stage. We must not pay good wages to a live performer who merely sings a ten-second coda at the end of a string quartet. That's bad economics. Additionally, what to do with the tacit singer until her possibly glorious coda presents a visual and social quandary. Bad economics and bad drama unite to form a powerful disincentive to compose that coda, but the issue disappears when one emancipates sound from the limitations of the concert hall. Composing for recordings instead of for live concerts closes some doors, but opens others.

What of the composer who had dreamed of having a flutist imitate some bird sounds at the end of the last movement of a quartet that has been limited to four strings? Can we hire a flutist to play for only one minute of a thirty-minute piece? Should the flutist stand backstage for the first twenty-eight minutes, and then come out to mimic the bird, or should the flutist sit next to the hard-working cellist and listen to the opening movements? The audience has had to listen to all of the movements; why should the flutist enjoy a twenty-eight-minute reprieve?

If this were a recording instead of a live concert, no one would care about the dramatic or economic comings and goings of the cello and flute.

If this were a recording, and if the composer wanted birdcalls, he or she could make a recording of some real birds and dispense with the flutist altogether.

If music—including music for standard ensembles—was conceived for recordings instead of live concerts, the music composed could be very different.

Superperformers and Mozart's Nose

> "At an evening party, Mozart bet a case of champagne that Haydn could not play at sight a piece he had composed that afternoon. Haydn accepted the bet and proceeded to play it on harpsichord only to stop short after first few bars. It was impossible to continue because the composition required him to simultaneously strike notes at two ends of the keyboard and a note in the very center. Haydn exclaimed, 'Nobody can play this with only two hands.'
>
> 'I can,' Mozart said, and took his place at the keyboard. When he reached that problematic portion of his piece, Mozart bent forward and struck the central note with his nose.
>
> Haydn conceded saying: 'With a nose like yours, it becomes easier.'"
>
> —E. Van de Velde, *Anecdotes Musicales*; N. Slonimsky, *Slonimsky's Book*

Hyperrealism can be applied to compositions with traditional instruments as well as to compositions using expansive sonic palettes. The player piano has already provided a view of the possibilities that become available once instruments and voices are liberated from the limitations of human anatomy. A singer who does not breathe will perform but a single phrase before dying, but by cutting and pasting, he or she can croon on for as long as we like.

If we accept the fact that recordings are routinely edited and enhanced, should we not also go a step further and allow pianists to overdub one hand at a time? Conlon Nancarrow's magnificent works for player piano show the variety and grandness of sound that can be had from just a piano. It's less amusing to overdub Mozart's impossible note than to play the note with one's nose, but it's all the same on a recording. In any case, hyperrealism aims for something other than more of "the same." It aims to turn performers into superperformers by removing the constraints of human anatomy (breath and touch).

Are We Being Thrifty or Just Cheap?

We were all taught that what counts isn't so much the material itself, but what comes of that material. The mandatory introductory lecture on Beethoven's *5th Symphony* dutifully traces the repetitions and transformations of a tiny motif. We are reminded that much is made of very little (why?). It's about economy of means.

Economy of means is important only when it is genuinely important. We need to conserve endangered species, and clean water and air. Nothing is saved when we save a note. Sometimes (often—especially in an information-rich age), less is not more; more is more. Why is it "a good thing" to make a great deal based on very little? Economy of means is by no means an obvious virtue. On the contrary, the rejection of bounty is a questionable act of nonerotic flagellation. Deprivation in itself is no virtue. It's a habit. We have been taught to value economy of means, but this lesson needs to be challenged.

"What Will Become of It?"

One of my father's signature remarks was "maybe something will come of it." When my first LP came out, he trotted out the old "maybe something will come of it" line, and I told him that this—the commercial recording—was the thing that had come of all the years of training and work.

I also remember an early composition lesson: "Don't write something unless it reappears in some way somewhere else." This twice-told tale invites any number of metaphors. I like the one that suggests parallels between repetition, motivic development, etc., and human reproduction. If something must be reproduced, it has no value of its own. Its value is established only through replication (my child makes me worthy).

In fact, the ability to record and reproduce sound has altered the need to repeat anything. If we are writing Broadway shows, we had best repeat those tunes often enough for anyone to walk out of the theater humming them, but those audiences are getting old, and so is the idea of validation through repetition. A wonderful phrase has a right to its own existence. We can always replay a recording if we want to hear a phrase again.

To Listen or Not to Listen

There is a great deal of talk about sensory oversaturation and the demise of music. Today, more music is heard by more people than has ever been heard at any time in history. Music is everywhere, accompanying movies and television shows, enlivening elevators and shopping malls. Surely no human being was intended to listen to the same pieces over and over again, year after year and decade after decade. Overexposure to any stimulus tends to reduce its power, but I think that the primary cause of a lack of responsiveness to music is the repetition of the same twelve notes—forever played by the same instruments and traditional ensembles.

Anyone scanning a radio dial with the intention of listening to something makes the decision to listen or not to listen in a flash. If one does not like country western music, it takes only a second to decide that we are on the wrong station. It's all there in a single timbral flash. The dial moves on until a blast of electric guitar (or whatever we like) hits us head on. Of course, in some sense, a flash of almost any kind of music reveals a great deal about what kind of experience we can expect. Based on our experience, a second of Wagner is enough to tell us what we will hear if we don't move on to another station.

We should not underestimate the power of the vertical sound itself. It takes nothing away from Beethoven's ability to manipulate materials in ways that ingeniously make much of very little, but some themes are better than other themes, and new audiences are entitled to have timbral preferences and a reasonable expectation to encounter new sounds. Scanning a radio dial is not a case of "what will become of it." It is an example of a decision based on the thing itself.

The phrase "sound effect" should be eliminated; "ethnic instrument" should be changed to "instrument." "Sound effect" is code for sounds outside the hallowed twelve notes. "Ethnic instrument" is code for a non-European instrument; the term is a remnant of cultural imperialism—

one that no longer expresses anything other than an historical bias. When sound effects come together in a film with vocal utterances (words or not words), and ambient and pitched sounds ("synthetic" or "natural"), the result thrills as much (and with greater freshness) as does any piece of traditional music. As long as we have ears and hearts and minds, music will continue to delight us, to move us, and to enrich our lives.

Very little in art must be one way or another, but a musical palette certainly can be different from piece to piece. Every act of composition might reasonably begin with a fresh and open-ended consideration of every available sound source. If someone has a commission for a string quartet from a reliable ensemble that will practice, and if this composer has a social or personal interest in giving and attending concerts, then he or she should write a string quartet. But if your quartet is intended to be heard on a compact disc or over the Internet, indulge yourself. Be extravagant. A soprano can provide one solitary high note, if you like, perhaps just there, at the end.

CHAPTER 9

TIME-TRAVEL

CHRIS DENCH

What Time Is

I think I know what "now" is. You think you know what "now" is, and between us we can manage to meet for lunch. Physicists, however, admit that they have no idea what "now" is. They are prepared to accept that they can utilize the concept of time extremely successfully when doing the complicated mathematics for Relativity and Quantum Mechanics, but as to how the moment of the now comes about, they have no more idea than you or I (so far as I know).

Why time seems to pass, and why it seems to pass from past to future, is another scientific mystery. Thermodynamic entropy is often invoked.

In *The Collapse of Chaos*, Jack Cohen and Ian Stewart describe the "now" thus: "the present, where our consciousness resides, is a moving boundary at which the context changes—a travelling catastrophe in paradigm space."

A general working definition in psychology identifies the "now" as a window of about six seconds which individuals perceive as the "present."

Another psychological view is that there is no such thing as "now"; it is a mental construct generated by our brains to enable us to function.

Julian Barbour, in *The End of Time*, suggests that there is no such thing as an "Arrow of Time," there is only a Metaverse which consists of every possible iota of time, or "now," in every possible permutation in which that "now" can exist, each one containing the past memories necessary for us to think that it is the latest in a sequence of "nows"—all existing statically "at once."

John Archibald Wheeler provided the only satisfactory definition of time that usefully addresses the "now": "Time is what prevents everything from happening at once."

* * *

As a composer I therefore create the conditions for time-travel. This is called Time Binding.

Time binding is fixing—to a greater or lesser degree—the internal life of an abstracted period of time, the Time Capsule.

Time binding can be achieved through any recording process—notation, the recorded media, oral instruction, and so on. Filmmakers, composers, writers, sculptors, and even many flat-plane artists bind time through their work.

As a composer, I am primarily concerned with time-binding through a fully written-out score. Other composers, especially performer/composers, may bind time through less completely prescribed mechanisms, such as recorded improvisation. If the improvisation is not recorded, the time is only bound for that one performance—it is not available for time travel.

Time, therefore, can be bound with increasing degrees of specificity. That is to say, it can be very loosely bound, as for instance in an instruction like: "sing the same note as the person sitting next to you." This would structure time in such a way that the performance would begin as a dense sound and gradually thin to a single note—which note would be entirely unpredicted. How long this process would take is also entirely unpredicted. On the other hand, it can be bound extremely precisely, as in Conlon Nancarrow's *Player Piano Study No. XXI*, *Canon X*, an acceleration canon in which one voice slows down, the other speeds up, and they cross in the middle; at the end one of the voices is moving at 112 notes per second. Being played back on the mechanism of a player piano, rather than by a human being, adds tightness to the binding.

Time can also be bound with increasing degrees of complexity. The spectrum of complexity is very broad; for example, from a specified period of silence (John Cage's *4'33"*) to a specified period of white noise (Lou Reed's *Metal Machine Music*). However, the complexity of bound time can be deceptive: Aphex Twin's *Come to Daddy*, while apparently showing extreme complexity at the rhythmic level, is timbrally not very complex. Also, the rhythmic complexity consists of regular rhythms in frequently changing tempo patterns, which, while complex in its detail, follows a readily understood if not predictable pattern. (It is, nonetheless, exciting.)

Time binding, then, can have more than one dimension. Elements like timbre, harmony, rhythm, can have different levels of complexity, and a time capsule may have a hierarchy of levels of time boundness. For example, a recorded track by Miles Davis from one of his albums between 1972 and 1976 will bind the horizontal aspect of the sound—the solo improvisations—tightly, while the vertical or harmonic element may only bind time loosely.

Clearly, the degree of boundness of a time capsule is directly connected to the information-richness of the music. I call this information-richness "knowledge."

Redundancy lessens the tightness of bound time. Redundancy in music most often takes the forms of repetition, predictability, uniformity.

Paradoxically, however, as music approaches total unpredictability, information-richness tails off. Without some redundancy, context cannot be established, and information declines back into mere sense-data.

There are of course other kinds of musical time-travel. Sets of variations on existing themes, especially those originally written by historically distant composers, subject those themes to a kind of time travel. Certain composers of the so-called Postmodernist persuasion have created works of music that are stylistic mosaics, juxtaposing (but rarely superimposing, which would be much more interesting) sections written in styles from different historic eras—composers such as Valentin Silvestrov and the late, great B. A. Zimmermann. The Anglo-Indian composer Klarenz Barlow (Clarence Barlough), requiring a central respite in his large-scale spectral composition *In Januar am Nil*, provided a brief interlude in which the musical style travels backwards through history at the rate of a century each 4/4 bar, from the present back to early medieval monody. These kinds of time travel require a degree of historical informedness from the listener to make their point, however.

* * *

Musical Score

A musical score is the embodiment of a time capsule. The score is a slice of time coded into graphic form.

Unlike time itself, the musical score does not need to be read linearly. It is not embedded in an unfolding arrow of time—although the process of using it inevitably is. Except in performance (including mental performance), however, the time process of using the score is not the same as the time bound in that score.

Composers and performers have the additional opportunities for time travel that score provides: the music does not have to be written or read in the order it was written down. Jumping from one spot to another in a score without passing through all the intervening "time" is a form of time travel.

Just as the score need not be read linearly, it need not be composed linearly. I may think of the central torso of a piece long before I think of a way to enter and depart it (and vice versa). It may not be obvious to the listener but a piece may encapsulate a certain amount of composerly time-travel. This can involve writing the music in one order and shuffling it to make an entirely new order—this can give the music a quite different psychological profile. There are a few pieces of my own where I decided, quite late on, that the best place to start the music was not the beginning. These pieces start somewhere in the unfolding argument, proceed to the end (which is not necessarily flagged), jump instantaneously to the beginning, and then continue to end at the point they started. Might one think of this as a kind of Möbius-music?

Although it is the score which records the music, it is the music itself which binds time. But is the score the music? This is an area that gets very philosophically fuzzy. Certainly for lots of non-notated or loosely prescribed music, the score is only a schematic of the sonic outcome; it provides necessary but not sufficient minimal information about how the time is to bound. Often an essential element is entirely absent from the notation—the ongoing tradition of performance practice, for instance, or the prevailing tuning system. This is true of rock, jazz, and a wide range of what we call "Early Music."

There is no doubt that before the score exists the music does not exist, so there is a clear precedence here. Trying to establish the relationship between different manifestations of the same music can be much more tricky. Is the *Clockwork Orange* version of Beethoven's *Ninth Symphony* really a version, or is it a new thing entirely? Or, when we listen to Charles Ives' *Concord Sonata*, or a disco version, or even a graphic representation "xxx—," is it really Beethoven's *Fifth Symphony* that is coming to mind, or simply a mental marker, an emblem, that we have ascribed to that piece? Are the abstract dots of a score acceptably the same thing as the sonic outcome? Prototype theory allows us to say that, within a certain statistical framework, the abstract patterns immanent in a score, or a performance, or a disco version, or an embellishment, or a Portsmouth Sinfonia–type incompetent performance, can be identified as being manifestations of the same piece of music.

So time travel does not have be a precise replaying of a stretch of bound time. A statistical resemblance will still bind the time, but less tightly. "Ah, ah, ah, uuuuuh," associates to the right mental marker but barely binds the time at all.

Memory

Memories can be many things but one thing they definitely are not is recordings of the past replayed in our heads. This is one of the painful truisms of our times. Memories exist solely in the present, and are the current manifestations of past traces that are constantly being modified as we revisit, reinterpret, and re-remember them. My personal experience is that, if I have not revisited a memory in a very long time, when it is unexpectedly prompted, it has a vague, out-of-focus quality, as if the resolution has degraded—because it has not been amplified by repetition. On the other hand, every time I revisit a memory I supply it with a new perspective (I have of course changed since last remembering) and amplify it by "rewriting." So that next time I revisit that memory it will have a changed "feel," a renewed quality—but an increased imprecision. In this way we constantly revise our memories and edit our personal histories.

Over time any memory is likely to become corrupt (in the data sense). As a regular insomniac, I have a sleep-inducing exercise: I listen, entirely in my head, to an existing work such as a Schubert sonata (sometimes, to really tire myself, I try to remember a piece of my own music note for note). This may even be a work I can play, and I have a muscular memory that accompanies the musical memory. But my recollection can be faulty, and over time I unknowingly incorporate minor alterations into my memory of the music, including my muscular memory. It can be a shock when I get out the score and play the work through at the piano only to discover that I've reinvented some of the music in memory.

Every time we re-encounter a piece of music that we are already familiar with, then, we "write over" our prior memory of that piece. We rebind the time, and when we revisit the memory we experience the re-bound (or re-re-bound, or re-re-re-bound) version. Each subsequent version may have a totally different emotional marker—and, possibly, different content.

So, sadly, I have to conclude that memory is not a form of time travel. Time travel is always an external phenomenon.

Forgetting

Memory, then, is an unreliable tool. Committing a chunk of bound time, a time capsule, to memory requires what Gregory Bateson called Collateral Energy. The more tightly bound the time capsule, the more energy is required, and the more difficult the trace is to internalize. Loosely bound musics are easily retained in memory, where tightly bound musics are increasingly hard. However, one could argue that this is in inverse proportion to the rewards from doing so. Tightly bound music has to be re-absorbed over and over again in order to maximize the resolution of the internal image, each time providing some intriguing addition of detail either forgotten or previously missed. Loosely bound information we absorb easily, retain easily … and degradation of memory is not important, it does not materially alter the character of the mental trace. Little is lost, but also little is gained.

Even so, we seem to be becoming increasingly lazy listeners. We obsessively re-listen to tribally mandated loosely bound music, while increasingly avoiding—and even disdaining—more enriching tightly bound musics. There is even a tendency to disparage the most tightly bound musics as somehow unnatural. Collateral Energy seems to be in short supply. Familiarity has replaced curiosity, reinforcement has supplanted questioning. And not just in music.

If we do not invest in experiencing tightly bound musics, we risk losing the skill. A vicious circle prevails whereby, by being unskilled at dealing with such sounds, we decrease their presence in our listening routines, thus making our skills even more rusty, and increasing the necessary effort when (eventually, if) we do make the attempt.

To lose the skill is not just to have increasingly hazy memories of more-complex music, and eventually none. It is to lose access to more than a thousand years of accumulated musical knowledge (information-richness).

Thus we, by small steps, impoverish ourselves and our imaginations.

CHAPTER 10

LITTLE STEPS

DAVE DOUGLAS

Booker Little was a trumpeter who played with and wrote for some of the strongest voices of his day, among them Eric Dolphy, Max Roach, Julian Priester, Reggie Workman, and Don Friedman. His music pioneered a way of writing for a small improvising group that, while uncommon and perhaps revolutionary for the time, was clearly an evolution from prevailing practice in harmony, melody, rhythm, and timbre. The 1961 sextet recordings *Out Front* and *Victory and Sorrow* (also known as *Booker Little and Friend)* represent some of Little's most emotionally powerful work. The pieces are additionally poignant because Little was living in great pain. He suffered from uremia, a rare (now treatable) blood disease that killed him a month after the final session, at the age of twenty-three.

This essay addresses a small but potent detail in that sextet music: Little often used the interval of a half step within his voicings, and the interval created a complex and sometimes ambiguous chordal harmony that pervades his work. Picking out this small detail had enormous impact on me, and it is an idea that continues to inform my own work. Below are some examples of this from Booker Little's music, a few ideas about ways it can work, and several examples of how I have used the idea in my own work.

There are many other beautiful things to hear in Booker Little's music! It is rich in emotional depth and expression, it has a broad tonal palette, and the players display many feats of technical mastery. There is also much novelty and ingenuity in the arranging, and the unusual forms of these pieces often have a lot to do with their expressive quality. It seems almost absurd to focus on one tiny intervallic idea in isolation, but I believe this practice was the kernel for much of this music's unique power and I hope the reader will bear with me and find something of practical value.

With *Man of Words* (Figure 1), Little uses a recurrent set of half steps to define the composition.

Figure 1. Booker Little, *Man of Words.*

The half steps are between the minor third and major ninth of the chords. This is the classic use of this interval in Little's music. The soloist, Little on trumpet, freely improvises over the repeating figure. This was a rare and radical concept of form in 1960, using extreme simplicity to create emotional complexity. The tension of the half step has a lot to do with that.

Quiet, Please (Figure 2) uses the half step to create the tension of a somewhat ambiguous harmony. Each successive half step has a different relationship to the root and chord.

Figure 2. Booker Little, *Quiet, Please.*

Forward Flight (Figure 3) uses several layers.

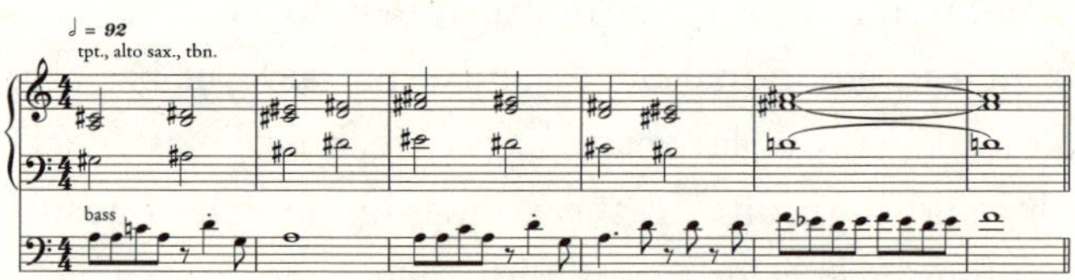

Figure 3. Booker Little, *Forward Flight.*

Half steps here represent movement against the prevailing harmony, creating tension and forward motion. The bass line clearly spells A minor, but the first chord in the horns rings out A major. With parallel structures Little moves further away from the root, creating a polytonal framework that is reflected in the development of the piece.

The interval can be put to wide expressive use, especially in small-group improvising situations. Little uses the interval most often between two horn players, trumpet, trombone, and/or saxophone. But the approach also has value in other instruments, such as guitar, vibes, piano and bass. Little almost always uses half steps within an octave and a half range (Figure 4):

Figure 4. Common range of Booker Little's harmonic use of half steps.

Below this range the half step is too muddy and seems to lose its harmonic effect. Above this range the effect is more strident and sharp, no longer carrying the effect of harmony. Below (Figure 5) are two situations where the half step works.

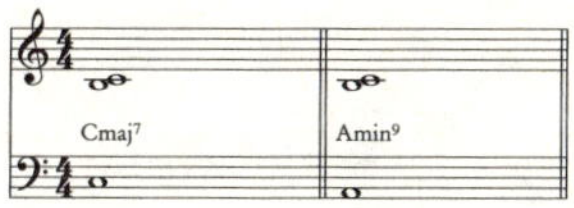

Figure 5.

In some cases the spelling of the chord can be interpreted in multiple ways (Figures 6, 7, 8, 9, 10, 11). The ambiguity of not knowing is often more powerful than a full iteration.

Figure 6.

Figure 7.

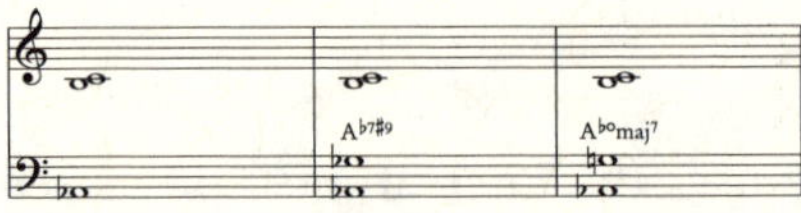

Figure 8.

Figure 9.

Figure 10.

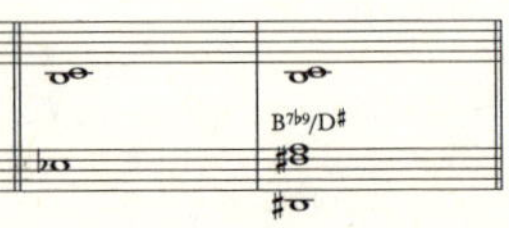

Figure 11.

In the case of Figure 11 there are numerous other potential ways of hearing the intervals. In my own writing for the recording *In Our Lifetime*, recorded in 1994 and dedicated to Little, I used the idea in various ways. In *Sappho* (Figure 12) the half steps are explicit, and intentionally ambiguous as to their harmonic references. In direct reference to Little's *Man of Words*, there is one soloist interacting with the half step material. In this case the material is played once.

Figure 12. Dave Douglas, *Sappho.*

In *Persistence of Memory* (Figure 13) the half-steps in the inner voices evoke the bittersweet qualities found in many of Little's compositions.

Figure 13. Dave Douglas, *Persistence of Memory.*

In *Three Little Monsters* (Figure 14) the half steps come at the end of the phrase between the horn chords and the bass. Close voicings descend to an expected resolution, only to be met with a more dissonant half-step relationship with the bass.

Figure 14. Dave Douglas, *Three little Monsters.*

Sometimes little things make a big difference. It seems to me that the possibilities for application of an idea like this are basically limitless. This small detail in Booker Little's work is a continuing source of fascination and wonder.

CHAPTER
11

FOR AND AGAINST TECHNIQUE

TREVOR DUNN

I really think it's important to be in a situation, both in art and in life, where you don't understand what's going on. —John Cage

Here at the dawn of the 21st century the idea of being an "eclectic" musician is old news. Fusions of all kinds, genre-shifting, and layering have been with us, at this point, far too long to calculate. Today, as a member of the audience, I'm not sure I could even hold a conversation with someone who hasn't spent quality time listening to Slayer *and* Webern *and* Mingus. It is hard to believe there are actually people who don't appreciate The Swans *and* Jo Stafford. As a professional musician I am expected to reference nearly any style conceivable, whether that means appropriating a "latin feel," differentiating between grind-core and speed metal, or knowing the changes to *Stella*. This, of course, is mostly my own fault; for two reasons: firstly, as a member of the audience, I am drawn to different styles (and this seems quite common among the musicians that I know) and so I've always been voracious, ready to consume and eager to learn or accept any gig; secondly, as a professional musician, I chose bass.

It is one thing to be lucky enough to have chosen an instrument that is constantly in demand and utilized endlessly. But it is most certainly impossible to become a virtuoso of *all* the genres that these demands lead one toward. The variety of techniques, feels, and musical languages in which one would need to be fluent in order to approach the diversity of one's record collection is overwhelming. In other words, the tastes of the 21st-century eclectic musician have far succeeded his proficiencies. Today, as important as any physical or creative skill are the abilities to adapt, interpret, and compromise.

Even before deciding on bass, The Beach Boys were a favorite pastime. Several of their records include the great Carol Kaye on bass. Later, a teacher would hand me a few volumes of Kaye's method book *Electric Bass Lines*, which featured exercises in "all rock styles" and examples of "booga-loo," "motown," and "shuffle-boogie." On my own I found Cheap Trick, with Tom Petersson's strange, wide-frequency tone made possible by eight- and twelve-string basses. It was through Rush and Geddy Lee that I learned how to play in 7/8 and through Led Zeppelin that I was introduced to the hemiola that I would later recognize in Stravinsky. In my parents record collection: Nancy Wilson, Thelonious Monk, Willie Nelson, Elvis, and Miles Davis' *Nefertiti* and *Sketches of Spain*. A second private teacher made me tapes of Sly and the Family Stone, with bass players Bobby Vega and Rusty Allen. And through college radio and peers in high school I discovered X, C.O.C., D.R.I, Venom, Exodus, Oingo Boingo, Stump, Die Kruezen, and Bad Manners.

(Initially I used a pick and later abandoned it completely for finger-plucking à la James Jamerson and Francis Rocco Prestia and thumb-slapping à la Larry Graham and Stanley Clarke. Still later I rediscovered the beauty of a plastic plectrum on flat-wound strings for that Owen Bradley sound, or on round-wound nickel strings for anything in the metal genre. I have since developed a way of storing a pick under my third and fourth fingers while I pluck with my first and second, just in case I need the pick in the middle of a riff.)

Then, entering my last year of high school, a teacher suggested I play the upright bass in symphonic band, and it wasn't long before I was hearing *The Rite of Spring*, Poulenc's *Organ Concerto*, and the works of Persichetti. In fact, I distinctly remember pilfering a Persichetti bass figure for my own death-metal piece I was working on at home. In the meantime, like all worshippers of Jaco Pastorius, I started learning Charlie Parker tunes. I also picked up a book called *Harmonics for Electric Bass*, by Adam Novick, which is a veritable bible of possibly the first extended technique.

I had been playing electric bass for about four years and thought nothing much of adding upright to my pallet. It's a bass after all, I thought. How little I understood. With no future in sight, college called. A bow, rosin, and two volumes of Simandl's *New Method for the Double Bass* were immediately jammed under my arm. I'll never forget my first lesson and the shame I brought on to myself by attempting a major scale with *electric* bass fingerings! One may laugh, but herein lies the crux of many problems to come. Certainly there is no glory in sounding off my open-mindedness as if to prove how versed I may be in diverse musics. I'm not here to win the blind-jukebox award. On the contrary, this brief history serves to show how utterly confused I have become. For in the moment of my flawed modal passage, a world of innocence came crashing to a painful end. It is here that I realized how completely distinct upright and electric basses are; how diverse the techniques; how obvious but so obscure the fact that for an electric bass *guitar* player, the world of the contrabass *violin* was indeed eclectic (see Figures 1 and 2).

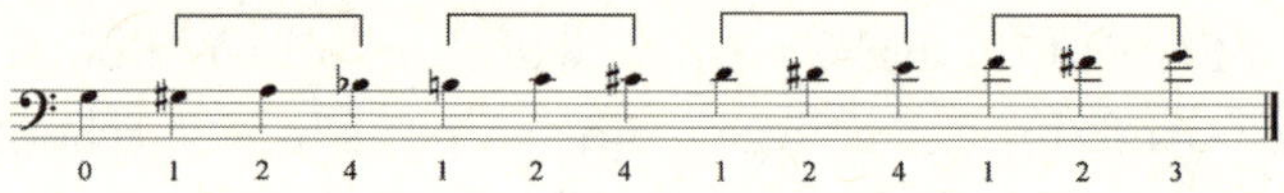

Figure 1. Chromatic scale for contrabass: typical fingerings/shifts (four positions).

Figure 2. Chromatic scale for electric bass: typical fingerings/shifts (three positions).

That didn't stop me; not with the help of professors turning me on to Harry Partch, Xenakis, Ligeti, Schnittke, and Peter Maxwell Davies' *Eight Songs for a Mad King*. I was starting to go mad. I took piano lessons, composition lessons; I joined not only the Big Band but also the Orchestra. Extracurricular activities: cutting my teeth in a bebop quartet, playing in a bar band, and starting an avant-rock group. When would I possibly have time to practice bass? Somehow, I found time. I picked up *A Contemporary Concept of Bowing Technique for the Double Bass* by Fredrick Zimmermann, *Simplified Higher Technique*, by Francesco Petracchi, *The Evolving Bassist*, by Rufus Reid, Simandl's *Gradus Ad Parnassum*, and methods by Francois Rabbath. I was additionally encouraged to read through anything I could get my hands on, so I looked into *The Artist's Technique of Violin Playing*, by D.C Dounis, atonal saxophone études by Siegried Karg-Elert, and unlimited transcriptions of cello music, including the Bach solo suites. (Studying music that is non-idiomatic to one's instrument is an excellent way to break out of monotonous routine and traditionally encouraged habits. Not to mention it strengthens one's sense of orchestration.)

Then I made my next mistake. Influenced by both the traditional range of bass in classical music, that of a low C, and the drop-C♯ tuning of the Melvins, I decided I had to have a five-string electric bass, an instrument that was emerging at that time. Again, I thought the transition would be simple. Ultimately, I reasoned, the low B-string simply adds a mere five additional notes to a typical bass tuned with a low E, those being B, C, C♯, D, and E♭. But I *had* to have those notes, and the manner of loosening a string well beyond its engineered tension was meeting its limits. Yet, how disturbing it is to find that your lowest string is no longer an E and how debilitating to the muscle-memory to find the entire physical plane of the finger board shifted. Remembering an interview with Jaco Pastorius, I began looking at *113 Studies for Cello Solo by Dotzauer*, which pair nicely with five-string electric due to cello notation. Another book that translates somewhat well to electric bass is Eddie Harris' *Intervallistic Concept*. And then I discovered another positive side to five-string technique. Because of lower notes now available in higher positions, I could reduce the amount of shifts in any given scale. (Compare Figures 3 and 4.)

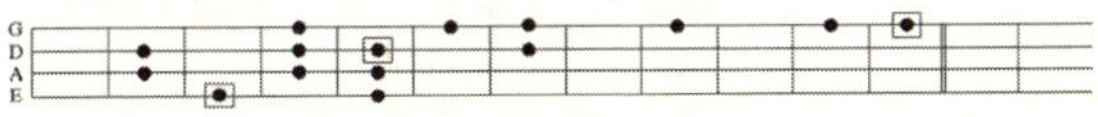

Figure 3. G Lydian scale in three positions for four-string bass.

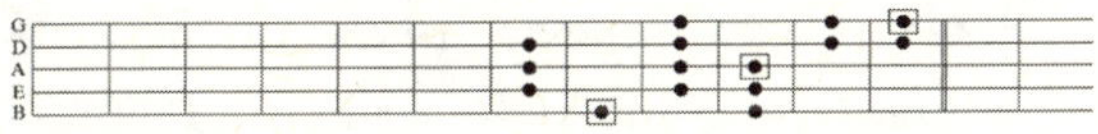

Figure 4. G Lydian scale in two positions for five-string bass.

This led to a re-examination of every scale I had ever learned and considerations of the most efficient way to adapt them from four-string to five-string. This, of course, has nothing to do with classical technique on the contrabass. In fact—and this is part of my point—nearly all of the books discussed (unless by the same author), and nearly all of the techniques employed are pretty much incompatible. That is, they are all unique to themselves, developed by individuals and mastered only by those sufficiently loyal and committed. It is obvious enough that exercises for alternate picking on electric bass and those for spiccato bowing for upright are not translatable, or that the left-hand patterns have little in common. Equally obvious are physical differences: the horizontal position of the electric's neck versus the vertical neck of the upright; the pizzicato fingers parallel to the upright strings but perpendicular to the electric; the inward curve of the right-hand thumb on the frog of the bow versus the straight supportive position against the pick-up on electric; the vast difference in the spacing between notes on the fingerboard. But even with one instrument there exist discrepancies in approach. Indeed, feuding schools of thought are legendary in bass history dating back hundreds of years. What we are left with is a melting pot that is to be decoded by the student. Ultimately, one must sift through all the dogma to find what works for one's body. This is not an easy task. It is a life-long journey deciphering what one or more teachers assign, weighing it against personal aesthetics and putting it to the test of what one's hands are ultimately capable of. Regardless of "schools," one is almost certain to wind up self-taught.

I say disparate techniques are "incompatible," but that is not entirely true. In recent years traditional upright fingerings have been annexed with borrowed electric patterns (see Figure 5).

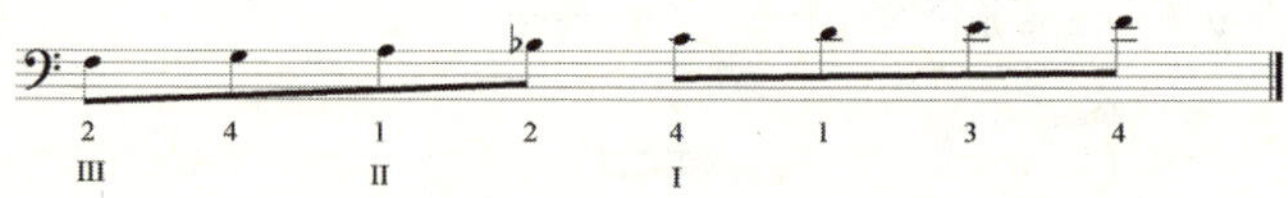

Figure 5. F-major scale for contrabass utilizing electric bass fingering (one position) beginning on the A-string.

Thomas B. Gale calls this the open-hand or "four finger" technique used in higher positions (also compare fingerings in Figures 1 and 2). With students of the electric bass I teach the four-finger position as a constant. Up and down the neck it is the most efficient way to get around the instrument. In my own playing, however, I noticed that, especially in live performances, the tendency to throw caution to the wind results in compromised technique. How many electric bass players actually retain this four-finger rigidity in the lower positions? In the heat of the moment I often find myself resorting to upright fingering, i.e., 1-2-4, reducing my left-hand range to a three-finger position. This occurs only as the music allows, but this type of relaxed technique is, as its name implies, a symptom of and a means to relaxation. I will continue to stress the value of the traditional fundamentals of a disciplined practice: long tones, shifting exercises, scales, arpeggios—slow, boring, tedious work. But I will also forego anything developed for what is intuitive as long as it works, and as we know, what "works" is nothing less than subjective. The point of technique, after all, is utter control over one's instrument so as to have no obstacles that might hinder expression. With enough concentration, microscopic analysis, and intent—repeated hourly, daily, year after year—one begins to find that in the heat of the moment muscle memory prevails, the body acts independent of the mind, ideas are realized.

I have also been fortunate enough to play with and learn from mavericks who never studied any kind of "proper" technique. Self-taught, self-studied, and often reacting *against* tradition, these musicians developed highly personal languages that exclude almost everyone. It is clear that their creative output could have existed no other way. Perhaps coming from a place even beyond music their inimitable verbiage challenges many preconceived definitions.

This is to say nothing of extended technique. Pioneers like Bertram Turetzky with his lexicon *The Contemporary Contrabass* and the master innovator Mark Dresser (see *Arcana*, vol. one) have championed an array of ultra-modern techniques that would turn Botessini's stomach. Well beyond the realm of tradition, some of these are legitimized bad techniques of yore. And so now I am to consider practicing what, for years, I tried to avoid. For me, the ultimate lesson is that any sound is containable. It can be studied, formalized, and reproduced at will. That, too, seems obvious. The mystery, then, is where will I find the time to conquer every tempo, every altered scale, every bowing articulation? Do I play behind the beat or on top of it? Sul tasto or ponticello? How much time can I allow to warm up before the gig? Should I eat before the gig? Have I adjusted my strap length correctly to accommodate the angle of my arm depending on the style of music? If I play a third below the root, will anyone care? Do I interrupt my practicing because I had an idea about a composition? Do I need to buy new picks? Have my bow re-haired? Should I play with my third finger since there is a blister on my second? Do I lay out or take a solo? Am I out of tune, and is that a bad thing? Should I play this middle C on the G, D, or A string? Can I simulate an arco tone with a distortion pedal and a volume knob? When are earplugs a hindrance? Is this playable?

And what are these physical differences doing to my body? How does this wavering between relative techniques affect my tendons, calluses, joints, and muscles? I know that after touring for six weeks with an electric bass my upright chops are completely shot. If I have the misguidance of booking myself a gig on upright, the day after I get home from such a tour it only takes about thirty minutes to destroy my right hand, leaving it wrought with blood blisters. Ideally I prefer three or four days to reacquaint myself, playing as slowly and controlled as possible. How sad and awkward the first day always feels. Vice versa, after focusing on my bowing and then jumping into cut-and-paste-metal rehearsals on electric, I instantly become aware of neglected muscles and reduced stamina. It's almost as if there are two physical planes to my being. One must step aside for the other, and this transition is always heartbreaking.

Christal Phelps Steele, Associate Concertmaster of the Indianapolis Orchestra, states, "In our business, there is much to learn about ergonomics, posture, muscle balance, back pain and overuse injuries. We are often left to figure out these occupational factors on our own. We have no team doctor or athletic trainer, specialized health professionals that professional athletes take for granted."*

But as sure as there is balance, there are positive repercussions. While one set of muscles and calluses is in demand, the other has a chance to recuperate. If I am lucky, my chances of acquiring repetitive motion disorder, tendonitis, or carpal tunnel have been reduced. More important is the mental stimulation, the spice of variety, as it were. The questions of which instrument or which style of music is preferred are unanswerable. I enjoy music that is barely audible and I enjoy music that makes my ears ring and I would go crazy if I had to focus on one or the other. And what a collection of people I have been introduced to! Music has taken me to strange and wonderful places, and I am sure that many of the social microcosms I have traversed will never cross each other's paths. I have become privy to more ideology than I care to absorb, but piece by piece, I absorb, react, reject, and accept. If there is one thing I hope to retain, it is curiosity. It is easy in this day and age, with worries of income, the drudgery of business, and the pain of excessive travel, to forget why one became interested in music in the first place. Despite any misgivings, as a musician in the 21st century I would be hard-pressed to ever find myself bored. The appetite I have been awarded and the unreasonable goals I have set are enough to remind me why I chose music, and that cannot be put into words.

* From the article "A Sporting Chance: An Athletic Trainer Saves a Violinist's Career", by Christal Phelps Steele. Published in *International Musician*, February 2007, p 13.

CHAPTER 12

PROCESS AND TIMBRAL TRANSFORMATION IN *16*

JASON ECKARDT

Much of my work is preoccupied with transformational processes. These processes facilitate gradual changes in various musical dimensions (such as pitch, rhythm, register, density, and amplitude) and also mark large-scale formal boundaries at their points of initiation and termination. This essay details the processes of timbral transformation in the first half of my composition *16*, scored for amplified flute, violin, viola, and 'cello.

The overall process of this opening section transforms unpitched sounds to sounds with pitch. When I began composing *16*, I mapped out the gradations between these extremes on three continua for vocal sounds, flute sounds, and string-instrument sounds. While movement across these continua as the processes unfold is not strictly sequential, certain areas within them denote subsections in the macrodesign of the section.

While compiling these timbral resources, it soon became clear to me that there were great disparities between the sounds' amplitude levels. Rather than limit myself to thinner textures or the simultaneous presentations of sounds with similar potential amplitude levels, I chose to electronically amplify all of the instruments. Because of the constant and kaleidoscopic shifting of textures, timbres, and amplitude levels that I imagined, simply adjusting the electronic amplification of individual instruments to fixed levels would not suffice. Instead, I decided that a technician would follow the score and adjust the amplification levels according to the notated dynamic markings. This solution allows for various timbral combinations impossible in a purely acoustic environment to be adequately projected in live performance.

Flute Timbres and Processes

Because traditional flute playing requires an embouchure in which the mouth is not completely affixed to the instrument, the vocal mechanism of the performer can be used in ways not possible on many other woodwinds. This vocal flexibility encouraged me to explore the flute's possibilities for alternate methods of sound production. The process that opens *16* involves the transition from vocalizations to traditionally produced flute tones.

The vocalizations are notated using the International Phonetic Alphabet. The IPA allowed great precision in communicating my musical intentions and also suggested vocal possibilities during composition. In *16*, the IPA phonemes are notated on a separate staff on which either the three middle lines of a percussion-clef staff denote approximate high, medium, and low articulations of unpitched phonemes (with "x" noteheads), or a traditional, five-line G-clef staff notates pitched phonemes (with standard noteheads).

The phonemes are divided into three categories: unpitched consonants, pitched consonants, and vowels. The phonemes are introduced into *16* in this order to reinforce the section's overall transformation from unpitched to pitched music. Throughout this process, additional timbral manipulations add variety: inhaled and exhaled vocalizations, glissandi between unpitched and pitched phonemes, and sprechstimme and sung phonemes.

While the transformation of phonemes progresses, a simultaneous, interwoven process is introduced using sounds produced directly on the flute. This process involves pitched, percussive flute sounds (key clicks, tongue rams, and lip pizzicati) changing into timbrally modified "traditional" flute tones (overly breathy pitches produced using an open embouchure, pitches with excessive vibrato, flutter-tongued pitches, pitches produced using alternate fingerings which distort their timbre and subtly affect their intonation, and multiphonics).

The flutist's embouchure position itself provides several timbral possibilities. Although the flutist vocalizes exclusively on unpitched phonemes as the piece begins, the flute is held in normal playing position, with no keys depressed. The residual noise of the breath passing over the blow hole produces a faint pitch (C♯4 on the B-key flute, the instrument *16* requires). This pitch is not part of the work's harmonic structure but rather a timbral component produced by the vocalizations. Unless otherwise instructed, the flutist is required to keep the instrument in playing position whenever phonemes are used. Therefore, there is always a sense of the flute being timbrally present, even if it is not immediately apparent. This subtle interaction between the flute and voice was the reason I chose to limit the vocalizations to only the flutist.

KEY TO NOTATIONAL SYMBOLS

FLUTE

- key click
- breathy pitch
- lip pizzicato
- tongue ram (sounding pitch)
- **s.v., m.v.** senza vibrato molto vibrato
- Normal playing position and blow hole covered by mouth with lips sealed around the blow hole.

STRINGS

- thumb slap
- thrown bow
- snap pizzicato
- **c.l.b.** col legno battuto
- **b.pc.** body percussion

Body percussion striking surfaces:

1. Back of instrument, near edge of rear belly, bridge side.
2. Back of instrument, between edge and middle of rear belly, bridge side.
3. Back of instrument, middle of rear belly.
4. Back of instrument, between edge and middle of rear belly, neck side.
5. Back of instrument, near edge of rear belly, neck side.
6. Back of neck.
7. On tailpiece.
8. Front of instrument, between edge and f hole.
9. Front of instrument, between edge and middle, neck side.
10. Rib, near rear.
11. Rib, near neck.

String Instrument Timbres and Processes

As with the voice and flute, the timbral transformation of the string-instrument music is plotted from unpitched to pitched sounds on a continuum. Since the voice's and flute's processes are intertwined, I decided that a similar procedural polyphony would be appropriate for the string instruments. I derived two subcontinua: one for sounds articulated on the strings and one for sounds produced using other parts of the instruments.

For unpitched, non-string sounds, the methods of sound production were divided into two categories: striking objects and striking surfaces. The former are limited to the musicians' hands (fingers, thumbs, fingernails, and knuckles). Striking surfaces are assigned to eleven areas of the string instruments, notated on a five-line percussion clef, using "x" noteheads:

1. Back of instrument, near edge of rear belly, bridge side.
2. Back of instrument, between edge and middle of rear belly, bridge side.
3. Back of instrument, middle of rear belly.
4. Back of instrument, between edge and middle of rear belly, neck side.
5. Back of instrument, near edge of rear belly, neck side.
6. Back of neck.
7. On tailpiece.
8. Front of instrument, between edge and f hole.
9. Front of instrument, between edge and middle, neck side.
10. Rib, near rear.
11. Rib, near neck.

Different combinations of striking object and striking surface provide variety in the qualities of timbre and attack onset and decay. In passages requiring these techniques, the performer is instructed to lightly mute the strings with the hand in order to prevent any pitched sounds emerging from sympathetic string vibrations.

I divided the string sounds into two categories: percussive and sustained. Percussive sounds include pizzicato (normal and "snap" versions), "thrown" bow whereby the bow is forcefully thrown onto the string to produce an indeterminate number of rebounds, col legno battuto, and a thumb slap similar to the technique used in funk electric-bass performance. Sustained sounds involve bowed strings muted with the left hand to produce a grainy, unpitched sound; bowing on the bridge; three degrees of increasing bow pressure that progressively distort the tone; bow position relative to the bridge and fingerboard of the instrument; col legno tratto bowing; ½ col legno tratto bowing (half wood and half hair drawn across the string); and natural and artificial harmonics.

Beginning with myriad forms of unpitched, non-string percussive sounds, the string instruments slowly progress to pitched sounds, beginning with pizzicati, then moving to thumb slap notes, thrown bows, and col legno battuto, before introducing the sustained string sounds which come to dominate the string-instrument texture.

The simultaneous presentations of the three processes (voice, flute, and string instruments) are not coordinated. Although all reach their completion at the same point—a point that also marks a large-scale formal boundary—they begin at different times and progress at independent rates. This structural counterpoint provides yet another polyphonic layer to those presented in other musical dimensions. Although the music in the first section is embedded with several intertwined processes, it moves toward its culmination as a coherent whole, with the individual strands clearly defined by their particular set of constraints.

I did not attempt to be exhaustive in my exploration of new timbral resources in the opening half of *16.* While there are other nontraditional string and flute sounds that appear later in the work, I omitted some relatively well-known extended techniques for artistic and sometimes practical reasons. For me, composing music is not an opportunity simply to compile lists or dazzle listeners with some exotic new sound. The challenge lies in confronting the compositional and instrumental possibilities and rendering them in an integral—not merely decorative—way.

CHAPTER 13

MORE FUN THAN CAPITALISM

Me and WB in Nerdy-Sexy-Commie-Girlieland

JEWLIA EISENBERG

Intro to Work

My work explores the intersection of text and the sounding body: lovely noise, complex ideas, and the particular emotional, erotic, and spiritual terrains that the voice can traverse. I explore the interplay of verbal and non-verbal languages and look for possible sites of translation.

A lot of my work has to do with these sites of translation as hubs of diaspora consciousness: vocal/text play as a diaspora home, a home without nation or land. I write/sing as an individual voice within a context of multiplicity—of musical sources, of authors, and of languages. So my music lives where Jewish and African diasporas collide, incorporating piyyutim and Pygmy counterpoint, doo-wop and niggunim, work songs and Torah chanting. The palette is drawn from the female body, including singing voices, beatbox, heartbeats and handclaps, sexbreath and silence. I'm interested in how the resulting music works to cross the membranous boundaries between people separated by space and time. The goal is not to blend every voice to the point of erasure, but rather to create a dialogic, multi-faceted whole—where differences can be transcended yet particularity is maintained.

There are different ways of evoking webs of connectivity and interaction that are heymish, different ways to create the non-spatial home. I do it with Walter Benjamin. WB was a philosopher, critic, urban observer, and nerd. He is known for his singular explorations of Marxism, theology, cities, fetishes, literature, hash, dreams, and performance art. In this piece, I'll be focusing on some of his ideas and frames that I find useful in my work. Most of the quotes and ideas below are from his fragmented, inspiring, unfinished work, the *Arcades Project*. I highly recommend it for a good time.

Porosity

In their essay on Naples, WB and red-diaper hottie Asja Lacis note the city's porous membranes of public and private, now and past, work and play, political and festive, personal and communal. This creates a space of anarchy and intermingling, so that "No form is so and not otherwise." Porosity shapes and disseminates creative culture. Susan Buck-Morss observes that the M.O. of the Naples essay—the integration of history, observed urban form, and personal experience—shapes the M.O. of the *Arcades Project*, and, in turn, my own work.

Montage/Layering

Montage serves a radical function for WB, blasting us out of the past to "make actual" the present. Montage reconstructs the way we experience the world—multi-sensate, not linear. Chopped up bits of images—and, I would argue, sound—affect us beneath the radar, where our conscious and unconscious are interwoven. We tune into patterns and similarities between two different things placed next to each other: a kitchen knife beside an eye, a Galician codex beside a work song. The ensuing shock of recognition is transformative, awakening, and can slam us intuitively into revolutionary consciousness or "Now-Time."

WB uses montage and layering in his *Arcades Project* and in his radio shows for kids. These have a pedagogic function but are anti-authoritarian—not teachy or preachy. They are filled with historical anecdotes, fun facts, fairy stories, and biographies, with room to be critical.

History and Tradition

"The same threat hangs over both the content of tradition and its receivers—that of becoming a tool of the ruling classes. In every era, the attempt must be made to wrest tradition away from the conformism that is about to overpower it."

History according to WB is hellish, brutal, cyclical barbarism. But it is possible to move from history time to messiah time with revolutionary action. "There is not one moment that does not bring its own revolutionary possibility." We can use traditional symbols to shatter tradition, revere the past in order to break from it. This is what's happening when I take the niggun for *Tzur Yisrael*, explode it, and use the fragments to build *Fortress*

Moscow. The symbols take a new shape, both personal and urgent. As with montage, the shock of tradition/revolution placed together can "awaken the powers of history," bringing us to the Now-Time. We all know that the present can transform the reading of past texts, but for WB, that transformative process is some combination of redemption and prophesy. As we shake up the old, we build a "tradition of new starts"—a nonauthoritarian system of cultural and text inheritance which births radical action.

Art

Making him the darling of lefty artists everywhere, WB argues that art can have a political effect and yet not be boring. He's not a cultural pessimist like Adorno—he doesn't think all art has to suck in the U.S. And WB's not just talking about hoch-kultur stuff, but also popular forms—mass culture not just as a font of false consciousness, but as a source of energy to overcome it. He exults in art that pushes between representation and reality, Brecht being a favored example. Though not framed as such, I read his "flaneur" character as being instructive for artists. The flaneur can be a wanderer, an observer, a socially rebellious bohemian. Or a sell-out—a flaneur can turn around and market flanerie to hipsters.

Because I work at the intersection of voice and text, I particularly dig WB's discussion of mimesis as a basis of a theory of language. I'm interested in the way he ties together lasting correspondences between magic, play, mimesis, and speech. Through use of the mimetic faculty, art can rock people out of the commodity-infused dream state where we usually live. Most of the time, people relate to each other on a dream level—they are unconscious, distracted. This dream level is shared, but not felt as social solidarity. Rather it contains infinitely produced individual experience via commodity fetishism—your iPod playlists, personalized ringtones, and customized sneakers. But art based in mimesis can reconstruct the capacity for collective experience. It can provide patterns of similarity that shock us awake, and it reconnects imagination to action. And that's why Meredith Monk is radical, man!

WB and Trilectic

To sum up my yikhes from WB: My music is porous and non-linear, making use of mimesis and montage. It is engaged with politics but also charged with spirituality. I get my hands on tradition to use it and shake it up. I am more interested in simultaneous fields of opposition that bounce off each other than in traditional dialectical relationships. Because this stuff is often hard to explain, I often just describe my music as Nerdy-Sexy-Commie-Girlie.

These ideas inform all of my work, but are explored most explicitly on my album *Trilectic*, which deals with the political/erotic connection of WB and Asja Lacis. Asja was a Bolshevik firebrand and an agitprop queen, most famous for her role as WB's radical muse. The heart of *Trilectic* is a setting of WB's *Moscow Diary* and of Asja's autobiography, *Professional Revolutionary*.

In *Trilectic*, I delve into ideas of porosity, mimesis, authenticity, and translation. Questions generated by *Trilectic* include: Can the idea of porosity be applied to the boundaries between people and texts over place and time? How does my private life interact with those of Asja and WB in the public space of a song cycle? What is the new site formed? With its use of mimesis, does this work serve a ritual function? Can there be an authenticity within montage? How does music shapes the afterlife of a text—how does it affect the reproduction of meaning? Does music change words in the same way a translation changes even the language into which one is translating? How can I give musical voice to the nonverbal languages—visual, spatial, emotional, or gestural—found in cities, or bodies?

With all these questions, both personal and theoretical, this became an album rich in dialectical relationships. *Trilectic* is situated between memory and experience, allegorical and crude thinking, Marxism and Jewish mysticism, historical moments and physical sites that contain both regressive and utopian possibility, in a place where past and future collide to blast open history into Now-Time.

Bibliography

Theodor Adorno, Walter Benjamin, *The Complete Correspondence*. Ed. Henri Lonitz. Translation by Nicholas Walker. (Cambridge: Harvard University Press, 1999.)

Walter Benjamin, *The Arcades Project*. Ed. Rolf Tidemann. Translation by Howard Eiland and Kevin McLaughlin. (Cambridge: Harvard University Press, 1999.)

Illuminations. Ed. Hannah Arendt. Translation by Harry Zohn. (New York: Schocken Books, 1968.)

Moscow Diary. Ed. Gary Smith. Translation by Richard Sieburth. (Cambridge: Harvard University Press, 1986.)

Reflections. Ed. Peter Demetz. Translation by Edmund Jephcott. (New York: Schocken Books, 1986.)

Understanding Brecht. (London: New Left Books, 1973.)

Susan Buck-Morss, *The Dialectics of Seeing*. (Cambridge: MIT Press, 1989.)

Asja Lacis, *Revolutionär im Beruf*. Ed. Hildegaard Brenner. Unpublished translation by Kristen Kopp, UMissouri. (Munich: Regner & Bernhard, 1971.)

CHAPTER
14

FIDDLING WITH SPUTNIK

How I Wrote *Lost Signals and Drifting Satellites*

ANNIE GOSFIELD

Some compositions embody a single period of a composer's life, and capture the present, shot through with glimmers of the past. I wrote *Lost Signals and Drifting Satellites* for violin and satellite sounds in 2003, and, in the process, considered a lifetime of past experiences, anchored by where I stood musically, technically, and emotionally at that moment.

I was raised in the shadow of 60s counterculture, when music, and the world, were changing. One of the most memorable aspects of my childhood was the flood of unusual sounds that were being produced at the time. As a very small child, I remember my older brother Josh putting his head between two speakers to listen to Steve Reich's seminal tape piece, *Come Out,* his experience enhanced by psychedelics. Another item on the Gosfield household hit parade was *Audio Collage*, a Folkways LP of musique concrète by Henry Jacobs, a legendary friend of the family who introduced my parents to each other in the 1940s. My own discovery of tape manipulation and altered sounds started with a reel-to-reel tape recorder that had been abandoned at my parents' house. The transport was broken, so I used two pencils to rotate the reels, which revealed the sounds of a couple having sex, recorded as a practical joke at a communal farm in Vermont. I quickly learned the ins and outs of manipulating the tape so I could control it to play backward and forward, and I spun the reels at different speeds to alter the pitch and speed of the moans and groans. Being exposed to all kinds of unusual sounds led to a lifelong habit of listening intently to things that weren't music, such as the radio tuned between stations, television static, and white noise, and instilled in my young ears an enduring link between music and noise.

In 2002, George Kentros, an American violinist who lives in Stockholm, proposed that I write him a new work for "violin and something." Up to that point, I had resisted writing pieces for live performers and tape,* reasoning that the format forced musicians to perform with an unbending, unsympathetic partner. In the worst case, the "tape" functioned like a collaborator who always played but never listened. But after many years' experience of working with acoustic and electronic sounds, I liked the idea of being able to combine electronics with a solo acoustic instrument without being dependent on samplers, computer processing, or any other potentially problematic technical issues. Ideally, this could be one of the simplest methods of mixing acoustic and electronic sources, resulting in a piece that could be performed anywhere in the world with just a violinist and a CD boombox, if that's all that was available.

* "Tape" in this case is used as a generic term for any pre-recorded accompaniment to a live instrument, because recorded tracks were originally played back on tape. Accompanying tracks for this type of "tape" piece are now most commonly played back on a CD or computer.

As I considered different approaches, and sifted through my collected sound sources, I found myself drawn once more to the sounds of detuned radios, and to different forms of radio transmissions. During my research, I became interested in the signals transmitted by early satellites, and learned the story of the launch of Sputnik, and how its sudden appearance captivated people all over the world.

In 1957, with the cold war in full swing, the race was on between the U.S. and Soviets to launch the first satellite. 1957 was declared the "The International Geophysical Year," in which sixty-seven countries met to research matters of the Earth, the Sun, and outer space. As part of this program, an international group of scientists adopted a resolution stipulating that satellites would broadcast their transmissions on a frequency of 108 megahertz. Laboratories everywhere prepared their equipment for the first broadcasts from satellites, without knowing which country would win this first chapter of the space race. On October 4, 1957, the Soviets launched Sputnik ("satellite," or "fellow traveler" in Russian), which fascinated and terrified much of the Western world. Sputnik transmitted radio signals on 20.07 Mhz and 40.002 Mhz, instead of the frequency previously agreed upon by the international commission. The Soviets chose a frequency within the ham radio band, which effectively took the satellite transmissions out of the hands of the world's established scientific community and brought them to radio amateurs all over the globe. The Soviets even asked amateur radio operators around the world to record when and where they heard Sputnik's signals. Tracking Sputnik became a nightly event; people set up bulky radio equipment in isolated areas all over the world (free from interference from large cities) to listen to the beep-beep sounds of a transmitter designed to measure the density of the Earth's outer atmosphere. The abstract signals were accompanied by a glimmer in the night sky. Sputnik was barely visible to the naked eye, yet millions watched this distant, twinkling dot as it progressed slowly across the horizon.

While this devoted group of people were listening raptly to the abstract beeps and hisses of satellite transmissions, Pat Boone and Doris Day were at the top of the charts, and popular culture had become more bland than ever. One inspiration for *Lost Signals and Drifting Satellites* was this odd dichotomy: In 1957 the rough energy of rhythm and blues and rock and roll was being cleaned up, commodified, and turned into a wholesome, salable byproduct, yet the otherworldly sounds of satellites drew people everywhere into their orbit. My fascination was to revisit the original odd, noisy, sound sources half a century later, and see what made them stand out from the pabulum of 1950s pop culture. I imagined people listening to Sputnik, interpreting these faraway, abstract satellite sounds in their own way, reading melodies into seemingly random beeps interrupted by white noise and interference, and creating their own relationship with a spinning, basketball-sized hunk of metal that circled the globe for just twenty-three days. This story of man and machine provided a perfect point of departure for a piece for violin, performed by a man, and satellite sounds, generated by a machine.

Working closely with a performer has always been an important part of my compositional process; each new piece reflects my own musical vision, and often reflects the musician's personal history and experience as well. After collecting a library of sounds and developing some basic ideas for the piece, I invited violinist George Kentros to my studio to improvise along with various sound sources. I recorded his interpretations of satellite bleeps, shortwave swoops, and machine sounds. Together we worked on techniques that would mirror and contrast the recordings of manmade sonic flotsam and jetsam. George developed some unusual techniques that produced noisy, shifting harmonics, which were a perfect complement to the sound of radio transmissions drifting in and out of tune. We discussed how to indicate these extended techniques in great detail. In the score, these very specific performance indications (such as "poco a poco sul ponticello, increasing pressure and losing pitch without scratching") are accompanied by looser directions (such as "becoming more noisy, like a radio losing reception"). Every violinist who performs the piece can interpret the directions in his or her own way, and find the melodies and beauty within the noise, just as those watching Sputnik did in 1957.

I always go through a transitional period when starting a new piece, in which I become comfortable within the confines of a new instrumentation. It's a lot like breaking in a new pair of shoes. After writing several pieces for larger ensembles, I was feeling the limitations of composing for solo violin. Because I was writing for just one instrument, I couldn't rely on the dynamic tension that occurs when a group of musicians interact with each other in performance. I was curious about the potential relationship between a single musician and faraway radio signals: Could I create a different type of dynamic tension between abstract sounds and a performer's interpretation of notes on paper? In spite of a few centuries' worth of great solo pieces for the violin, I had to find my own way. Setting this lone, high-pitched instrument against a backdrop of satellite transmissions evoked for me the inherent loneliness of an individual watching the night sky.

My experience as an improviser has led me to explore texture, timbre, and unlikely combinations of sounds when composing. Instead of mapping out a form in advance, then filling in the details, I prefer to take a more improvisational approach when starting a piece, by playing piano or, in this case, imagining the violinist's fingers on the fingerboard. *Lost Signals and Drifting Satellites* posed a new challenge: While I was free to gather all kinds of sound sources, and work with a variety of techniques for the violin, I had to eventually commit to the fixed, recorded component of the accompanying track. This recorded "phantom collaborator" would represent the vast sonic possibilities of the night sky, littered with satellite and shortwave noise. It would also reflect my own experiences and sampling aesthetic, and act as a "virtual Annie": a more portable version of myself, free of the physical burden of a sampler, or the expense of an airline ticket. Performing a virtual duet anywhere in the world became as simple as mailing a score and CD of the recorded electronics to another musician. The recorded component of the piece existed first as an improvisation that I played on a keyboard sampler, designed as a sonic landscape to accompany the violin. As the piece developed, so did the recorded part, and bit by bit I would negotiate between the phantom collaborator and the notated violin part, tweaking, tuning, and altering the electronic sounds (multitracked in ProTools) so that they would contrast and complement the violin without stealing too much of its glory. I modulated the pitch of the satellite sounds, which mirrored the shifts in frequency caused by the Doppler effect that occurred as Sputnik circled the globe. I also included recordings of Vanguard and other satellites, shortwave broadcasts, and a good measure of machine sounds.

Translating the recorded track into a notated part on a score was another challenge. A good deal of the satellite sounds are layered, sustained, and create a bed of finely tuned noise that is metrically forgiving to the violinist. As long as the performer has a general idea of where he or she is in these sections of the piece, it's fine to get a few beats ahead or behind. Crescendos and entrances of new sounds are notated as cues in the score, just as instrumental cues would be, and serve as signposts to the violinist. There are also sections that are more rhythmically demanding, in which the violin interlocks with machine and shortwave sounds. I transcribed the rhythms of the satellites, shortwaves, and machine sounds, so the violinist can follow the score, but every musician hears the patterns in the noise differently, so turning these blips and bleeps into rhythmic patterns on a page always felt a little arbitrary. Writing a piece for violin and tape was becoming surprisingly labor-intensive. In order to demonstrate exactly how the sounds had been carved into beats and measures, I created a practice track for the performer that includes a metronome. The metronome is never used in live performance (it would impose a kind of rhythmic rigor mortis that would not be appropriate to the piece), but it is a very useful guide to navigating the meters and rhythms within the piece. After a few run-throughs with the backing track and metronome, the violinist will recognize the route, at which point the metronome becomes unnecessary. There is also a cadenza, and as the satellite sounds fade into the distance, the violinist has free rein to interpret the music without being tied to the tape.

Lost Signals and Drifting Satellites combines many elements that I have been developing over the years: a combination of acoustic and electronic materials, the use of non-musical sounds, and a collaboration with a specific performer. After a period of shying away from solo pieces, in which I preferred the clamor and din of a crowd of musicians, I warmed up to the idea of writing for just one player. My experience since has led to a series of solo compositions, each written for a specific musician, that incorporate a lexicon of extended techniques that each soloist had developed. The series includes *The Harmony of the Body Machine,* for cellist Joan Jeanrenaud, which couples her incredible technique with machine sounds; and *Marked by a Hat,* for Marco Cappelli and the ten detuned sympathetic strings on his custom-designed "extreme guitar."

Every new composition leaves its mark in a composer's life: not only in the path leading from one piece to the next, but as an entity in which process, melody, harmony, rhythm, and noise band together to take on a life of their own, disguised as notes on paper, digital information, or just some space in a musician's memory. While researching *Lost Signals and Drifting Satellites,* I dug deeper into the history of radio transmissions, which eventually led me to develop an opera inspired by the encoded radio transmissions of the Danish Resistance in World War II. Like every composer, my continuing body of work is informed by what came before it: Should the next composition be more strictly or loosely notated? Will I concentrate on a player's virtuosity, or get down and dirty with noisy racket? The unpredictable trajectory continues, as one short piece for one musician leads to an opera. After years of resisting, I finally wrote a piece for live performer and tape. Now *Lost Signals and Drifting Satellites* can be performed by violinists all over the world; all they need is a violin, a CD player, and an ear to the sky. The static, sputter, and concealed melodies of the satellite transmissions are echoed by the violin, which drifts between extended techniques and traditional writing for the instrument. Like a radio that is gradually losing and gaining reception, the music shifts between two worlds, hovering between notes and noise, and ultimately drifts into faraway static.

Related Discography

Lost Signals and Drifting Satellites, performed by George Kentros, *Lost Signals and Drifting Satellites* (Tzadik, 8007). An audio excerpt can be found at: http://www.anniegosfield.com/signals.html

CHAPTER
15

BOOK OF TONO-RHYTHMOLOGY

MILFORD GRAVES

We are immersed in an evolving period of collision vibrations that requires a network of adaptive processes. Music involves a quality of nonadhesive resolutions that are required to redirect destructive vibrations (frequencies) from exhausting biological motion. The responsibilities and task of the musician should include the following:

1. To know and understand the possible origin and history of total music without cultural limitations. Is music a cognitive process: the energetic pathways that come from the primordial beginning of how we were conceived as human motion factors? These factors can include the inherent qualities of metabolic motion that are integral to biological activity on the subcellular level. Subcellular constituents and events are resonant energies and morphological constructs of cosmological events. Or, is music a derivative of the collective-intellectual process of the institution?

2. To know why you are doing what you do. Are you following or have allegiance to concepts that are deviant to cosmic-biological events of nature? Or, from a mutant process derived from a lack of connection with spiritual energies for creative growth?

It is not prosperous to not know that you do not know, but profess to know. However, it is prosperous to know that you do know.

3. Physiological transduction: The referential here is mechanotransduction and how sound is transported through the hearing system, which, in particular, involves the tympanic membrane, organ of Corti, and the basilar membrane. It is important to have an understanding of the dynamics of ion channel activation and frequency differentiation of incoming sound that occurs in the cochlear complex. This will provide for a synchronicity of what is imported into the hearing system relative to ionic bio-electrical harmony.

To deal with a functional aspect of what has been stated concerning the hearing system, the following should be understood to construct a music that initiates a biological process for greater flow of cellular energy for mind expansion and innovation:

Neuronal activity in the brain will produce a relative magnetic field with induction of hydrogen atoms in the corresponding area with emission of radio signals. Oxygen-rich blood will increase neural activity with a relative increase in a magnetic field. Changes in blood flow-oxygenation is called hemodynamics. Before doing a perusal of the hemodynamic process, it is important to understand a system of thought known as Correlative Thinking. Correlative Thinking (CT) is of Chinese origin. In brief, CT is an analogical process of incorporating the imagination to create image-functional relationships. CT should function as a comparative to rational or logical thinking which is grounded in analytical procedures. The harmonic relationship between hemodynamics and neural activity involves the consumption of oxygen by nerve cells. After a time delay of approximately one to five seconds (5,000 milliseconds), commencing from the initial uptake of oxygen into a nerve cell, an increased rate of blood flow will occur in a relative area of the brain. The hemodynamic complex wiill peak between four to five seconds. See http://www.rep.routledge.com/article/G001SECT2 for more information on CT.

The emission of radio signals from the interplay of hydrogen and magnetic fields from neuron activity in the brain should be understood as a fractal activity (reduced-size copy of the whole) as related to organ activity which has a frequency rate in the extremely low frequency (ELF) range. Optimal frequency range for harmony between the brain and heart is between 3 and 30 hertz.

To further institute and embellish what has been iterated so far, the human mind-body complex can be considered as a receiver of energy transmissions from sources from without and greater than itself.

These sources can come from earth and cosmic activities, which include the following:

1. Cosmic microwave background
2. Cosmic/solar energy: electromagnetic energy
3. Cosmic plasma energy
4. Energy and variable forces as defined by nonwestern cultures
5. And what we do not know.

So, there must be a continuous flow of blood throughout the material system of the living body. What we are talking about is motion. Music is motion; it is life itself. There is no life without motion. Motion and the flow of blood are one in the same. Music shapes the atoms and molecules (nitrogen (78%), oxygen (21%), argon (0.94%), and carbon dioxide (0.03%)) in the air by the fact that music produces sound, which is a manifestation of variable changes in atmospheric pressure causing harmonic touching of the aforementioned atoms and molecules.

In this respect music is a motivator for the transport of the essential activators of the life force—in particular, oxygen. The sequence for a continuous looping of the required life force involves a dynamic interplay between cosmic events (electromagnetic activity), magnetic field enclosures of planetary bodies, atmospheric pulsations evoked by music (sound production), and the cooperative participation and respect by humans for cosmic-earth laws. *Music perpetuates oxygen and fortifies breath.*

Things to Know and a Way for Musicians to Function According to Correlative Thinking

Color: The three primary colors of the visible light spectrum deduced by the optic nervous system are red, green, and blue. See Table 1 below for properties of the three primary colors.

Color	**Wavelength**	**Frequency: 10^14 Hz**	**Energy: electron volts**
Blue	450–495 nm	6.1–6.3	2.8
Green	495–570 nm	5.3–6.1	2.4
Red	620–750 nm	3.7–5.0	1.8

Table 1: Three primary colors of visible light spectrum.

The following frequencies for the three primary colors were derived from the deductive process of octave relationship for relevancy of organ events. See Table 2.

Color	Frequency	Music Note	Offset: cents	# Octaves reduced
Blue	13.429257	A	-40.85	44
Green	7.567280	B	-33.89	45
Red	9.734435	E♭	2.09	45

Table 2: The music notes are nontempered frequencies.

Point of View: The adaptive angular motion of the cardio-hemodynamic system should not be regulated by a hearing mechanism, which is dogmatized by a music scalar system constructed on the 12th root of 2 (1.059463094).

From a medical perspective, the elements of calcium, potassium, and sodium, which are involved in the electrical activity of nerve impulsion, when tested (photometry) in the laboratory produce the colors of red for calcium (Ca), violet for potassium (K), and yellow for sodium (Na). See Table 3 below.

Color/ Element	Frequency	Music Note	Offset: cents	# Octaves reduced
Violet	11.79500	F♯	34.49	44
Yellow	16.48459	C	14.30	44
Red	9.734435	E♭	2.09	45

Table 3: The receptors in the eye will combine the spectral colors of red and green to produce yellow.

The Trio of the Ultraviolet Radiation Spectrum

The following data on the ultraviolet radiation (UVR) spectrum is reflective concerning frequency specificity when producing music. The trio or the three wavelength bands of the ultraviolet spectrum are divided into bands called UVA, UVB, and UVC. The subdivisions are arbitrary.

The following should be known about UV radiation from a composer/musician point of view:

1. UV radiation originates from the sun.
2. The Stratosphere ozone layer acts on UV radiation bands as follows:

UVA: This band, 320–400 nanometers (nm), is not absorbed by the ozone layer. UVB: This band, 290–320 nm, is mostly absorbed by the ozone layer; however, some reaches the Earth's surface. UVC: This band, 100–290 nm, is completely absorbed by the ozone layer and oxygen, unless there is a defect in the ozone layer.

3. Synthesis of vitamin D3 occurs in UVB between 290 and 315 nm. Initiation of Vitamin D3 production in the skin is caused by ultraviolet radiation with a frequency between 29,000,000,000,000,000 (twenty-nine quadrillion) to 31,500,000,000,000,000 (thirty-one quadrillion, five hundred trillion) hertz. See Table 4 for relative reno-cardiovascular frequencies for harmonic relationship between kidney, heart, and neurodermal complex (emanates from the embryological ectoderm layer).

Wavelength nm	Frequency: Hz	Music note	Offset
290	25.757174	A♭	-14.02
291	25.845992	A♭	-8.09
292	25.93481	A♭	-1.44
293	26.023628	A♭	4.47
294	26.112446	A♭	10.37
295	26.201263	A♭	16.25
296	26.290081	A♭	22.10
297	26.378899	A♭	27.94
298	26.467717	A♭	33.76
299	26.556535	A♭	39.56
300	26.645353	A♭	45.34
301	26.73417	A	-48.89
302	26.822988	A	-43.14
303	26.911806	A	-37.42
304	27.000624	A	-31.72
305	27.089442	A	-26.03
306	27.17826	A	-20.36
307	27.267077	A	-14.72
308	27.355895	A	-9.09
309	27.444713	A	-3.47
310	27.533531	A	2.11
311	27.622349	A	7.69
312	27.711167	A	13.24
313	27.799985	A	18.78
314	27.888802	A	24.31
315	27.97762	A	29.81

Table 4: Ultraviolet Radiation Band B (UVB) for production of Vitamin D3.

Note: relative to different disciplines, UVB can be from 290 to 315/320 nm.

Frequencies in Table 4 are found by octave reduction process to harmonically vibrate with cardiomyocyte activity.

Understanding Rhythmology Through Cardiac Motion

The metronome is for a machine and for those that seek a constant, quantized groove.

The motion of the heart, with its multi-vectors and variable movements, functions with adaptogenic polymeters. Figure 1 is an xy graph (LabVIEW) of ten heart-sound cycles, showing variable waveforms of the right ventricle of the heart.

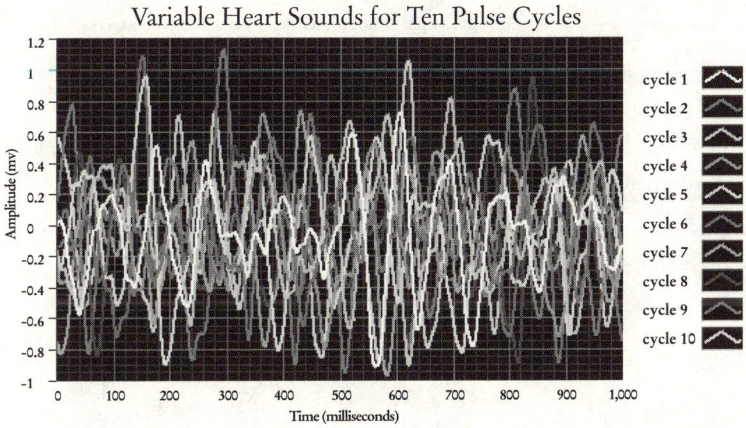

Figure 1. The waves are an overlay of the sequencing process from cycle 1 to cycle 10. The relative time, frequency, music note, and offset values for each cycle are listed in Table 5.

Variable Vectors from Within the Heart

TIME: milliseconds	Frequency: Hz note	Music	Offset
978	11.651066	A♯	13.24
982	7.676107	B	-9.17
962	9.435077	D	48.01
998	4.757707	E♭	-37.30
982	9.783141	E♭	10.73
949	9.798639	E♭	13.47
930	9.456499	E♭	-48.05
980	11.014091	F	15.90
999	11.685543	F♯	18.35
947	9.588517	E♭	-24.05

Table 5: The sequencing of heart-sound motion does not prescribe to a sine wave with circular integer decisions.

The real school of music and how to properly learn music is to listen to your inner self. Music is not played with an external instrument, it is played with your universe-connected mind.

From a point of space and time, the dynamics of rhythm should be related to the neuro-cardio functions of the heart. See Figure 2.

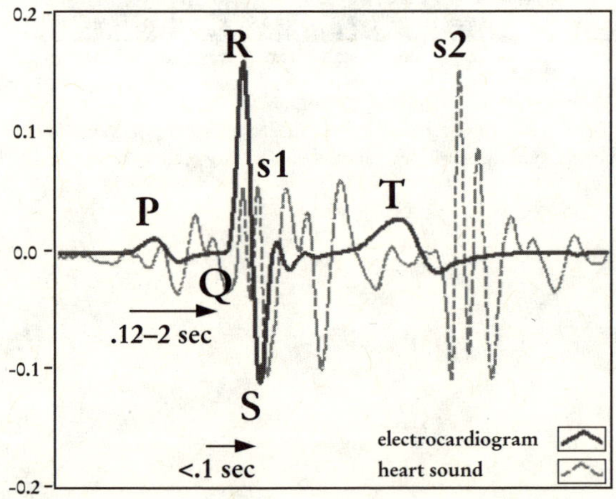

Figure 2: One pulsation of the heart. The electrocardiogram represents the passage of electrical impulses through the heart. S1 and S2 is where the first and second heart-sounds are located.

Relative to what is known as heart-rate variability (HRV), the heart does not and should not have a metronome beat (pulse duration is equivalent to a measure in music) to beat sequencing structure. When producing music, the factors of HRV should be fully observed because music stimulates the autonomic nervous system (ANS).

The ANS is the coordinator for heart motion, with the objective of maintaining a balance between mind and body functions (homeostasis).

In closing, the following holism and thought processes can serve as a means of producing a composite music:

1. Probe into a relativistic understanding of the connection between innovative music and quantum physics.

2. The flowing and looping frequencies of cosmic and solar energy that passes through the human body on a micro-time schedule.

3. Consider what is happening between the extremely fast pitch changes of energetic music in relation to the CASIMIR effect.

4. Other concepts that should be explored relative to developing new innovative concepts of music composition are: Einstein-Rosen Bridge, parallel universe, black hole, Big Bang, Big Crunch, Schumann resonance, and Dogon philosophy.

The present situation in the universe requires that a musician be totally aware of what is taking place on the greater cosmic environment of Vibration.

CHAPTER 16

CONFESSIONS OF A SENSUALIST

CARLA KIHLSTEDT

When I was very little, there was a physical feeling that came over me now and again. I called it the biglittle feeling. It was a contradiction. It was a black hole. It was a suspended state. It lasted sometimes for five seconds, sometimes for twenty, never more. It was subtle, like when you put the eraser of a pencil just between your eyebrows, but not quite touching your skin—another sensation I indulged in as a child. It was the feeling of being the bridge between two adjacent things entirely opposite in scale, weight, heft, and intention: a tractor tire and a sewing needle, an elephant and a feather, a house and a dandelion seed. I never knew what brought it on, I could never predict it, and I could never make it happen, but I looked forward to it as if it were a strange pen-pal that were coming to visit, but would only let me hear her voice. It was my own private tornado.

* * *

My violin teacher from age ten until about fourteen or fifteen was a large narcoleptic man named Berl Senofsky. He was a fantastic violinist, and an incredibly compelling musician. He was the first American ever to win the Queen Elizabeth Competition in Belgium, and had been the concertmaster of the Cleveland Symphony under George Szell. He had fingers like bananas and eyelids like a sleepy ostrich. I can easily say that I learned everything that I know about making sound on a violin from this man.

For months I played nothing but long tones on open strings. Months … until it made me cry (ah, the glory of the classical pedagogy!). In the end, what he was trying to make me understand was significant, and utterly inarticulable. There was a day—I think I was eleven—when he had been trying to get me to understand what tone meant (weight, speed, balance, emotion, intention, expression, restraint, color). He hung his gigantic bear-paw from my bow arm as I played, I'm sure yielding a fantastic crunch of a sound. When he took his hand away, and I played the same passage (Prokofiev F-minor violin sonata), he shouted, "Ha! That was it!!! Did you hear that?!"

* * *

I cried the first time I heard Sofia Gubaidulina's *Offertorium*. I had never heard so many textures coming from an orchestra. She is a sound sculptor.

* * *

A musician is: a cartographer, a cook, a scavenger, a diviner, a preacher, an auctioneer, a hoarder, a thief, a diplomat, a dictator, an historian, an oracle, a travel agent, an organizer, a storyteller, a chemist, an alchemist, an epiphanist.

* * *

I spent five weeks in a castle in Umbria (Civitella Ranieri), where I listened to recordings of the voices of American championship cattle auctioneers. I used them as the basis for the soundtrack for a dance piece. The different perspectives that made up that constellation of ideas: for Jo Kreiter (the choreographer), it was a socio-political statement about the abuse of female sexuality at the service of capitalism and marketing, and the personal intimacy which is sacrificed in the equation. For me, it was rhythms and language, it was somewhere between preaching and singing and speaking in tongues. It was a traditional folk art form.

More than usual, I was a collage artist in the making of this piece. I have always loved putting images together, and letting the dialogue between them emerge. I have done it all my life as a hobbyist with visual art. I learned this from my grandmother, who made collages well into her seventies, some political, some purely fanciful and surreal, and some a little bit of all three. (There is a fantastic collage at my sister's house of the plinth of the Statue of Liberty, but instead of Lady Liberty standing tall, there is a nude woman who bends forwards at the hips, her body entirely disappearing back in between her own legs.)

In the auctioneer piece, as on my art desk, I laid out the various elements and watched and waited for convergences. Violin, voice, piano, several auctioneers' voices, the Oxford English Dictionary definition of the word *ravish*, the bells from the castle chapel. The auctioneers each implied a certain music; they each had a tonality and a sense of phrasing, a harmonic world, and a rhythmic language of their own. I listened for days until I could hear the implied music around their monologues. I was more archeologist than composer. Of course, a different archeologist would have found an entirely different music there.

* * *

It is like being a mapmaker, or a pre–computer era oceanographic cartographer. You need both data and intuition, and you have to let them feed and balance each other. You start with curiosity, and let the answers you find lead you to the next question. You have to be willing to put things together that you have no proof will get along. You set the general parameters of your territory. You survey the topography of the area. You use what you have learned from other landscapes like it, but are willing to throw all your previous knowledge away when new evidences surface.

* * *

It is a matter of mapping spaces that have existed without me and will continue to exist whether or not I explore them, but somehow, this simple act of curiosity seems to make the world breathe.

* * *

I spent the week practicing quarter-tone scales … as slow as possible. Then once those intervals felt distinct and open, I went on to one-sixth-tone scales. It seems that you could climb endlessly into smaller and smaller intervals until you were like *Alice in Wonderland*. They would just expand around you like gigantic furniture.

* * *

One can talk endlessly about the social/political/cultural implications of various "types" of music, about our particular coordinates in cultural history, about aesthetic trends and developments, and although these approaches help us understand something about what it is to be human, and although you cannot escape the influence of such ideas and perspectives, I leave that to the historians among us. For me, these ideas play out in my work whether or not I am aware of them. Often I am too myopic in the act of music-making to take in such "big-picture" concepts. They are there for inspection after the fact of artistic creation if I want to step back and look from afar, to see what I've done and how it fits in the great stream of music that is being conjured at any point. I need a certain amount of myopia when I write, or improvise, or practice, or perform. The moment that I'm seeing it all from above, almost like a documentary, is the moment that I've lost my personal, and often very tenuous, connection to the actual thread of the music I'm finding.

* * *

A friend who cooks, and cooks well, said yesterday that she's just realizing how courageous it is to use almost no spices or seasonings ... to just let things taste the way they are, unadorned, has made her into a much better chef.

* * *

Difference tones. It's all about difference tones. I can get them going between certain notes on the voice and violin. I stayed up all last night in the barn (at the Headlands Center) swimming in difference tones. They make most people nauseous. They make me high. They change the whole way that I hear harmony, because they're present whether you are "hearing" them or not.

* * *

In the best of worlds, I am trying to find what the music needs, and not what I want. Each piece has its own logic. Sometimes it's a logic of symmetry and balance, and sometimes it's an irrational system of impressions and reactions. Sometimes it needs to remain limited and closed to reach its potential, and sometimes it needs to be exploded from within.

CHAPTER 17

SECRET INSTRUMENTS, SECRET DESTINATIONS

LUKAS LIGETI

At an ungodly hour one morning in 1992, I was awakened by the phone. At the other end was a voice, saying, with a distinctly German accent, "Good morning, this is the Goethe Institute. 'Es geht um Afrika.'" In German, that means, "This is about Africa," or, ominously, "Africa's future is at stake."

I was studying composition at the Vienna Music University in Austria. The evening before the unexpected phone call, I'd gone to see a concert featuring German musicians; it was boring, so I read the program notes. The saxophonist had been on a "tour of West Africa for the Goethe Institute." Darn, I thought, wouldn't it be nice to tour in West Africa? But it's not going to happen. There is no institution in Austria that sends musicians to Africa. The Goethe Institute is for Germans, and I'm not German, so that's that.

Next morning, that phone call came. I figured I was still dreaming, or someone was playing a joke on me. I hung up. It rang again. "Sorry, we've been disconnected. I'm from the Goethe Institute. We would like to send you to Africa."

Flashback. Given my family name, many people assume I was set to be a musician by the time I was five years old. But, some isolated piano lessons aside, I made my first attempts to learn music at eighteen on percussion, settling after two years or so on drum set and composition. My starting point was, for all practical purposes, a clean slate. I had not listened to much music from the age of eight; now, I began listening to all kinds of music simultaneously. My father and I would swap tapes sometimes, and he was listening to African traditional music at that time, some of which he dubbed for me. Also, I attended some musicology lectures at the University of Vienna, and the most interesting ones by far were those by the ethnomusicologist Gerhard Kubik, whose analyses of the court music of the

Kingdom of Buganda, located in what is now Uganda, completely changed my world view.

I listened to Cuban and Ghanaian drumming, Kwela (the southern African townships' answer to American big band jazz), and other styles. African forms, rhythms, and melodies found their way into my earliest compositions, and in 1988, some months after starting to listen to African music, I wrote a piece called *Pattern Transformation*. Scored for four players on two marimbas, it was a first step toward developing my own voice as a composer. Using techniques adapted from the music of Buganda, I constructed a crazily polymetric landscape, achieved through complex hocketing and interlocking between the musicians. But, obviously, no Western-trained musicians would have practiced this approach to meter, while African traditional musicians did not read music, so I thought the piece unplayable. Then, I heard about a Hungarian ensemble called the Amadinda Percussion Group. The amadinda is a xylophone used in the music of Buganda, and sure enough, these Hungarians had become as enamored with this music as I was, and had mastered its special technique of interplay. They premiered *Pattern Transformation* in 1990 and have since played it all over the world; the Goethe Institute heard about my African-influenced music, and invited me to Côte d'Ivoire to work with traditional musicians.

While I had listened to lots of African music, I had never played any myself, and the prospect of actually going there seemed so distant I'd never given it any thought. Now, suddenly, there was an opportunity to go. The African musicians would be no better prepared to play my music than I was to play theirs. How could I collaborate with them?

The most feasible approach seemed to try to find a type of music that could not have been thought up by them or by me alone, a music that required our combined backgrounds and skills sets: something new. And that was fine by me anyway. By 1992, I was near the end of my student days in Vienna and was itching for a new experience; my plan was to work on electronic music, with a special emphasis on live performance, to investigate what would happen if I applied my nascent drumming skills to electronic percussion, a field that was then, and has remained, somewhat neglected by the experimental music community but continues to intrigue me to this day. The idea of using electronic drums in Africa seemed promising. Trouble was, apart from some tape-splicing at the university's electronic music studio, I had never worked with electronics, so I told the Goethe Institute that I'd like to take along someone specialized in electronic music. They told me it would have to be someone from Germany, but I knew no one there. I asked them for a recommendation; they were surprised I had never heard of Kurt Dahlke, aka Pyrolator.

It turned out I actually had heard some of his music. During my senior year in high school, I occasionally tuned into the radio while doing my homework and was always happy to hear some Neue Deutsche Welle (NDW), a German style of "new wave" or early "synthi-pop," a DIY mixture of punk and disco with homemade electronics and clever German lyrics. Kurt had been a founding member of the seminal NDW band Deutsch-Amerikanische Freundschaft (D.A.F.) in the late 70s and, after leaving that outfit, cofounded Der Plan, probably the most experimental group of the genre, really a performance-art collective influenced by the Residents, Genesis P-Orridge, the Düsseldorf art scene, and more. In 1979, Kurt and his friends started the recording studio and label AtaTak, and, over the years, he produced hits such as Andreas Dorau's *Fred vom Jupiter*, rock bands like Fehlfarben (currently experiencing a revival with Kurt on keyboards), and glitch-electronica experimentalists like Oval. He also became a proficient performer on several electronic instruments such as Don Buchla's Thunder and Lightning. I caught up with Kurt at a recording studio in Arnhem, the Netherlands; we decided we could work together and have continued doing so ever since.

In 1993, I purchased my first computer and an electronic percussion instrument called the DrumKat, and Kurt and I put together a duo program to present during our two-and-a-half-week stay in Africa. Finally, in February of 1994, we boarded an Air Afrique plane bound for Abidjan.

Much of my knowledge of African music was at that time still based on Gerhard Kubik's work in Buganda, but while it does display some core concepts of African music in an especially clear and extreme way, this music is a very special, unique case, and does not have terribly much in common with the traditions of West Africa, many thousands of miles from Uganda, where I now found myself. Still, to better understand the conceptual background I brought into the collaboration, some explanation is in order.

The court music of Buganda goes back hundreds of years, but the kingdom and its traditions were so severely impacted by the totalitarian regime of Milton Obote in the 1970s that his successor, the particularly bloodthirsty Idi Amin, had little left to destroy. Kubik first came to the region in 1959 and learned to play the music just before it effectively disappeared, to resurface only after relative normalcy returned to Uganda in the final decade of the 20th century.

Baganda court music is played on a variety of instruments, including the amadina xylophone and the ennanga, a harp. The amadinda is played by three people; the music is pentatonic and an amadinda has twelve bars, ten of which are played by two players sitting opposite each other, covering a two-octave range. The third player limits himself to the top two bars, which are not touched by the other players and sound two octaves above the two lowest bars. A piece begins with the first player starting a melody in parallel octaves (with both hands hitting simultaneously), in even "quarter notes"—very fast, and usually of a length divisible into two as well as into three parts, for example, twelve or twenty-four notes. The melody is repeated, over and over again, with no variations. At a predetermined point, the second, opposing player sets in with a countermelody whose characteristics are somewhat similar to the first. Both melodies have leaps and jumps; for reasons that will soon become obvious, the stepwise progressions of European "vocal" lines are not opportune here. The two melodies are played at exactly the same, fast speed, but not in rhythmic unison. Rather, the second player plays his melody exactly in between the notes of the first, interlocking with the opposing player. Putting the two melodies together, a very fast pulse results, 500 or more impulses a minute. How can player two syncopate so quickly as to be able to play his notes exactly between player one? The answer: he doesn't syncopate at all. Try playing offbeats at such a tempo and keeping the time steady; you will see that you soon "lose it" and slow down, skidding into rhythmic unison with the downbeats. Rather than using such an approach, the second player listens to the first and internalizes the tempo. He then starts playing, quasi-syncopating once to slip in between the opposing player's notes. And from that point on, he inverts his metric perception, convincing himself that he is playing on the beat, while the other is syncopating. By experiencing the beat as occurring at different points, the two players are able to maintain equilibrium and play their exceedingly fast, interlocking structures without drifting out of sync.

This idea—that there is no necessity for a unified concept of meter within an ensemble, that players in an ensemble can have a relative notion of the beat—is unknown in Western music, and indeed in most types of music around the world. It is, for the most part, exclusive to certain forms of Central and East African music; it does exist to a certain degree in Gamelan, but not with the same rigor and structural necessity as in amadinda music. To me, this was a completely fascinating, inspiring, and liberating concept, and has become the foundation of many of my experiments ever since.

But there is much more to the ingenuity of Baganda music theory. Players one and two are striking the same repertoire of bars, the ten lowest ones of the instrument, from opposite sides. The melodies both contain leaps and jumps, and are interlocked at an extremely fast tempo. The result of this interplay is that the listener's ear soon loses track of which note is being played by which musician. A new aural image emerges: that of a resultant pattern, of the combination of melodies. And now, your brain creates new internal subdivisions, reordering this very fast resultant pattern in different ways; for example, by frequency band. Soon, you begin hearing a melody in the upper range, another in the middle range, and another down low. None of these resultant melodies are played by any individual musician; rather, they are embedded in the deep structure of the music, emerging only when the brain has reordered the aural image resulting from the fast interlocking of the basic melodies. Gerhard Kubik therefore called these resultant melodies "inherent patterns."

One of these inherent patterns is situated on the two lowest-pitched bars of the amadinda. That's where the third player comes in, doubling this melody on the top two bars, two octaves higher. This can be quite complicated. Imagine the first and second players' melodies have thirty-six and twenty-four notes respectively; that would make the entire overall pattern 144 pulse units long before it repeats. Each inherent pattern is the jagged result of the component melodies' jumps and leaps, so the pattern on the lowest two keys is long and rhythmically irregular: quite a burden on the memory. So how is it possible to exactly replicate this on the top bars? It turns out that, while amadinda music is instrumental, a hidden vocal component exists. The same pieces can also be played on a harp called ennanga, and here, the player's hands interlock, one hand effectively representing each of the first two amadinda players. And then, the harp player sings a melody and lyrics, and the sung line retraces one of the inherent patterns—the exact pattern that, when played on xylophones, lands on the bottom bars. The rhythm of this melody follows the rhythm of the lyrics. So, in order to play this pattern on the amadinda, our player three must know the song's lyrics and imagine himself singing. Provided he starts imagining the lyrics at the right moment, his resultant melody will correspond to the inherent pattern played on the xylophone's lowest bars.

Composing a piece for amadinda is akin to finding your way through a maze: melodies have to be constructed so that interesting inherent patterns result, while the rhythmic contours of traditional lyrics are implied. But the complexity goes further. Since this music is pentatonic, and the steps between pitches are, for all practical purposes, equal, a piece can be transposed four times from the original without losing its intervallic gestalt. But while you play these transposed versions, the amadinda as an instrument always remains the same, with the same pitches available. So while the intervallic relationships between the melodies remain intact, a different inherent pattern will land on the bottom bars in each transposition; consequently, a different pattern will have to be replicated on top. And while a piece may have its preferred version, any transposition can theoretically be played, and the corresponding patterns must be memorable somehow. It's a composition technique by no means less sophisticated than fugue writing; a technique of creating the sonic equivalent of a sculpture which can be experienced from many different sides.

My initial reaction to all this was twofold. I started writing *Pattern Transformation*, and, at the same time, began applying what I had learned to my drumset playing.

Pattern Transformation, for four players on two marimbas facing each other, is based on a pulse of well over 400 beats a minute, written as eighth notes. The piece opens with a chromatic canon, the initial "theme" starting and ending with the note "c"; for maximum density, all eighth-note pulse units are played. The structure then thins out; the theme of the canon is dropped; the chromaticism is transformed into a pentatonic environment (of course not an equidistant pentatonic one as on the amadinda; we are dealing with Western marimbas here), and the music becomes less dense. Eventually, the musicians are playing quarter notes instead of eighth notes, but they are not playing these quarter notes in rhythmic unison. They are interlocking. Two musicians play on the "downbeats" while the others are on the "offbeats," but those who play on the offbeats perceive the music as if their notes were the downbeats. And, indeed, the music can be heard either way. I do use conventional meter and barlines, but that's just to facilitate reading. The musicians aren't actually thinking of barlines, they are just feeling the fast basic pulse and multiples thereof; while the basic pulse remains constant, various multiples of it are played at different times. Sometimes, a musician will play each pulse unit for a little while, and then slow down, which actually means playing at the same speed but playing every other, then every third, then every fourth pulse unit, etc. Another musician might be doing the exact opposite. To the listener, it may sound fairly rubato at times, but since there is here an underlying unified sense of tempo at all times, the players remain totally coordinated. All metric relationships are tightly determined, and when they come into unison, this unison is immediately totally together, because the musicians were never actually apart, they just sounded as if.

Perhaps it comes from a pop-music influence, but this tightness, this underlying order even when things appear to be chaotic, is very important to me. That doesn't mean I object to free meter, rubato, or to the absence of any metric foundation. But something that has always fascinated me is the contrast between chaos and order. And I like phrases that are totally strange, seemingly chaotic, but are then perfectly repeated, or phrases that are played very sloppily and very precisely at the same time, with the heterophony that results (these ideas led me to develop a few years later the practice of what I call "secret instruments"). In any case, so as to create these very distinct contrasts between chaotic looseness and total tightness, the tightness had better be really tight. An efficient way to do that is to also have the disorderly sections be tight in a subliminal way, inaudible to the listener but always tangible for the musicians.

The most extreme interlocking in *Pattern Transformation* occurs when each of the four musicians plays every fourth pulse unit, but offset by one pulse in relation to the previous player. Every pulse unit is played, but each pulse is played by only one musician, and they take turns. I revisited this form of hocketing a few years later in my piece *Groove Magic*, facilitated by my secret instrument setup.

To play *Pattern Transformation*, percussionists have to learn to interlock at high tempos, divorcing themselves from the concept of a unified meter or beat, yet adhering to a unified tempo, much like in amadinda music. Nevertheless, it is music for Western-trained musicians. There is no spoken-word element inherent to this music, and the rhythmic relationships are constantly changing, which requires reading. My dangerously optimistic hope was that musicians would be able to combine traditional African and traditional European skills and give rise to a new kind of musicianship, but in Vienna at the end of the 1980s, that was still a somewhat unrealistic scenario.

It's more than a little surprising that the ensemble that would first realize this dream for me came from Budapest. While Vienna was fairly conservative in a way, it was still one of the great centers of music-making in Europe, with musicians from all over the world studying or visiting. It was a last stop, a dead end before arriving at the Iron Curtain, yet it was resolutely part of Europe's free West, where information was readily available. Hungary, on the other hand, was behind the Iron Curtain, and, while home to greatly skilled musicians, not exactly the ideal place for studies in exotic traditions. Still, it was in Budapest, of all places, that a group of young percussionists had come together in 1984 to form a quartet and had somehow discovered the amadinda, even naming their ensemble after the instrument. They were as surprised to see a composer build on the techniques of Baganda music as I was to find musicians who could play it. As a result of their many performances of *Pattern Transformation*, numerous other ensembles also took it up, and so it has, perhaps, made a small contribution to expanding the possibilities of percussion ensembles and the ways musicians in Europe and America think about meter.

The other immediate reaction to my discovery of amadinda music was the creation of a novel and personal approach to playing the drumset. I asked myself whether I could use interlocking patterns to create the impression of several simultaneous meters and tempos. For any jazz drummer, "independence" is a loaded word; a player strives for independence between their limbs, so as to execute several rhythms at the same time, for example a swing pattern on the ride cymbal, a steady "two and four" on the hi-hat, and various polyrhythmic punctuations on the bass and snare drums. However, as the great jazz drummer Bob Moses points out in his book *Drum Wisdom*, independence is actually an illusion. Listeners are tricked into thinking that drummers are able to control their limbs individually, but actually they are playing a limited vocabulary of prefabricated licks featuring sufficiently complex rhythmic relationships between the limbs so that the impression of independent control arises. Indeed, Moses proceeds to instruct readers in a "non-independent" concept, in which the practicing drummer is well aware of the fact that his four limbs are very much interdependent and seeks a way to produce the maximum impression of polymetrics with the minimum amount of independence.

But conventional drum-set playing, while derived to a significant extent from an African rhythmic ancestry, does not include the concept of relative meter. I attempted to develop a drumming technique using this concept, harkening back to the ennanga harp, where inherent patterns are produced by one player alone. My right hand plays a repetitive pattern, circling around the drum set in a steady stream of, say, quarter notes. I could begin by hitting the ride cymbal, then my right rack tom, located to the immediate left of the cymbal, then continue to a cowbell suspended on top of my bass drum below and to the left of the rack tom, and then move my hand to an even lower position, further to the right, to strike my floor tom. Then I could return to the ride cymbal and the beginning of my pattern. I now have a pattern of four notes—four pitches, four timbres. I can then construct a similar pattern for my left hand; let's make it even simpler and make it a three-note pattern. I start with my left rack tom, which is to the left of the previously mentioned right rack tom. From there, I continue to the cowbell suspended on the bass drum—the same cowbell already included in the previous pattern. Then I continue to my snare drum, down and somewhat to the left, mirroring the down-and-right motion of my right hand from the bell to the floor tom. And from the snare, I lift my arm and land back on the left rack tom. While this is a pattern of only three sounds, the motion described by my left arm is relatively similar to that described by my right. So I now have two patterns, which I can interlock. A complete metric cycle takes 4 x 3, or twelve, notes, but the patterns interlock, so it really takes twenty-four pulse units. But I have yet to use my feet, which could be integrated into, or superimposed to great effect on top of, the hand patterns. For example, I could play the bass drum every fifth pulse unit. Every other time I play it, it would come together with the right hand; every other time, with the left . The result would be a pattern 24 x 5 = 120 pulse units in length, still fairly easy to execute. I could now add the hi-hat on every seventh pulse. This gets challenging, but is still quite manageable compared to various technically demanding aspects of conventional drumming. And I now have a pattern with a length of 120 x 7, or 840, beats.

I now had a very economical and manageable way to play polymetric structures that have simple basic ingredients but quickly explode into great complexity. But how do I keep track of where I am in my pattern? In most Western music, this is done by counting; in this music, however, while there most definitely is tempo, there is no clear "one," no definite beat, making counting a schizophrenic and pointless undertaking. I do not use meter, melody, or timbre to maintain my bearings when playing these structures; rather, I use position. I conceive of this type of drumming as a choreography, a kind of dance on the drums, and by following the shapes, the forms of motion described by my body, I can feel my way through the patterns, using the relative positions of my limbs to keep track of exactly where I am at any given time.

This way, I was quickly working with much longer structures than exist in Baganda music, largely due to the availability of my feet to create additional polymeters. Playing even longer cycles is no problem, either by using more-complex patterns of motion or through other means, for example adding the aspect of striking the drums in different ways and superimposing this "parameter" on top of a pre-existing pattern, an approach somewhat reminiscent of serial music. Either way, inherent melodies quickly emerge; the drumset being an instrument of indefinite pitches, it would probably be more appropriate to speak of timbral melodies, "Klangfarbenmelodien." In the example above, both hands play the same cowbell, resulting in an obvious one-note inherent pattern. Or one could listen to the relationships between instruments of similar timbres: a 4:3 relationship emerges between the left rack tom, played by the left hand as part of a cycle of three notes/hand positions, and the right rack tom, struck by the right hand as part of a cycle of four. Since the hands are offset from each other by one basic pulse unit, the emerging 4:3 doesn't sound like the 4:3 we are conventionally accustomed to, with the two lines coming together on every third hit of the slower tempo or every fourth of the faster one. They never come together, and, indeed, this 4:3 is not a 4:3 between two different speeds. Both hands play at the same speed. Yet the time between two hits on the left tom is still shorter than between two on the right tom. It is an illusionary type of polymetrics, a polytempo structure accomplished not through actually playing different meters or speeds but through playing motion patterns of different lengths at the same speed.

Next, I began searching for ways to notate this drumming style. The drumset is often used in music featuring little notation, and no unified drumset orthography exists, though a five-line staff is often used for convenience. This quickly proved to be an inadequate approach; drummers are used to reading simple rhythms featuring obvious repetition, with an immediately apparent sticking. What I was writing down looked more melodic and altogether difficult to oversee. Using two staves, one for each hand, provided some relief, but still, sightreading was challenging. The solution for my problems came when it occurred to me that I was playing more based on position of my hands on the instrument than on sound or pitch: a tablature notation therefore seemed appropriate. I drew an aerial view of my drumset and started drawing vectors to represent my patterns of motion. Next, I had a small stamp made of my aerial view, and proceeded to stamp images of my drums on paper, writing down one right hand and one left hand hit per image. Around that time—late spring of 1988—I met John Zorn, who had come to Vienna to teach his game pieces in a workshop; I'd just started taking drumset lessons and was beginning to explore jazz and the New York Downtown scene. It was none other than Zorn who suggested I use a single image of my drums and write the entire pattern into it: R1, R2, R3, L1, L2, L3, etc. I followed his advice, which saved me lots of stamping. The only drumset tablature I've come across to this day, my notation proved extremely efficient. But, like any tablature, while it told me a lot about the positions of my hands on the instrument, it did not say much about rhythm. For the moment, that was not an issue, because I was always playing steady, even "eighth notes."

A few years later, I started trying to develop an analogy for this type of playing using electronics, and also sought to introduce it in various contexts, ranging from free-improvising groups to African collaborations; nevertheless, the changes I made to my technique were only slight and gradual. Recently, I've become more interested in pushing my ability to play drums in this way and in taking on the extreme technical challenges that soon emerge after the relatively easy, straightforward applications have been mastered. I began altering my patterns so that my straight-eighth pulse is interrupted or changed, and am currently working on possibilities of incorporating rhythmic notation into my tablature. I also had the desire to incorporate more space and rests into my patterns. It turns out to be quite difficult to play rests in this style: the limbs are moving along, hitting things; telling them to hold back in specific places is challenging. My solution was the invention of what I call the "non-sounding percussion instrument" or "silent block," an instrument designed to make as little sound as possible upon impact. I started out with a Jam Block, a plastic temple block which, manufactured by the company Latin Percussion, is relatively inexpensive, very lightweight, and has a mechanism so that it can be fastened to drum stands; it also has a horizontal surface on its topside. I then searched for the type of foam that would make the absolute minimum amount of sound when struck by a drumstick; it would have to be sufficiently soft to be quasi-silent but sufficiently hard so I'd feel an impact when playing it. I then glued generous amounts of this foam onto the horizontal surface of a Jam Block. It worked. Placing several of my silent blocks in different, strategic positions around my drumset, I was able to incorporate rests into my playing while maintaining the feeling of playing constant patterns in a relaxed way. In March of 2006, I tested my concept in a recording session with John Oswald, Henry Kaiser, Michael Snow, and Casey Sokol at the Canadian Broadcasting Company in Toronto. In this recording of free-improvised music, my drumset was close-mic'd and I occasionally played very sparsely. I already knew that my modified jam blocks worked well when I played loudly and quickly; they were not individually audible between all the sounds produced by the other components of my drumkit. But what would happen when I played slowly and the microphones were only a few inches away—would the result be a sound, or an unsound? It turned out that even the slightest resonance from other parts of the drum set, as well as even the most pianissimo utterings of other instruments, covered up my silent blocks to such an extent that they were not perceptible. My invention had passed its acid test.

In late 1992, I received my first composition commission, a piece for small chamber orchestra to be performed by the London Sinfonietta at a festival of Austrian contemporary music in London in April 1993. After having written *Pattern Transformation*, I was lucky to meet the Amadinda Percussion Group, but now I would write for musicians unfamiliar with the African rhythmic techniques that had become so important to me. And yet, I wanted to somehow use methods of ensemble interplay based on my polymetric ideas. It seemed to me that many of my problems would be solved if it were possible to "conduct" the ensemble in multiple, albeit synchronized, tempos, which, while impossible with a conductor, could be done with electronics. As a drummer, I enjoyed playing to click tracks (prerecorded metronomes) in the recording studio; perhaps I could work with multiple click tracks in concert. Around the same time, I had the opportunity to spend a day at STEIM, a computer music research center in

Amsterdam, and one of their recently developed programs was called Polyrhythm. Initially designed for the Den Haag Percussion Group to help them rehearse rhythmically complex passages in the music of Xenakis, Polyrhythm was basically a sequencer designed exclusively for the input of metronomic tracks, each in its own meter and tempo, up to ridiculous levels of complexity, allowing for time signatures unnotatable in any conventional way, tempos in the decimal ranges, and practically unlimited tempo and meter changes within a track; however, each track could only produce two sounds, one on the "1" of every bar and one on the other beats. Polyrhythm was not written for some obscure mainframe system, it was designed to run on the Atari, the most popular personal computer at the time. This was exactly the tool I needed, and the idea of composing a piece based on the capabilities of this software—rather than a piece ideally playable without it, for which the software was merely a crutch—inspired me. I bought the program, and though I didn't own a computer yet, this was the time I also started working with electronic percussion, and to these ends had purchased an Akai S-1000 sampler, which could store about half a minute's worth of sounds, quite a bit by the standards of 1992, and had eight individual sound outputs. I conceived the following system: My piece would be for eleven musicians. Sometimes, all musicians would play at the same tempo; sometimes, the tempos would diverge. There might be eleven different tempos. Or all musicians could play at the same speed but their beats could be offset from one another by small increments of time. Each musician would listen to an individual click track via headphones, but all the clicks would always be precisely coordinated because they would be played by Polyrhythm, which would effectively conduct the ensemble. From the computer, the information would be relayed to my Akai sampler, where each track would be routed to a different output. As my sampler had only eight outputs, I needed to incorporate a second sampler into the setup to take care of the clicks for the remaining three musicians. From the sampler outputs, the sound would go to headphones worn by the musicians. Having musicians wear headphones in concert is a controversial proposition; they would certainly complain about not hearing themselves or each other; dynamics and intonation would be a problem, the latter especially for the strings. To alleviate these problems, I opted for open, "Walkman-style" headphones, and gave each musician an individual headphone amplifier so they could regulate their monitoring volumes individually. I eventually found small headphone amps to clip onto the musicians' clothing, giving them control over the volume from the comfort of their seats. And because each musician had an individual track in the sampler, it was possible for me to change metronome sounds according to individual preference.

In writing the piece, which I entitled *Groove Magic*, I opted for a time-proportional notation, so that I would always be able to see exactly how the various musicians' parts interrelate. I am not the kind of composer who can write a piece part by part. Lutoslawski and some others have done that, but it's an alien approach to me, because I am always most concerned with the sound of the finished piece. I am not interested in randomness. Perhaps this comes from being an improviser; improvisation is, of course, far from random; it is, however, an exercise in loss of control. I love improvising, but when I compose, I want to maximize control; I want the music to sound exactly like I imagined it. In *Groove Magic*, I was interested in very exact coordination, a surgical, pop music–like precision. While not as complex as in *Groove Magic*, some polymetric and polytempo layering does occur in late-20th-century composition in the works of Xenakis and others, but there is always a certain looseness involved. My approach was closer to Conlon Nancarrow's, and I had the computer to help me achieve the tight synchronization I desired. No matter how many tempos occurred simultaneously, I was always conscious of how the parts lined up and had these relationships exactly in mind when composing. And when they did come together, it would be with a "bang"—the parts would suddenly converge, with no latency or hesitation.

Having no computer at my disposal, I composed the piece on paper. While my notation enabled me to keep track of what was going on in an optical/acoustical sense, I had to be mathematical about keeping abreast of each part's progress in time; otherwise, I'd never be able to untangle the mess and bring the parts back together again. I used a pocket calculator and notated the cumulative time of each part in the margins of the music paper, a somewhat Stone Age–like method. It worked, but before I knew everything was alright, there was a scare. I installed Polyrhythm on my friend Norbert Math's Atari and entered all the data. But when playing back the clicks, things quickly began sliding out of sync.

And there was another issue. All parts contained long rests at various points during the piece. Still, I had to "through-compose" all click tracks; otherwise, there would be no way for me to bring a track in exactly where I needed it after the rest. But that did not mean that I wanted the metronomes to actually sound during a long rest. I didn't want my secret instruments to cause any noise pollution. They were to be inaudible to the audience; only the musicians, the insiders, the tribe members executing the ritual, were privy to the metronomic information, while the audience would hear the outside of the structure, the facade, and, while observing this strange ritual, would wonder how this duality of exact coordination and apparent chaos could have been achieved. Alas, Polyrhythm did not allow one to mute or unmute a track; it had to play straight through.

Norbert and I procured an early-model Apple PowerBook running the Cubase sequencer program. While constructing rhythm tracks as complex as what I had composed would be very difficult with a 21st-century sequencer program, it was completely impossible with 1992's version of Cubase. On the other hand, the Mac's processor was far stronger than the Atari's. We played the eleven tracks one by one on the Atari, recording each one into the Macintosh. When all tracks had been recorded, we tried playback in Cubase and were relieved to see that everything now lined up exactly as intended. And it was now easy to mute redundant click information, as every impulse of the metronome was a separate piece of data in Cubase, and individually editable. Each musician would receive two bars of countoff before starting to play. At the end of a passage, when the musician had a rest, the click would stop and remain silent until two measures before the next entrance, at which point it would resume with a countoff. This way, musicians only had to concentrate when they had to play; counting bars through long intervals of silence was unnecessary.

In numerous performances, my click track setup turned out to be very robust. I was often asked why I didn't just record the clicks to multitrack tape. I've never been attracted by tape music; an interactive element is missing, even in the case of a "secret conductor": using the computer, sounds can be changed, the tempo can be adjusted in rehearsal, etc. It is simply a much more flexible way to work; the slight chance of the computer crashing during performance is a risk I'm willing to accept.

Groove Magic proved to be a great success, and I got no complaints from musicians about playing with headphones. Still, I often heard, "This is a great piece. I'd love it if you composed something for me/my group. But without a click track, please." And my polymetric drumming was not easy to integrate into situations that ultimately called for more conventional grooves. Slowly but surely, I decided I'd have to start my own group to continue developing these approaches. Today in 2007, living as I am in New York City, a place full of open-minded musicians, the time for this has finally come. But in the meantime, my life went in other directions, allowing me to continue my roads of polymetric discovery in unanticipated ways.

Africa was calling. Bernd Pirrung, the director of the Goethe Institute in Abidjan, Côte d'Ivoire, had put out a call to the local scene, inviting musicians to come to my workshop. 150 musicians showed up the first day; Kurt and I couldn't possibly work with that many people! So we decided to play some of our duo pieces for the local musicians to hear—our strangest-sounding, most inaccessible pieces. The strategy worked: the next morning, fifteen people showed up to work with us. The objective of our workshop was not clearly stated, but I insisted on having a concert at the end; I wanted us to have the pressure to come up with a tangible result. During the workshop's initial days, this objective seemed difficult to achieve.

Most people who come to Abidjan either love it or hate it. Save for Lagos, Abidjan is the largest city in West Africa, and the (naïve) idea many people have of Africa is a rural one. From independence until the 1990s, Côte d'Ivoire was one of Africa's most stable and developed countries, due in part to Félix Houphouët Boigny, the country's long-time president (until 1993), placing the economic emphasis on agriculture rather than on industry, at least until world market prices for the country's main products—cocoa, coffee, and palm oil—started falling in the 1980s. Côte d'Ivoire certainly wasn't a model democracy—Houphouët was something of a benevolent dictator—but the atmosphere was remarkably free. The relationship with France and the West always remained positive—no ruinous dabbling in Marxism here, and no romanticized nationalism of the type that caused decades of misery in Ghana, Guinea, and other neighbors. Côte d'Ivoire was a "globalized" country before globalization existed. Anyone was welcome to settle; residence permits were unnecessary. (This ended, alas, during the last years of Houphouët's tenure, ushering in the gradual trip down the slippery slope that resulted in political chaos and a stalemate on the verge of civil war starting in 1999, as yet unresolved.) But during the country's "golden years," there was even a period when resident foreigners could vote in local elections—a trailblazing idea at the time. Côte d'Ivoire's economy benefited greatly from this openness, and people from all over West Africa came. During the 1990s, perhaps up to twenty percent of all citizens of Burkina Faso lived in Côte d'Ivoire—Burkina was the Mexico to Côte d'Ivoire's U.S.—and communities of Malians, Guineans, and Senegalese were extremely significant. Add to that Liberian refugees, more than 100,000 Lebanese (who are to West what the Indians are to East Africa, having controlled much of the commerce for many years), tens of thousands of French, a visible community of Chinese and Vietnamese, and many others, and it is no wonder Abidjan was often referred to as the "Paris of Africa"—though to me it always felt more like Africa's New York. Plateau, the city's central and administrative district, has skyscrapers and is situated on a narrow peninsula, a little like Manhattan; an important port city (with the requisite cargo areas, mariners, and drug trade), Abidjan has water everywhere, but it's built around a lagoon; much like New York, the Atlantic Ocean is present but often forgotten, on the outskirts. The comparison with the U.S. can be taken further. Very few people lived in what is now Côte d'Ivoire until about 400 years ago. Then, gradually, people started migrating in from the surrounding regions—the Akan from the east (Ghana), the Kru from the west (Liberia), the Mande and the Voltaic tribes from the north. Côte d'Ivoire has no ethnic majority, and wandering around Abidjan is an excellent way to experience the traditions of the country's different peoples, as well as those of West Africa as a whole. But it is also a very big, very chaotic place, with much technological infrastructure by West African standards (in all my travels, I have never seen another region as infrastructure-deprived as West Africa), leading some Westerners to complain that this is not the "real" Africa. I find this attitude patronizing. If people come to Africa in search of traditional huts, no problem—they will find them in the countryside. But Africans are no different from people anywhere else in the world; they want to be affluent, they want their creature comforts, they want their VCRs. To claim that a household in Abidjan is less authentic because there is a VCR in the living room is, to me, frankly, offensive.

Likewise offensive are the expectations of many "outside" fans of African music that they will hear something "authentic." What is authentic, anyway? I greatly respect the work of musicologists—after all, much of my musical house of cards is based on it. Still, traditions emerge only to disappear after some time, giving way to other, new traditions. I don't especially enjoy talking about traditional musicians; for lack of a better term, I do it anyway, and when I do so, I mean musicians whose worldview and musicianship is sufficiently rooted in a certain tradition so that they can be identified with said culture. It does not mean, however, that they feel—or should feel—any need to protect these traditions against "attacks" from "foreign" cultures, or that they should be expected to confine themselves to forms of expression already present in their cultural environment. Moreover, I do not believe in the claim to a cultural context based on ancestry. I have never understood the phrase "my culture." I am the son of Hungarian Jews who, after nearly being killed by both Hitler and Stalin, immigrated to Austria. I had a very international upbringing, went to international schools, and now live in the U.S.. I can proudly say I have no "my culture." Even if my case is extreme, pure cultures do not exist, and those who feel their ethnicity or birthplace gives them "possession" of a certain culture would be well advised to consider where such false pride and narrowmindedness has led in past epochs of history. I've met Africans who are clueless about African history; Europeans who are clueless about Europe; Africans who are serious experts on, say, Italian literature, and Americans who know all about Japan but nothing about football. Culture is not in your blood, it is in your mind and your thoughts, and every individual has their own thoughts and their own way of understanding the world. It makes no sense to group people together according to superficial characteristics. There are no majorities in the world: we are, each and every one of us, a minority of one.

As a newcomer to Africa, coming not to learn the music of my collaborators nor to convince them to learn mine, the main question I asked was, What can we create, what can we learn, from the pooling of our minds? What can we, a group of individuals, each with his or her own background knowledge, learn from each other, and how can we inspire one another to tap into our creative intellect? Obviously, for such a collaboration to be successful, the right group of people has to come together. Narrowing down the group of participants by playing inaccessible music proved to be a useful approach; those who lacked the openmindedness to deal with something unknown simply took off. The musicians who remained had some sort of motivation; they were curious and unafraid.

What did these musicians have in common? In a way, I would say, not much. They came from all over West Africa. Some played at weddings or circumcision ceremonies in their community; others worked the city's club scene, where a fairly commercial form of jazzed-up funk/fusion was the order of the day; some worked mainly as theater musicians or were determined to play their own music, steeped in the traditions surrounding them, but open to any influence. Not surprisingly, there were about as many native languages as there were musicians. Dioula, a Mandé language used mainly for business purposes, is the region's African lingua franca, but, in the end, the language of choice was the usual one for Abidjan: French, with some Dioula thrown in, plus an occasional word in Wolof, Malinké, Balante, Peul, Crioulo, Moré, Baoulé, Agni, and so forth. Many of the participants came from long lineages of musician/storytellers, known as griots or djeliw in Mandé languages. None of them had had a great amount of schooling; some were entirely illiterate, while some read and wrote well in French; others did not, but read the Koran in Arabic.

In hindsight, and after having worked on several other cultural exchange projects, I can say that this group, which with minor changes came to constitute the ensemble Beta Foly over the next six years, was a stroke of extremely good luck. They were expert musicians whose mission was not to defend "their" culture against outside intruders, but to take a situation as is and try to make the most creative best of it; to try anything that came their way, but never to lose their identities. In 2000, I composed a piece for Miami-based musicians from various Caribbean islands, and while it was an interesting collaboration, I felt a certain rigidity and an element of distrust I eventually attributed to what I would call "double-diaspora syndrome." Much Caribbean culture is based on African roots, so in a way Cuban music, for example, is already the music of a diaspora. Then, these musicians ended up in Miami, where their main function was to entertain a community of other displaced people who were nostalgic about their homes. Their mission was to keep it basic, to cultivate their roots. The sudden appearance of a rootless cosmopolitan whose official commission was to mix things up was greeted with reserve and hesitation.

Not so in Abidjan. But while I was itching to interact with these musicians, something else had to be developed first: a consensus among the African musicians. In the beginning, we tried playing together a bit. We jammed, and fell into a kind of world music/ethno rock. It was fun to blow that way; many exchange projects go down this path of the least common denominator. This seemed superficial to me, so I encouraged the musicians to play together; I retired myself to the position of onlooker so they would not feel the need to accommodate me. The musicians shared a certain approach to music, and even had some melodies, some songs in common, yet their interests and priorities differed, and there were stumbling blocks—for example, their instruments' tunings occasionally seemed incompatible. I asked questions, both to further my understanding and to prevent things from getting comfortable. I'd ask them to repeat sections so I could see how their parts intertwined, and how they approached playing their instruments. I also provoked mildly. There were two balafon (traditional marimba) players at the workshop, Kaba Kouyaté from Guinea and Aly Keïta from southern Mali; their instruments were tuned differently, forcing one or the other to sit out any given piece. I persuaded them to play together and see whether, through the conflict of tunings, new harmonies, new compatibilities, could be achieved. After a few days, a group dynamic among the musicians started emerging, and I developed ideas for pieces and for ways I could integrate myself into the ensemble. In about eight days of hard work, we composed and rehearsed a collaborative repertoire, and presented it in an extremely well-attended concert which went off surprisingly smoothly. By then, we all knew we wanted to continue; an ensemble had formed, and it already had a name: Beta Foly, meaning "the music of us all" in Malinké. As I left Abidjan, I felt I had found a home, with a community of people to work with and where much interesting music could be made.

I returned a year later to record a demo cassette; in 1996, we recorded the CD *Lukas Ligeti & Beta Foly*. Released in 1997 by the German label Intuition Music, our CD contained compositional contributions from many of the band members and was essentially a compilation of experiments in the combination of African and Western approaches to music-making. We used the computer as a compositional tool as we had no notation or common tradition to build on. Electronic instruments—in my case, the DrumKat percussion controller, and in Pyrolator's, the Don Buchla–designed instruments Thunder and Lightning—were used both in recordings and in live performance. Some of my pieces (*Adjamé 220*, *Guinée imaginaire*) were almost completely scored; elsewhere, I only provided a basic concept. *L'escalier du temps* and *Langage en dessin* were polymetric improvisations where I recorded a drum part in my motion-based style before the other musicians contributed improvised takes. Since the studio was small and few microphones were available, the entire album had to be done by overdubbing, with not more than three musicians playing at the same time. *Langage en dessin* was recorded using a click track in a way similar to *Groove Magic*; I had introduced this method during the initial workshop in Abidjan. Much African music is based on the way individual parts interrelate and interlock; it is sometimes hard for musicians to play their part of a piece in isolation. Because playing with headphones creates a certain isolation from the other musicians, this method could be seen as counterintuitive in an African setting. I was curious to see what would happen. I began by giving an ensemble of six musicians a polymetric structure with six different click tracks, but the musicians ignored the clicks and fell into a rhythm, playing together. I asked them to pay more attention to the click, whereupon they played in total isolation from each other, listening exclusively to the secret information. So I asked them to find a compromise between the two extremes, and it worked almost instantly. The musicians quickly became very creative in the way they listened to each other, but adhered, elastically, to the clicks at the same time. I also used other headphone-conveyed information, such as speech. For example, we created hocketing structures using spoken word as a "click track," with each syllable as a "pulse unit." This sounded incredibly jagged and strange and was immensely fun to work with. I later expanded on this approach in other improvising groups. In the polymetric-drum-driven pieces on the CD, I asked the musicians to hone in on one component of my drum set and construct rhythms cuing off of this component. For example, Amadou Leye M'Baye, the sabar (Senegalese drum) player, could listen to my ride cymbal and derive a rhythm and tempo from that, while djembé player Lassiné Koné would refer to my snare drum and Tiémoko Kanté would play his bolon (a plucked-string bass instrument related to the kora) in accordance with my bass drum. Every now and then, I'd change up my rhythms, tipping the musicians off into chaos until they regained their bearings. In *Sound of No Restraint*, by contrast, we sought to emulate the approach of Korean musicians in our African environment. We listened to recordings of p'ansori and other Korean music and became inspired by the flexibility of tempo, using breath, rather than a firm beat, as the foundation. Much of the piece was free-improvised, but now and then, each player would hear six clicks in their headphones; on the sixth, they had to play a strong accent, followed by a few seconds of silence. Different players could have their accents at different moments, but sometimes, the whole group came together. The result sounded nothing like Korean music, but nothing like any known African music, either.

In another piece, *Balarama*, I made the aforementioned incompatibility between the two balafons my guiding principle. I sampled both instruments and detuned these recordings in various ways. Playing my electronic drums, I triggered the sounds of the balafons and made their tunings converge, little by little, over about five minutes. Even when tuned identically, a timbral difference between the two instruments' samples remained. I played this piece as a duet with Aly Keïta, who contributed his live balafon, whose tuning was obviously stable. The resulting tensions in intonation created interesting harmonic possibilities. Meanwhile, Pyrolator had his own duet with Aly, entitled *Brontologik 3.44*. Based on a synthesizer he had helped create years prior, he wrote a program in the computer language Max. Aly played his balafon; a microphone recorded him and fed the sound into a computer which analyzed and followed Aly's pitches. On the basis of the data thus generated, the computer composed melodies, accompanying Aly with a piano sound in a delayed response. For *African Loops*, Pyrolator and I sampled all musicians playing or singing short phrases; Pyrolator then assembled some of these recorded snippets and made a piece in an electronic dance music (techno? house?) style. On top of that was superimposed a vocal part by Yero Bobo Bah, a Guinean singer, dancer, and percussionist. *African Loops* might possibly have been the first attempt to fuse West African traditional music and electronic club/dance music; in the last few years, this type of fusion has become quite popular, particularly in Mali, and my current band, Burkina Electric, is part of this movement as well.

These experimental approaches contrasted with pieces like Lamine Baldé's *Tras di sol*, a typical example of singer-songwriter music from Guinea-Bissau, or *René*, by Tiémoko and Bobo together with Guinean flutist Babagalé Kanté, in a traditional style from Guinea's Fouta Djalon plateau. But the atmosphere was never completely traditional, as something experimental—be it only a solo featuring an unusual take on the piece's melody—always entered into the mix.

Beta Foly visited Europe for tours every year between 1996 and 1999; since then, the group has been "on ice"—it's costly to tour with such a large ensemble; also, the deteriorating political situation in the Ivory Coast hasn't helped. But Africa has remained a prominent part of my musical life.

In 1997, I participated in a project in Zimbabwe and met with musicians of the Valley Tonga tribe living near Lake Kariba. Their "Ngoma Buntibe" music, originally used in burial ceremonies, is played by a large ensemble of horns and drums; each horn contributes one pitch to the fabric of the music, and the arrangements contain incredibly complex hocketing. While this general approach exists in several central and southern African cultures, Ngoma Buntibe is particularly daunting and confusing to listen to and has not been documented or analyzed extensively by musicologists. The Zimbabwean composer Keith Goddard found it reminiscent of avant-garde classical music from Europe of the 1950s and onward; at the same time the music, albeit totally arranged, sounds deceptively free and conjures up images of free jazz. My short stay with the Tonga did not allow me to comprehend this music's structure, but I did gain one valuable insight: that danceability of music depends on the cultural environment of the dancer. The villagers had no problem dancing to Ngoma Buntibe, while I was clueless. I could imitate individual drum parts, but how they fit together, indeed how to identify any metric regularity at all, remained a mystery to me. I think that, in order to dance to music, one must identify the sounds or parts—drum or whatever—that provide the rhythmic backbone. Just about any music can be danced to, as long as one has the key to its "secret code." I would even include ametric music, if one has a hotwired connection to the music maker's head! After all, most music is made through motion; even the fingers of an oboist playing rubato constitute a type of dance.

My trip to Zimbabwe led to a brief stay in 1998 in Mozambique, where I was lucky enough to hear the Chopi timbila (marimba) virtuoso Venancio Mbande play with his ensemble (more than a dozen timbilas of different sizes) at his home. My melodic imagination had been greatly inspired by the music of the Mandé people since my first visit to Abidjan; this was now joined by Chopi music, which, while completely different, also touched me deeply. Its influences are noticeable in many of my compositions to this day. In 1999, in turn, I had the privilege of spending several weeks in Cairo, Egypt, collaborating with musicians from the Opera orchestra and with Nubian traditional musicians, exposing me to music from the region where Africa and Arabia meet.

Around the same time, Beta Foly traveled to Ouagadougou, Burkina Faso, for some concerts. Several of the group's members were from Burkina, and Maï Lingani, a singer who had participated in our CD recording, was living here now. In Ouaga, I found an extremely lively music scene, with bands playing at outdoor clubs in the middle of the night. They all seemed to play a similar repertoire of African pop standards mixed with kitschy American pop and jazz fare. Lying in my bed in the town's center at 3 a.m., I would hear four bands, at four different venues in four different directions from me, playing *When the Saints Come Marching In* in four different keys, at four different speeds. Just walking around Ouaga with a microphone on a weekend night is a viable way to create a great sound-art piece. Maï had made enormous progress as a singer in the two years since I'd last seen her in Abidjan; she had established herself in Ouaga and had recently won the country's most important music award. We subsequently worked together on several projects, including her debut solo album, *Entrons dans la danse*, voice/electronics duos, and even a concert playing together via a phone line, with her in Burkina and me in Austria. For some people who haven't been to West Africa, it's hard to imagine the lack of infrastructure there, while others assume the conditions to be totally primitive. Neither is the case. Working with technology in Africa is entirely feasible, albeit always an adventure. I'm fascinated by working in electronic music in Africa because I see many things about African culture that make it especially well-suited for electronic experimentation.

Over the past two to three years, ever since an Austrian NGO asked me to "do some concerts with musicians from Burkina Faso and electronics," the band Burkina Electric has been my main Africa-related project. I invited Maï, Burkinabè guitarist Wende K. Blass, Pyrolator, and the Austrian composer Rupert Huber, best known as one-half of the Vienna downtempo electronica duo Tosca, to join me. Burkina Electric continues where we left off years earlier with *African Loops*—electronic dance club music, related to Western DJ culture, but using elements of traditional music, in this case from Burkina Faso. The group consists of vocals, guitar, drums, and electronics; we also added As, a dancer from Ouaga, to the group, as well as, usually, a second dancer and a backup singer. Our music, composed collaboratively, includes the sounds of many traditional instruments, but only in sampled form, and always treated and processed in unusual ways. Soundscapes recorded in Burkina are used; in fact, many of our songs have their origins in recordings we made whilst walking around in Ouaga. Our pieces are anchored either by traditional rhythms from Burkina, or rhythms of our own invention, inspired by these traditions.

Rhythms such as the waraba or the ouennenga, from the traditions of the Mossi people, are relatively simple, yet firmly outside of what is considered "danceable" in a Western club environment. We hope to supply listeners with the "secret code" needed to dance to these rhythms; the dancers are very helpful in live shows. Our experience has been that audiences may be confused at first; twenty minutes into the show, they are up and dancing. The most relevant thing about some of the rhythms we use is that they can be experienced both in two and in three, a feature of many African rhythms. As soon as this duality is accepted and the simultaneity is felt in a physical, visceral way, dancing is no problem. While these rhythms do have a clear "downbeat" once in a while, there is still a great deal of freedom in how to experience them, and we capitalize on that. I play drumset and the Marimba Lumina, a Buchla-designed percussion controller similar to an electronic marimba; Pyrolator again plays Lightning. All our pieces contain much freedom for improvisation; in concert, we mainly use Ableton's Live software, which allows us to change songs greatly from one performance to the next. Pyrolator has written software in Max/MSP's Jitter programming language to manipulate video footage shot in Burkina Faso. While Burkina Electric is clearly a pop band, we try to develop our own production values by combining the aesthetics of African traditional music with a fairly experimental approach to electronic pop.

My solo electronics playing, meanwhile, has also incorporated many of these same ideas. Using electronics, I wanted to preserve the idea of playing percussion. A drummer is concerned with starting sounds; then they tend to decay quickly, so ending them is not usually a concern. With electronics, that can be quite different; what that would do to my technique was only one of the many questions I asked myself as I delved into electronic percussion around the same time I first went to Africa. The DrumKat was conceived more or less for recreating a standard drum kit . That wasn't at all what I wanted to do, but the instrument still proved very useful. Much of my initial work with electronic percussion was an expansion of my motion-pattern-based drum-set playing, going where I could not go with normal drums. I could program one of the DrumKat's pads so that a different sound would be triggered every time I hit it. Using patterns similar to the ones I played on the drums, I was soon creating structures that would take thousands of beats until cycling back to the beginning. Indeed, there's a piece in my repertoire that would need about 75,000 years! A desire to be able to improvise more melodically led me, in 2005, to concentrate on the Marimba Lumina as my main electronic axe. A highly sophisticated instrument, it allows for very flexible programming. For example, it is played using four color-coded mallets, and the instrument knows which mallet is striking it, so it's possible to program it completely differently depending on which mallet is used. My first concert with the Lumina was in September 2005 at the Unyazi Festival in Johannesburg, South Africa, the first-ever festival for experimental electronic music on the African continent. In 2006, I had the opportunity to spend some more time working in Johannesburg and enjoying its unique atmosphere, which feels like Atlanta and Lagos simultaneously and inspired me to think about why I'm so attracted to the combination of African music and electronics.

In many African languages, the words for "playing" and "dancing" music are identical. Electronic music has introduced an unprecedented detachment between motion and sound into music-making; audiences can't follow most electronic music performers' movements, not to mention connect them with the sounds they are hearing. Yet I think that live electronic music performance has huge potential as live music in its full kinetic sense, and Africa should be great terrain for this. Here, playing music is not taught exclusively via sound, but also via movement. Traditional African musicians could find new ways to perform electronic music and, in so doing, come up with ways to render electronic music far more interesting for live audiences. Likewise remarkable is the connection in Africa between music and language, with the rhythmic and tonal inflections of poetry embedded in many melodies as described in the above example of amadinda music. Electronics is an ideal environment for the combination of media; just as with dance, the proximity of music to poetry can open undiscovered artistic avenues, while the fact that similar structures are often explored in African music and visual art could lead to new analogies between electronic sound and visuals, with novel approaches to VJ-ing.

Much African music is cyclic and based on "additive" structures; in many ways, it is "digital" music, having at its heart a web of fast elementary pulse units. This way of thinking is quite close not only to basic ideas in computer architecture, but also, more practically, to how most sequencing software is conceptualized (though much of this software also uses bars and barlines, an entirely European concept). Most music software is made for pop songwriting, which obviously derives to quite an extent from African models. So could most electronic music today actually be considered African music? And how would one conceptualize a sequencing program specifically geared toward an African way of musical thinking?

Timbral aesthetics is yet another area of difference between Africa and the West. In Europe, musicians and instrument builders have long pursued "clarity" and "purity" of sound, while in many African regions an instrument is incomplete without attached objects—be they spiderwebs, bottle caps, or whatever—that create a mirlitone effect. In a way, African instruments already "have their effect pedals built in"; sound processing, an essential part of electronic music, has been present in African music for a long time. Can this be used to creative ends in electronic music?

Furthermore, while Western-style orchestral instruments are largely identical worldwide, instrument construction and tuning in Africa varies from village to village, much like in electronic music, where different artists may be working with similar hardware or software platforms (wood from the same trees; the same traditional tunes) but customize these environments so that no two of them are the same, making it difficult for a musician to use the computer of a colleague. Like computer musicians who build their own environments, many African musicians build their own instruments; for them, this aspect of electronic music should be a natural fit, while non-Africans working with electronics can seek inspiration from the extreme multitude of African tuning systems, timbral variations, etc., and use their electronics to find new avenues for harmony and timbre not viable with conventional Western instruments.

Then there is my personal fascination with interlocking structures and the creation of consonances, dissonances, and harmonies made not from a multitude of simultaneous melodies but from a simultaneity of rhythms and tempos. While physical, acoustical properties of music are constant regardless of culture, the ways they are used in the conceptualization of music vary greatly from culture to culture. A fitting analogy is the area of ethnomathematics: while the basic laws of mathematics are the same everywhere, the way this knowledge is exploited is not. The book *Ethnomathematik, dargestellt am Beispiel der Sona-Geometrie* (Spektrum akademischer Verlag, Germany, 1997), by the Mozambican mathematician Paulus Gerdes, has been exemplary for me in this regard. Using the geometrical analysis of southern African sand drawings, Gerdes points to ways of using traditional craft, acquired by children at a young age, in curriculum design for African elementary schools; for example, how basket-weaving could lead to a new way of teaching geometry. Similarly interesting, the American mathematician Ron Eglash in his book *African Fractals: Modern Computing and Indigenous Design* (Rutgers University Press, U.S., 1999) argues that African art contains some very direct and clear uses of fractal geometry, be it in large-scale designs such as settlement architecture, or on a smaller scale in textile design, or, in an even more confined dimension, in hair braiding.

And, of course, there are countless social and sociological questions and implications, and the incredible possibilities and promise that technology, especially the Internet, holds for Africa, a continent suffering from a chronic lack of access to information. Bringing electronics to remote areas of Africa can motivate people, no matter how far off the beaten track they live, to find ways to seek out access to information; playing unconventional music can inspire people to think outside of the box and thus empower themselves to solve problems that have proven uniquely resistant to any within-the-box approach. One of my most moving experiences was playing solo electronics in the beer hall of a village in Zimbabwe where electricity had arrived only three weeks before. My audience, about 200 elementary-age children, were some of the most concentrated listeners I've ever had. They must have thought I'd come directly from Mars. When I was done, they kept sitting there, silent. I was as astonished as they were, and just sat there as well. Finally, one child broke the silence: "Can I go to the bathroom?"

I think I have a lot left to do in the field of experimental and electronic Africana. It has, for me, been an extremely satisfying road to travel, both artistically and personally. Largely off the beaten track for experimental musicians, it is still, in many ways, avant-garde music's virgin territory. Spending time in this incredibly diverse, culture-rich continent has changed my way of thinking, and listening to its music has warmed my heart and stimulated my mind. It has provided me with lasting friendships and neverending inspiration. Africa has crept into all of my work, and I'm happy it is there.

CHAPTER 18

A CONCEPT OF TIME

JOSÉ MACEDA

Editor's Note: This is a substantially edited version of José Maceda's article originally published in the journal *Ethnomusicology*, volume 30, number 1, in Winter 1986. The original thirty-eight-page text applies these ideas about musical time in descriptions and transcriptions of specific Southeast Asian musics, including *kulintang* and other gong and vocal music traditions from the Philippines, *Pii Phaad* music from Thailand, Javanese gamelan, and other musics from the region. My intention with this edition is to provide a more accessible introduction to the historical, theoretical, and philosophical underpinnings of Maceda's view of the time in Southeast Asian traditional music, which also influenced his own compositions. —Chris Brown

Introduction

A concept of time in China as this was manifest in Chinese science was the object of discussion in a lecture delivered by Professor Joseph Needham and published as *Time and Eastern Man* (1965). According to Needham, the Chinese viewed historical and biological time as a succession of events, cumulative, linear, and algebraic, rather than geometric, a system where "like causes bring like effects, as it was then so it is now, and so will it be forever" (ibid: 16). Contrary to a Christian West, where the world outlook is "a unique present with an open future which would be affected by the action of the individual," the Greco-Roman world recognized a cyclic view of time where "time would return yet again to its beginning and all things will be restored to their original state" (ibid: 46). In effect, although both China and the West lived a linear concept of time, both were also influenced by a cyclic view. In this matter, Needham concluded, "on the whole China was a culture more of the Irano-Judeo-Christian type than the Indo-Hellenic" (ibid: 52).

In contrast to China, the region of India and Southeast Asia was absorbed in another concept of the world, another measure of time, not a linear, cause-and-effect entity of logic and matter, but a metaphysical world with a profound respect for nature and the divine for whom temples, stone monuments, and stupas were constructed, a life replete with rituals and ceremonies, in constant communication with spirits and deities with whom man corresponded to maintain an equilibrium with nature. In this part of the world, time was recorded less in writing events and more in the erection of stone symbols, shrines, the recounting of oral literature and practice of old beliefs and traditions. A very old custom of using bamboo tubes as a receptacle for cooking rice in the fire may be paralleled by a corresponding use of bamboo as a musical instrument, with both usages still alive today. Cultivation of rice since past millennia has not changed much and a secondary burial practiced in the region since thousands of years continues on today (Fox 1970).

While reflections on time in the scientific world of China and the metaphysical universe of India have their respective references for discussion, speculations on time in music of both regions have for a base of study not only the sound of the music itself but also its structure, its instruments, and its symbolisms, a product of perception more subtle than conscious thought in written documents. In the early 1940s a concept of space as a division of time was illustrated in music, in an analogy between physical space in the universe, the solar system, and the circumnavigation of the world on the one hand, and a concept of musical space in the renaissance, the discovery of equal temperament, harmony, and the expression of that musical space through the use of a wider range of instruments on the other (Lowinsky 1941). In Southeast Asia such historical associations between events have fewer sources in writing, but ideas about a relationship between musical time and culture may also be viewed as philosophical concepts which find expression in a respect for nature, infinity, and the divine—notions which are an intrinsic part of life in this part of the world.

Drone and Melody

In Southeast Asia one musical element concerning time is the concept of a vibrating medium which, in the suspended gong, the metallophone, the whole gamelan ensemble, and other gong ensembles, is allowed to vibrate freely with one stroke, without further control of the fingers, the hands, or human volition. Unless the vibration is stopped, the gong will vibrate by itself, unlike a bowed string or a wind instrument whose sounds stop the moment the bowing or the blowing stops, that is, under the direct and continuous control of the human will. A gong sound is at liberty to vibrate by itself. Other non-gong percussion instruments made up of plant and animal materials are similarly free to vibrate by themselves once they are struck, and the rapidity of the decay of their vibrations characterize their sounds. The discovery of bronze and its use as musical instruments brought about another concept of time, for the freedom of vibration in instruments with short decays became one of long duration, a new aesthetic value which the court societies of Southeast Asia favored, gradually leaving a native music played on bamboo and wooden instruments to remain mostly in villages and rural areas.

A sense of mystery pervades gong sounds associated with rituals, ceremonies, and communications with spirits; and a fundamental element that characterizes these sounds appears in a concept of drone or ostinato, as this is present in many if not most gong ensembles of Southeast Asia. Drone may be understood to be not only a sustained sound, a continuation of the long vibration of gongs, but also a constantly repeating phrase of one or more pitches played by one or several instruments for the duration of the music. The continuous and repeating sound may be an identifiable pitch or not, a series of pitches making a phrase, or it may form a group of repeating sounds. Moreover, several instruments may each play a repeating sound, and together they constitute a drone. The repetition may form irregular or regular beats, a sound or sounds grouped into one, two, or four beats.

A more important element of drone concerns music ensembles with a large number of instruments repeating rhythmic phrases, each instrument acting separately, at the same time as the whole group behaves together as a drone. In these ensembles the indefinite pitches of different sizes and types of gongs, drums, and cymbals produce a variety of timbres. The pitches are lost in the harmonic series and what is left is a homogeneous blend of the sound and the pulse of the music. The pulse and the timbre make up the drone. They are the markers of time, not the pitch. A melody instrument may accompany the drone ensemble, but its pitches move independently of the pitches of the drone instruments. This concept of drone differs from drone in Indian music or ostinato in Western music, both of which are centered on pitch, rather than pulse or timbre.

A musical counterpart of drone is melody, which may be taken as a succession or permutation of pitches, events in time in many musical ensembles in Southeast Asia (Maceda 1974). A bilateral relationship between drone and melody describes not only the music but also the thinking behind the music, for different combinations of drone and melody represent an expression of a group of people, perhaps a reflection of a social organization, a representation of values, and a view of time. While time may be measured by pulse in a drone, it may also be represented by pitches in a melody, except that, where pulse or beats in a drone are repeated regularly, melodic pitch occurs in time irregularly, often avoiding the regularity of the pulse. A melody that moves around a principal tone differs from one which uses several tones, having no preference for principal or secondary tones. Furthermore, an elasticity of intervals between pitches creates nuances between these intervals comparable to a view of chromaticism in Western culture and music (Clement 1979).[1]

Perspective in Time

Many examples might be offered for music from Southeast Asia which is based on repetition or drone with melody. The isolation of important musical elements, especially drone and melody as just explained, show their usages in time and identifies a music of Southeast Asia in relationship to other musical cultures in Asia and Europe.

A view of time in the music of Southeast Asia does not differ as much from music in China or India as it does from Europe, where musical perspectives see musical principles in another perception of the world. The music of Southeast Asia covers a very long span in time, extending from prehistory to the present, a period of thousands of years. This extension of time is important because it points to a slow change rather than fast development as exemplified especially in European music. One unifying factor in the music of Southeast Asia is the element of repetition, which has become a musical form itself, one which may be called drone, ostinato, or punctuation in solo instruments as well as complex ensembles including the *gamelan* and the *pii phaad*. Repetition and pulse, an element of drone, are measures of time which are anchored in most instrumental musical forms in Southeast Asia. While in India, drone is a tonal center, in Southeast Asia, drone is a pulse, a

1. Catherine Clement refers to Claude Levi-Strauss' ideas on chromaticism which may be symbolized in rainbows, poisons, potions, odors, colors, or in ambiguity, women, and some animals. "That the analysis of South American myths would have led us to make of the poison for fishing or hunting a combinatory variant of the seducer, poisoner of the social order, and that between nature and culture, one or the other appears like two modalities of the reign of small intervals, is well to convince that the philtre of love and the philtre of death are interchangeable for reasons other than those pulled out from simple opportunity and leads to reflect on the profound causes of chromaticism in Tristan" (p. 411: translation by José Maceda).

regular repetition of percussion instruments, principally gongs, drums, and cymbals. Drone is a center of time which controls melody and the space around which melody moves. It is a pillar which supports music itself, like a law of nature, an equilibrium between man and nature. Drone expresses notions of infinity with an inner life made alive by simple beats and timbres, colors of indefinite pitches of low-sounding bossed gongs and diffused, scattered sounds of flat gongs, bamboo, and wooden percussions.

Drone exists by itself as a musical form in solo instruments or a group of instruments practiced by many cultural-language groups of people over a wide area in Southeast Asia. Their use in rituals is well known, which include ceremonies after harvest, weddings, peace pacts, communication with spirits, dances, offerings by the rich, feasts to honor the spirit of rice, state affairs, and religious celebrations. Music in the form of repeating beats is an expression of all these events. The mere sound of musical instruments denotes the occasion and the ritual.

To speak of the indefinite pitch of gongs, drums, cymbals, and a whole range of percussions made of plant materials is an inadequate description of the sound colors they produce. The sounds of bamboo and wooden instruments still used in rural areas can only be described by an enumeration of each of these instruments. They represent a view of the sound spectrum not in fixed pitches, but in timbres difficult to capture in written symbols like pitch sounds. Gongs have definite and indefinite pitches. Flat gongs make brilliant ringing sounds, and dampening them with various techniques alters their quality without identifying these qualities individually as in instruments with definite pitches. Similarly, as with suspended gongs, although some big gongs may have the pitches of their harmonics identified, many gongs produce a diffused pitch or timbre, with the whole ensemble functioning more as a color group rather than a pitch group. The timbres describe the ensemble, and time divides these timbres into beats and pulses. Timbre, pulse, and indefinite pitch are the principal sound qualities that drone instruments play with, a measure of time as rich in sound qualities as the use of identifiable fixed pitches in melodies.

Another measure of time lies in melody or in space where pitches can be conveniently identified, written, and analyzed. Written melodies can thus be seen while drone colors can only be heard. The melodies in various ensembles have a quality of indefiniteness in their flow and direction, with changing anchors in tonal centers, principal and secondary tones. In the

Malay peninsula, Sumatra, and village Java, a solo melody provided by a string or wind instrument moves around tonal centers, and the intervallic relationships between these centers make up the melodic structure. In the Phu-Thai ensemble of Northeast Thailand, the short melodic phrase is clearly heard, repeated incessantly, but minute changes, variations, extensions, and unpredictable entrances of each variant spread and diffuse the melody in time. A listener plays an endless game of finding out which melody one instrument follows in another, as it avoids, duplicates, or waits for the melody of any of the four other instruments pursuing the same ends.

The use and the maneuvering of pitches to construct melodies demand techniques which are dependent on culture. They do not just happen. The choice of pitches and their arrangement becomes very particular in the gong ensembles of Java, Thailand, and Mindanao, where gongs or metallophones, not wind or string instruments, make up the melody. In these ensembles melodies are limited to five tones of their scales, four out of five of which tones are in a fifth interval relationship with each other, making a bipolar opposition of fifths possible between two pairs of tones, rather than just one pair, thus making the opposition weak or redundant, for any of the four tones in the two pairs could be the stronger or weaker tone.

In the Javanese *gamelan* an opposition between the first and the fifth interval may be seen in *cengkok* in the form of unstable and stable degrees, or in Thai fifths where they are treated as pivot points. A technique of bipolarity came into use in the Magindanaon *kulintang* as played by Amal Lemuntod, which was a contrast to a wandering use of tones in the *kulintang* of the Sama of Sulu.

The music of Southeast Asia fills time along notions of continuity, infinity, and indefiniteness in a non-secular, metaphysical world, and hierarchy in a secular world. The musical techniques used in musical forms prefer melodic ambiguity, repetition, and diffusion to an identification and isolation of things as these are brought about by a system of logic known as causality.

The principle of causality is a mode of thinking whose origins date back to various works of Aristotle. In an article on music logic, Charles Seeger sees classical, formal Aristotelian logic as a technique that deals with structural concepts of laws of thought involving "identity, contradiction and the excluded middle" (1960: 232). In addition, the philosopher Jacques Derrida considers Western thought as always

> structured in terms of dichotomies or polarities: good vs. evil, being vs. nothingness, presence vs. absence, truth vs. error, identity vs. difference, mind vs. matter, man vs. woman, soul vs. body, life vs. death, nature vs. culture, and equal entities. The second term in each pair is considered a negative, corrupt, undesirable version of the first. In other words, the two terms are not simply opposed in their meanings, but are arranged in hierarchical order which gives the first term *priority*. (1981: viii).

It was at the time of the Renaissance, when Greek thought, Aristotelian logic, and causality were gaining favor in Europe, that a harmonic musical expression was taking shape, similarly employing this hierarchical order in the dominant and tonic relationship where the tonic is given priority over the dominant, a concept which provided a strong and convenient base for rapid musical development. Such an opposition had a linear, either-or relationship, different from the many choices of tonal centers open to five tones of pentatonic scales of gong ensembles in Southeast Asia. In Europe, instead of a pentatonic structure with built-in fifths and gapped-scale melodies, two disjunct tetrachords superimposed one on top of the other supplied the base for a diatonic-melodic relationship. Structural points or tones had to be chosen from seven tones of the scale, unlike the five tones in gong ensembles which were treated from the very outset as points of equal importance. While in the *gamelan*, *pi-phaad*, and *kulintang*, fifth polarities between all the five tones were prospectively of equal importance, in Europe only one set, consisting of the first and fifth intervals, was isolated from seven tones and given special preference as dominant and tonic intervals. A harmonic treatment between these two poles underwent a process of change involving other fifths and tones of the scale in complex modulations, always in bipolar oppositions.

The dominant-tonic dichotomy is a precise tool of identification as causality is in logic, and a whole range of musical forms from the Renaissance or the medieval ages to the present would not be able to identify themselves without this basic opposition which they contain embedded in every phrase or melodic progression of these musical forms.[2] It appears then that the principle of causality is basic in Western music, and in science, Professor Needham sees a connection between time, science, and causality. He says,

> There can be no doubt that time is a basic parameter of all scientific thinking... It lies at the root of all natural knowledge, whether based on observations ... or upon experiences ... The appreciation of causality, so basic to science, must surely have been favored by a belief in the reality of time (1965: 48–49).

However, in another instance, he considers it somewhat debatable that syllogistic logic would have helped the growth of the sciences, even as he observes how

> the failure of Chinese culture to develop systematic logic on Aristotelian and scholastic lines

may have been the effect of a Chinese preoccupation with historiography and linear chronological time (ibid: 15).[3]

In music, the historical role and development of syllogistic logic in the form of dominant and tonic which, even after its dissolution in atonality, still employed bipolarity in serial music—in *fff* and *ppp*, very high and very low pitches, clusters and single tones, sounds and silences—appear evident and undeniable, but an equivalent principle seems to be more diffused in Western science. And yet, to the question that Professor Needham posed, "Why has modern science ... not developed itself but in the Western world?" (1973: 5), a partial explanation that parallels bipolarity in music may perhaps be traced to a thinking in the Greek classical period, in an Aristotelian logic that was acknowledged and understood by European thinkers, like harmony was discovered or formulated out of this system of bipolar reasoning. This mode of deduction

2. Actually, the oppositions are not merely dominant and tonic, but complicated offshoots of that relationship. In the first prelude of J.S. Bach's *Well Tempered Clavichord*, the beginning arpeggi–C: I, II_7, I, VI_6, G: V_7, I_6–are an expression of cause and effect, which leads one statement, one arpeggio into another, in a logical and strict harmonic process. Statement II_7 is in opposition to Statement I for which a resolution later to I is made via V_7. A direct resolution would have been I, V, I, the original cause and effect bipolarity, but in I, II_7, V_7, I the statement II_7 colors the resolution, at the same time as it is still a part of the logic. The next statement C: VI_6, a fifth of II_7, serves as a bridge to G: V_7, also a fifth of G: I_6, showing the importance of the fifth as a pivot or as an opposition to another statement. The last arpeggio I_6 is expressed indirectly in the first inversion, and hence is a weak opposition to the dominant G: V_7.

While in Debussy's *Piano Studies*, the dissonance-consonance dichotomy is still clear as in the *Octave and Chord Studies*, in Strawinsky's *Rite of Spring*, they are merged within ostinati patterns, so a whole passage appears like a massive drone of opposing harmonies, as in *Danses des Adolescentes* and *Rondes Printaniéres*.

3. In Asia it is not only in China where logic (see "Chinese logic" in *The Encylopedia of Philosophy*, vol. 3, pp. 523–525) was cultivated, but also in India (see "Indian logic," *ibid*, pp. 520–523) where it was especially developed. There is a partial similarity between Indian categories of substance, "quale," action, generic character, ultimate difference, "inheritance," and those of Aristotle (*ibid* p. 522). However, the point sought for is that although a logic cultivated in Asia may have affinities with that of Greece, it has not been made the unique focus of musical structure as it has been in Europe.

Apart from a bipolarity in logic, there is also an opposition in *yin* and *yang*, *linggam* and *yoni*, and a dualism in Papua New Guinea, Timor, Sulawesi, and other parts of Southeast Asia which are not at all the same oppositions in Greek reasoning and in logical oppositions employed in Western music.

became the early basis of a development of very complex systems of thought in Western science which music mirrors in its many and subtle shades of technical-musical expressions. Indeed, musical suspensions, passing tones, modulations, double-sharps, and diminished fifths are scientific tools whose uses and placements in precise slots in music compositions are based on a thinking in dominant-tonic bipolarity.

This is not to say that there may not be other more important factors which may be ascribed to a unique development of science in a relatively short time. Max Weber raised questions similar to those posed by Joseph Needham, but his interests lay in explaining how religious elements contributed toward a rise of capitalism in the West (1930). On the other hand, Michel Foucault was concerned with an archeology of human sciences, an order of words and things that made man the object of his own knowledge, an end in itself, a unique feature of European culture (1966).

In Southeast Asia, it is precisely this absence of a development of a musical technique equal to bipolarity or causality which prevented that music from expressing in precise terms oppositions in anything—in ideas, emotions, abstractions—a technique unfamiliar to the region, which is exploited fully by European music. In melodies without any clear and purposeful pitch oppositions, the thinking is not oriented toward closure, for identification and precision would narrow a view, and may lose its contact with other perspectives, especially a concept of the larger space, infinity, a metaphysical construct of the universe. Such music hinges on non-confrontation, an avoidance of issues, problems, and questions which can more pointedly be solved by a bipolar reasoning. The techniques of causality never really took hold in a music of Southeast Asia, and not even in China, in spite of the influence of the Mohists. It is as if its acceptance would have limited time to a dichotomy of events, and would have made causality responsible for succeeding acts of opposition inherent in this system of reasoning.

While Southeast Asia accommodates with nature and places music in a relationship between nature and the metaphysical world rather than human events, Europe confronts that physical world, and with a use and control of logic and reason, a tool of identification and precision, associates a music of dichotomies to a vast array of human perceptions impossible to isolate in techniques without bipolar oppositions. The Southeast Asian tradition of thousands of years lives in a separate time from the modern world—with a minimum of wants and constraints, a sense of peace, and no tensions brought about by clear goals, timetables, and exact calculations—now overwhelmed by a complex, controlled, and efficient world. It thinks that while such a world gives comfort, solves problems, and alleviates suffering, it feels at the same time that in that world there is less room for qualities like patience, sorrow, doubt, and humility, and other spiritual attributes which are spurned by the righteousness of logic and precision. Furthermore, a confusion arises out of a conflict of values in these two traditions, for example, in an application of economic theories that bring about extremes of overdevelopment and underdevelopment, or in an adoption of musical techniques that result in a harmonization of native tunes and an expansion of small instrumental ensembles into large orchestras.

In reality, structures such as drone and melody, and dominant and tonic are mere objects enlivened only by human experience in the very musical forms they produce and in their integration with human beliefs and emotions. Increasingly the universal access to past tools of music production and to the emotions they engender makes it possible for modern society to peer into them and test their relevance in the contemporary world. The thinking behind the organization of music of old human traditions is a guide to a search for new musical expressions, or new life-styles, without which, or without a human basis for music making, electromagnetic hardware and a prepared software of musical production alone would be insufficient to give life, meaning, and a humaneness to any musical expression they convey. In this sense the time of the past is as modern as the present, and a linkage between the two times may be found in a balance which holds the speed and precision of logic and science within boundaries of an equilibrium between man and nature.

Bibliography

Catherine Clement, "Le Lieu de la Musique," *Claude Levi-Strauss, Textes de et sur Claude Levi-Strauss reunis par Raymond Bellour et Catherine Clement.* (Paris: Gallimard, 1979.)

Jacques Derrida, *Dissemination*. Translation by B. Johnson. (Chicago: University of Chicago Press, 1981.)

The Encylopedia of Philosophy, "Time," Vols. 7 and 8 (126–139). "Causation," Vols. 1 and 2 (56–66), 1972.

Robert Fox, *The Tabon Caves: Archaeological Explorations and Excavations of Palawan Island, Philippines*. (Manila: National Museum, 1970.)
"Manunggul Caves." (*Filipino Heritage*, 1, 169–173, 1970.)

Michel Foucault, *Les Mots et les choses; une archéologie des sciences humaines* (Paris: Gallimard, 1966.)

Edward Lowinsky, "The Concept of Physical and Musical Space in the Renaissance," *Papers of the American Musicological Society* (57–84), 1941.

José Maceda, "Drone and Melody in Philippine Musical Instruments," *Traditional Drama and Music of Southeast Asia* (246–273). (Kuala Lumpur: Kementerian Pelajaran Malaysia, 1974.)

Joseph Needham, *Time and Eastern Man*. (Royal Anthropological Institute of Great Britain and Ireland Glasgow: MacLehose University Press, 1965.)
La Science et le'Occident. (Paris: Seuil, 1973.)

Charles Seeger, "On the Moods of a Music-Logic." (*Journal of the American Musicological Society*, 12, 224–261, 1960.)

Max Weber, *Protestant Ethic and the Spirit of Capitalism.* Translation by Talcott Parsons. (New York: Scribner and Sons, 1930.)

CHAPTER 19

"MICRO-RITMIA": HYPER-HUMAN MUSIC

ERNESTO MARTÍNEZ

Two musicians sit down in front of their instruments, they "get connected" and they start to receive rhythmic beats through their headsets. It is a sonorous code, an audible clock that they have learned to obey with precision.

Like "human machines" these two musicians are geared together, they form a precise system which is basically dualistic: each one plays an instrument similar to that of the other, producing different sounds that become forged into one. In the same way, two anatomies are forged into one. They themselves form the final link in the chain, as if they were peripheral elements that communicate with the outside world through the compositions and improvisations they create. They have in their hands a powerful tool which allows them total control in the execution of twenty or more "events" or beats per second. This is a fundamental sonorous chronometer that they have learned to follow with precision, marking the exact point where each note, each silence, or each chord must fall. Their improvisational freedom remains intact. The timing and the textures produced are unthinkable in conventional execution which has been limited by individual human anatomy, the rules of which in this instance cease to operate and disappear. The two players form what could be called a "hyper-anatomic unit," giving rise to the term "hyper-human music."

Until recently the textures thus produced were the exclusive domain of computers. Indeed, it is a space stolen from the field of cybernetics and transported back to our habitual world of muscles, chords, pipes, tensed membranes, and live performers.

Background

Upon completing my studies in the National School of Music in Mexico City I encountered a musical world which held little attraction or interest for me. I felt it offered me nothing, nor was I able to offer it anything of importance. Two of the main options were dodecaphonic or chance music. I continued searching for two or three years without any kind of production, and in the meantime found work, as I still do today, tuning pianos. During this time I met Conlon Nancarrow and became familiar with his music; the impact was strong and ongoing. It wasn't until I discovered the technique which I now call "micro-ritmia" that I began working again as a composer. In 1994, I began a more dedicated phase of experimentation with real musicians thanks to the participation of three other Mexican musicians, Eduardo González (composer and pianist) and, more recently, Alejandro Huerta and Juan Mercado (percussionists). We have lived intense experiences in composition and improvisation which have both challenged and motivated us. In a little less than ten years, we have been able to make our old instruments speak in new ways, and we have entered new worlds, such as that of hyper-velocity in live performances. Today there is ample testimony of these events in two recordings (*Micro-Ritmia*, México 1997, Lejos del Paraíso, CDGLP83, and *Mutaciónes*, New York 2004, Tzadik TZ 7096, www.tzadik.com). In the following pages I will try to deepen and clarify these concepts.

The Human Clock—Beats Per Second

As it turns out, "micro-ritmia," the technique which I thought I had discovered, (as I found out later) had already been around for some 800 years and continues to be a living tradition in places like Bali, Africa, and Bolivia, and in the Middle Ages was known as "hocketus." This age-old technique is based on the alternate execution between two musicians where each produces his/her own sound and then waits for a turn in the cycle of the ensemble to intervene again. In these ensembles there are often numerous musicians participating. The group executes instruments of the same type in different ranges to achieve a unified sound as if it were a much larger instrument. Clearly, among many players there is the creation of a sonorous tissue, interwoven with great complexity. This is intrinsically collective music. Nevertheless, in the model which I conceived, there is an element which could carry this ancient technique to unsuspected and surprising arenas: the synchronicity of two musicians mediated by audible signals communicated through headsets, as if they were a human clock. As it were, a type of "motorized hocketus."

In its elemental form, "micro-ritmia" basically requires two musicians—each with a musical instrument of any type, but both with the same type as the companion (except for the human voice)—two sets of headphones, and some weeks of practice. The sonorous base which both musicians hear through their headsets is the fundamental key to their coordination and the possibility of reaching potentially greater musical resources. We are talking about a clock formed by audio beats. The greater the number of beats per second, the greater the velocity. The beats heard on the headsets form a grid upon which the musicians can oscillate between hyper-slowness and hyper-speed. If one sound is articulated for every beat there will be hyper-speed and, to the contrary, if the sound is articulated every "x" number of beats, the speed is reduced. The perfect analogy is found in MIDI technology, where clocks calibrated to a specific number of beats in time (BPQN, beats per quarter note) determine the definition of sonorous events. Those in charge of reading these pulses and converting them into music are the so-called sequencers. In "micro-ritmia" the receivers of the impulses are the executors themselves. Their performance is analogous to a sequencer.

This is an important point because what it means is that a human player (musician, dancer, etc.) who learns to synchronize with an audio beat can cross into and transit sonorous regions and worlds which would otherwise be inaccessible to him or her. Similar to a prosthesis, or a diver's suit, or a seat on an airplane, it is a "plus" which enables us to conquer worlds, unexplored oceans that we could not reach using our natural capabilities.

The clock which emits the beats per second is fragmented according to the number of participants. If we have, for example, sixteen beats per second, we need two players, one of whom receives and acts on beats 1, 3, 5, 7, 9, 11, 13, and 15, while the other executes beats 2, 4, 6, 8, 10, 12, 14, and 16. If the speed is increased to, say, thirty-two beats per second, it is necessary to have four musicians utilizing the following fragmentation: A) 1, 5, 9, 13, 17, 21; B) 2, 6, 10, 14, 18, 22; C) 3, 7, 11, 15, 19, 23; and D) 4, 8, 12, 16, 20, and 24. The production of the beats needs to be constructed with precision in the presence of bass, medium range, and high-pitched sounds (a simple click won't work) so that they form a realistic "acoustic counterbalance" to the musical instruments being used by the musicians. They form two opposing sounds which must be perfectly balanced: the sounds from the headphones vs. the sounds of the musical instruments. Aside from these elements there are also at least two centers of gravity which come into play, forming the gravitational centers which are the beats giving rise to individual temporality. It is thus difficult to retain the synchronicity since each musician places his/her notes between the hundredths of seconds of the other player, never at the same time. Listening to all the elements at once is transcendental for the execution of "micro-ritmia." It is worthwhile to note that the method doesn't propitiate or force the musician to play his/her instrument more rapidly. Speed is achieved through synchronicity; synchronicity as a collective effort, as a summed potential as a synergistic manifestation.

There are two aspects I would like to underline: first, the skill required of the musician in following the beats with precision can be acquired through several weeks of practice, after which, in our experience, one achieves an environment that is experienced as a comfort zone by the musicians. It has been surprising to discover that it is possible to adapt naturally and without problems to the demands of millionths of seconds of precision.

Once the initial stage that requires consciousness and concentration is interiorized and conquered, the brain assimilates these new experiences and within a fairly short period of time the practice becomes automatic. When the participation becomes almost automatic the musician reaches the level at which the technique becomes natural; it then becomes possible to concentrate on the purely musical aspects, favoring artistic expression without being concerned about keeping up with the beats.

Second, once the skill level makes it possible to couple the notes with precision (even in slower tempos), the musician can then gear the level of execution to speeds over thirty beats per second. We have not yet found an upper limit.

Improvisation

In order to improvise or compose using "micro-ritmic" principles, it is essential to consider two elements that benefit the sound fusion between performers:

1. Close Region. Each performer should place his/her notes in the same region as the rest of the ensemble, not beyond a fourth. To achieve this during improvisations, one performer will act as a leader, and the others as followers. The leader decides the zones where the improvisation will take place. Clearly a game of follow-the-leader.

2. Double Tone Color. Since repeating the same note reduces the sense of speed, it is recommended to think in terms of double tone color, i.e., the same note with different tone color, two notes, two chords within the same tonality, two modes, bitonality, atonality, etc. Of course, it's also important to be open to the possibility of what might happen if one fails to observe these rules, perhaps producing interesting results.

Anatomy

Music which uses tuned sounds, as in the great range of known musical instruments, has been created with the idea of being executed predominantly individually. The human hand as an anatomical element has, among others, the following characteristics and limitations:

—ease in executing scales (adjacent notes)
—ease in executing notes that skip other notes going in the same direction
—ease in executing repeated notes
—ease in alternating hands
—difficulty in executing broken melodic lines
—difficulty in executing two or more notes simultaneously (intervals or chords) in ascending, descending, or broken movements that are not static
—difficulty in executing jumps
—at high speed the only touch possible is legato.

Broadly speaking, these characteristics have predetermined most of the concert music produced to date. This anatomical disposition, as well as any other means, has its limits, some of which are the following: In the execution of "easy" anatomical movements (points one through four), the speed reached is already maximum. On the contrary, in the execution of "difficult" anatomical movements (points five through seven), the speed drops dramatically. Here we can see clearly the relation between texture and speed and we can deduce the anatomical implications in the evolution of music. In synthesis, we can say that we are accustomed to hearing musical textures that are coherent to individual human anatomy; we will never hear passages with rapid chords, neither in fast broken melodic lines or fast staccato passages.

How to surpass these restrictions?

Hyper–Anatomy

If the human hand possessed eight fingers on each hand, the music which would have arrived in our times would have been created with ad hoc musical instruments and that music would be radically different. So, if we were to change human anatomy, we would be forced to create new musical instruments that would lead us inevitably to the generation of new music. This is the point I would like to approach: in "micro-ritmia," there is a drastic alteration of anatomy because it becomes essentially a dual phenomenon (two musicians form an anatomical unit, a "hyper-anatomy") and the conditioning elements mentioned earlier disappear while other new ones arise with other new limitations. Some of the new characteristics are:

—the seven points mentioned above fall within "easy" execution.
—the speed in each one of these points is doubled, tripled, etc.; at high speed the most favorable forms of touch are staccato and "tongue" (which intrinsically imprint greater sonorous energy and favor precision).
—there is ONE melody executed between two musicians.
—there is ONE bass executed between two musicians.
—there is ONE accompaniment executed between two musicians; melodic, rhythmic, and harmonic functions are drastically altered and are thus converted into an area of research and investigation.

Hyperión

This is a keyboard nylon-stringed instrument which I have been designing and perfecting over the past two years; it attempts to respond to the needs of hyper-anatomy and to explore one step beyond the hyper-velocity sensation. Let's take a look.

I have been able to observe that the most precise, energetic, and fast movement that human beings possess is that of the wrist, and, more concretely, it is the alternation of wrists. This intrinsic capability of humans not only is not exploited in keyboard, holles, keys, or fret instruments; it is in fact inhibited, for a curious reason: to take full advantage of this motor resource (the alternation of wrist movement), it is necessary that the sounds emitted by each wrist be close to that of the other, which is to say that they must be interlaced in the same region with a range not greater than one fourth, as mentioned earlier. What occurs if the distance is greater than a fourth is that the effect of melodic fusion disappears and there is the perception of two isolated musical events, thus causing each to be heard out of sync with that produced by the other wrist and at half the speed. To the contrary, if they remain at close range, the speed is doubled and the sounds produced by both wrists are perceived as a unit. This is the key point which sustains "micro-ritmia": alternating sound events (two musicians) produced by similar timbres (two instruments of the same type) in regions close to each other to produce the sensation of unity.

In the "Hyperión" we find that the alternation of wrist movement is privileged through this instrument since its range, which extends along three octaves, has a tendency from bass notes to high notes, repeating the same schema toward the center of the instrument, thus allowing the attack on the same sonorous region while maintaining the arms separated and avoiding the inherent obstruction between the hands which is experienced on the piano. This allows us the incorporation of a valuable motor resource as the preponderant element in musical discourse, adding the benefit of being able to fuse both hands in one melodic-rhythmic line. Thus it is possible to think, in this sense, of a "micro-ritmia" (produced by both hand-wrists) individually or as a soloist.

I think that the capability of the human ear in capturing sounds of different densities, speeds, timbres, and dynamics is absolutely unsuspected and reaches far beyond the advances made by all societies put together in terms of auditive stimulation. I am fascinated by the recognition that even an untrained ear can capture a whole branch of high-speed sonorous events, allowing each event an important place and meaning in musical syntax. In this sense, it can be said that our muscular structure has evolved to levels considerably below our auditive capabilities. This gives rise to the idea of generating methods which on one hand stimulate our ear to a greater degree and generate new sensations and new levels of energy, and on the other hand produce new advantages in human musical execution. This has become my principal motivation in continuing with these experiments.

I believe that another important part of the project consist of developing didactic systems that are simple and that facilitate practice and learning in these areas, which are vast in themselves. The demand and interest shown by musicians is beginning to emerge slowly, and thus it seems fundamental to place these techniques in the hands of those who may be interested.

It is also useful to note that the practice of these techniques will favor and assist any musician in countless every day music situations, producing an extremely valuable didactic benefit. As an example, the live generation of complex rhythms, timbres, and spaces using eco chains and processors, is a field that I am enthusiastically exploring in parallel and as a direct result of "micro-ritmic" experiences.

Finally, as a last thought, I would like to propose that perhaps the history of music can be read as akin to the "note density," moving from the austere times of plain chant to Mozart who was accused in his day of writing "too many notes," to recent-day Nancarrow, harvesting 127 sound events per second from his automatic piano players. I am sure that the human brain perhaps needs more time to digest more dense textures, but it can suddenly jump to a higher level and start to build images and sensations that become significant and meaningful to listeners. The brain learns, develops, and generates new understandings.

All of this is in the hands of composers who take on the task of creating evocative and seductive music that, in turn, expands the palate of images and sensations available to the sensitive listener. This is our motivation.

In the meantime, staying faithful to the advancement of this challenge, we are in the final stages of producing a whole family of "Hyperións" (bass and tenors), that will form a fundamental part of our third album and which will help us explore more fully the hidden sonorous energy in the world of micro-spaces.

For María Cristina, Mariana, and Esteban

Querétaro, Qro. México, Winter 2006,
Translation: Kathryn E. Seib Vargas

CHAPTER 20

THE SCIENCE OF FINDING

LAWRENCE D. "BUTCH" MORRIS

Who cares if music we are listening to is improvised or notated?

I certainly don't. There are enough issues to get in the way of one's musical enjoyment than to stratify the conditions of music, music making, or the sheer joy of it.

I do believe that both are skills that have been, will, and need to be broadened in the coming age to understand the breadth of their usage and capacities.

My interest lies in that area between the two: where the interpretation of the symbolism that generates notation meets with the spontaneity of improvisation; and in the evolution of the ensemble, and of the individual and collective identities and expressions that constitute music, musicianship, and music making for a far greater expression in the sonic arts.

At the same time, I have also recognized an overriding need to locate in music an essence that can, by its various operations, present questions, prompt definitions, explanations, and expressions of and to what I feel, hear, and think—transformed into coherent, often poignant information.

For more than twenty years, through Conduction I have had the privilege to engage and enjoy, from the inside, this intermediate space between notation and improvisation, acquiring new skills and perspectives while doing so.

The context, of course, has been polarized by history and practice: musicians and musical communities bound by notation, and musicians and musical communities bound by improvisation. Yet between them is the space where a potential for new life, an expansive range of expression that has gone untouched, prevails; and where ideals and ideas incubate for the continuum of the "musical" canon.

Conduction®: a vocabulary of ideographic signs and gestures *activated to modify or construct* a real-time musical *arrangement* (of any notation)

> or *composition*. Each sign and gesture *transmits generative information for interpretation* and provides *instantaneous possibilities for altering or initiating* harmony, melody, rhythm, articulation, phrasing, or form.

Conduction concerns transmission, communication, and expression; a common ground where all culture and style cohabit, not only by way of their distinctiveness, but also in how each contributes, in an ensemble, to a unique encounter. More intimately, it concerns a capacity of musicianship for new skills with new principles.

The vocabulary of Conduction is symbolic information (directives: signs and gestures) that carry definition and meaning to propel musicians toward substantive understanding and achievement. It provides the precision and the focus needed to navigate music's vast terrain.

The principles of Conduction foster, enhance, and evoke the analytical reasoning of each musician's history, knowledge, intelligence, experience, instinct, intuition, expression, will, and fantasy as fundamental requirement.

In Conduction, the art of composition and the immediacy of performance become interdependent—while the language of music cultivates and integrates all vernaculars and traditions open to, and in, the ensemble.

Results are ever present: enhanced musicianship; discovery of structure and substance in the arc of the performance; the evolution of a social logic based on new reciprocities between human and music, and between composer and conductor, conductor as composer, instrumentalist and conductor, instrumentalist and composer—and audience, attaining new levels of momentary logic and new clarities about the character of the work itself.

Now, this bridge that Conduction builds between notation and improvisation fuels interest. For with it, I can identify, embrace, and exploit the weaknesses and strengths of both together and depict, in the process, core limitations in either. Conduction also requires its realization in physical, rather than theoretical, form to facilitate (new) kinds of augmentation. The logic of circumstance(s) dictates the maximizing of encounter, and the musical and social structures that grow from such encounter.

Conduction is vivacious in that it draws on the full expanse of musical design while asking of its musicians that they refine their capacities beyond style and cultural aesthetic or social difference.

There are as many rewards as questions here but none, it seems, as significant as that which opens pathways, both individually and collectively; pathways shuttered previously by custom or fear. And I refer to the exclusionary focus of most musical traditions and to the fear of compromising identity.

Conduction, however, is not in contestation with given forms as much as it seeks to supplement them with a greater appreciation of possibility—a capacity for dialogue uniquely spurred by the moments and movements that appear and vanish.

At the same time, by stripping away predispositions to value this or that in music, we also construct a mirror to the kinds of relationships that subsist in society, and the wherewithal of music to challenge and transform them; a community in microcosm that functions via this dynamic.

Conduction is neither method nor process, but practicum that *reveals* only in practice and through all its metaphorical concepts.

A sonic arena utilizing every tool in its arsenal to construct, deconstruct, and reconstruct with and from the basic properties of pitch, duration, intensity, and timbre. Primed by an "Extra Dimension," which motivates us to engage and respond within, as beyond, all territory, Conduction invokes a continuum that thrives in a real-time transmission of relationships and meaning; the spontaneity and precision that we need to ignite and combust order and organization within sonic thought.

From the Conductor's Perspective

Conduction is the art of "environing," the organization of surrounding things, conditions, or influences. It is a technique to capture and discover sonic information, structure and substructure, meaning, implication, and expression (as we construct together)—all primary values in our pursuit of coherence and poignancy, and the immediacy of place.

From the Perspective of the Instrumentalist

The musician learns that Conduction is ensemble skill, and that Conduction's criteria drive attentiveness, discrimination, understanding, perception, and execution.

Each Conduction sign has definition, yet within that definition each musician is obliged to qualitatively define its "content." The descriptive (vocabulary) thus generates prospect; and by virtue of the definition attached to each sign, each interpretation evolves by progressive self-development through historical and momentary orientation.

To contribute to Conduction, the musician reveals explicit content within the evolving work. As such, musical flexibility and potential expand as we explore a new condition of liberty to foster individual and collective freedoms in real time.

A state of risk, certainly; a distillation of immediacy, no doubt; the incarnation of a step in the evolution of music that each musician embodies: this is a goal.

Conduction is an art that flowers in contradiction (for some), ambiguity (for others), and encounter (for all involved). By constructing, deconstructing, and contrasting composition at will, we forge an intermediate space, both intensive and extensive, for the evolution of ensemble music, and for a new virtuoso thus versed.

In this way, Conduction opens a range of possibility previously unknown, just barely known, or in what we know all too well. After all, Conduction is a way to explore music as we make it—a probe to mine music and the ensemble at its most basic levels.

All in all, what we have here is the evolution of a model of empirical form; a way to contribute to the musical continuum as possibility and a (new) musical responsibility where the collective determines the experience of symbolic sonic stimuli; where all forms of notation, improvisation, style, and thought combine to establish a unique constellation of momentary logic (improvisation); where consciences can mature in a perfectly working precision that can never reach what is traditionally known as perfection.

Further: Concepts of Comprovisation* or Induction, or Conduction, for that matter, are no more ludicrous than the concepts of improvisation, notation, (musical) instrument construction, electronic gadgets, practice methods, or cave drawings ... these are techniques to probe and document.

* See John Zorn, *Arcana: Musicians on Music* (Granary Books/Hips Road, 2000, v.)

They all give or have given us food for thought that has led us out of one Dark Age after another. There is nothing more ludicrous than to believe that a way to make a musical expression is ludicrous. And to believe such would account for why we may be in the darkest age of all (and don't know it).

Comprovisation (a hybrid meaning composed-improvisation(s)) is a term that I first used to identify the direction of my chosen musical expression. It still holds water and has future uses.

However, Conduction, the term I have used since 1985, is more exacting in its intent and content in terms of definition, meaning, and action. Conduction also leads to "the kind of ambiguity" necessary to establish a common ground that grants to music making an "extra dimension."

Let us not forget that Conduction lends itself to the extra-musical: transmission, energy, convection, radiation, currents, potential differences, heat, substance, electricity, guidance, excitation, temperature differences, and impulse, among many more.

To foster meaningful interdependent architectonic relationships between music, musician, and audience is indeed a real-time action whose resources are adaptable to a limitless scope of production.

I, for one, am curious, *and* desperate, to know what is behind every idea we can possibly find and have about the creative self, and how the creative self so richly contributes to the "science of finding."

CHAPTER 21

THE PERFORMING DIRECTOR

JIM O'ROURKE

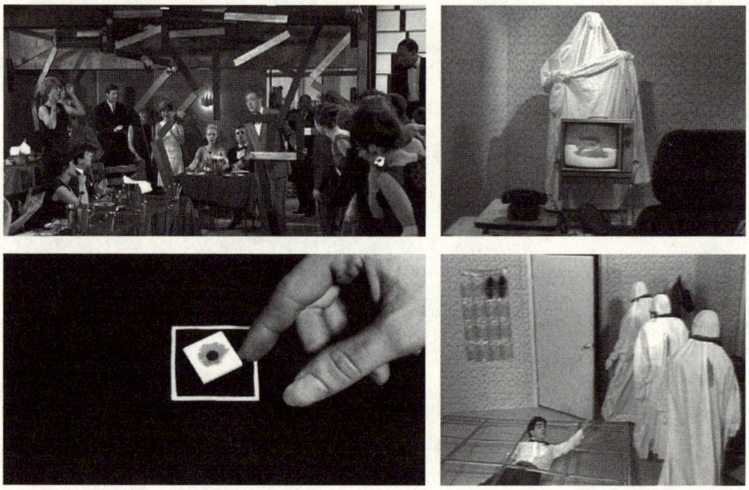

In Fall 2006 to Winter 2007, Jay Sanders and I began a series of focused email exchanges around what we saw as a vitally underrecognized current of performance-based art, and one for which we share a mutual fascination. Centering on artists Michael Smith and Stuart Sherman, along with John Zorn, and the films of composer Mauricio Kagel, we were interested in articulating our impressions of this work and its broader importance to us. Filmmaker Jacques Tati looms large in our discussion, as does Tony Conrad. The inner workings of these artists' performances, films, and videos seem highly prescient to a contemporary shift in the cultural reality of artmaking, and of the cultural landscape, an shift that's fast forming and still highly illegible.

Stuart Sherman began as an actor in Charles Ludlam's and Richard Foreman's theater productions. In the mid 1970s, he began to stage small-scale solo performances, which he called *Spectacles*. These were performed in theaters and art spaces, but also in parks, on street corners, ferries, etc., in

New York and worldwide. Looking almost like magic shows, Sherman manipulated a host of small everyday-item props atop a card table, developing a hermetic personal language. He worked also in film, video, and larger performances before his death in 2001.

Michael Smith's earliest works were audio pieces in which he developed a deliberately slow, deadpan comic timing, which he began applying to performances around 1975. His performances would typically take a basic theme: *Comedy Routine*, *What's in the Refrigerator*, *Down in the Rec Room*, which amounted to a stage-set of rudimentary props. As the only performer, he would gradually make his way through the set, performing a series of droll gags, all the while narrating in his inimitable style. Smith extended his work to video around 1980, which allowed for further dystopic enactments of the "everyday," and developed the character "Mike" (played by Smith), who stars in most of Smith's works.

* * *

Jim: I was thinking about the shift in video art in the late 70s, when television/local cable/PBS studios became available to these artists. I was wondering about the balance between how these facilities, with their built in possibilities to emulate "TV", effected a change in direction for artists like Michael Smith, and, say, Dara Birnbaum, and how much of it was a cultural shift. The handling of commercial landscape, the daily landscape, in Mike's work has a functional similarity to filmmaker Jacques Tati's *Playtime* and *Traffic*, but I was wondering if the roots actually do converge. There's definitely a different tone, I think. Tati is dealing maybe more directly in response to his changing environment, where in Mike's work, the feeling of rootlessness is there. There's the element of working through the possibilities of small reconfigurations, which I can completely see in both Mike's and Stuart Sherman's work.

Jay: Well, Mike readily acknowledges that he is actually very into Tati, who seems to be a real secret source for numerous artists. In both their work, there is that kind of wonderment at the everyday—that deadpan "coming-up against things" and having to deal with them in a blatantly perplexed manner. And your comment about "small reconfigurations" seems the key to all this work we're both interested in. Tati is a master at staging relationships between himself (as the actor/character) and the objects he encounters—heightening certain qualities that make the world and its contents appear otherworldly. And I think Sherman's very good at that too, "making the ordinary extraordinary" (to borrow a funny phrase from one of Mike's tapes).

Jim: But "making the ordinary extraordinary" is kind of key to Mike's work, don't you think?

Jay: And it's a great summation of Tati.

Jim: Well, I think one key element of Tati is that he takes a few extra steps beyond both expectation and what was thought to be the possibilities, and then when he goes past that point, it is in some ways such a simple change of perspective that it is dazzling.

Jay: Similarly, Stuart Sherman talks about each of his object manipulations as a kind of "provisional construction." These strange, highly rehearsed actions bring his prop-objects together very quickly and in odd transformative ways, then all the bits and pieces collapse back into the clutter of ordinary everyday life.

Jim: The word "extraordinary" has always struck me as such an internal conflict. I mean, "extra-ordinary" may be instead thought of as what you find beneath the surface of something labeled as "ordinary," because you're not really seeing IT, you seeing a representative object of "ordinariness."

Jay: With Mike's early videos, he starts with the highly artificial look of a bright TV sitcom set. It's a media version of the "ordinary." He keeps things fairly vacant, avoiding overt cultural references. But like you were saying, he's occupying a "commercial landscape." It's claiming an artistic space at that moment in the late 70s, early 80s, when a new media space was forming and the vocabulary for that space was becoming legible. It's highly contemporary for that moment. And I don't think anyone else had Mike's foresight to spoof that stuff right then, to take control and manipulate it so adequately—taking that late-night cable TV dead-air feeling and then pushing it even more, slowing the pace way down to get his catatonic spaced-out tone. It effectively deflates the expectations that would typically go along with this "look"—for wit, more frenetic action, some basic plot, etc. The slowness and highly composed aimlessness he achieves ironically both deadens any kind of conventional development and, at the same time, opens up a new kind of space which puts more weight on the subtle structural devices Mike is using—pauses, his flat speaking-to-himself vocal delivery (Smith plays "Mike" the main character, in his videos), and repetitions and permutations of all sorts. It's like he takes "normal" to such an extreme that it tips upside down into surreal. It parallels some comedy styles at the time, but again, without the reward system or the payoff. It's just self-consciously very unhooked.

Jim: This is gonna sound dumb, but I remember when I was like twelve or so, how the TV show *Police Squad* introduced me to that way of seeing things. I remember really questioning everything I was watching, and in general it rarely acknowledged what it was doing, and this sleight of hand you could say really made me aware how much "gravity" is involved in acknowledging what you are doing is for an audience. And around the same time—'80, '81—I first saw Mike's *Secret Horror* video and it blew me away. The ending especially, as I was so heavy into Robert Downey Sr. then, especially *Putney Swope* and *Greaser's Palace*. That use of "dead time" was very-eye opening for me.

Jay: It's a major step into a different kind of aesthetic space. In *Putney Swope*, the language, the script, and all those weird repetitions ... that kind of empty time-space and then someone stutters a line over and over and over. It's actually a little scary the first time you see it. You're like, "Jesus. This thing is a big empty chamber," but it's also really exhilarating.

Jim: It sounds silly, but the "how many syllables, Mario" gag in *Putney Swope* was a life-changing experience for me, I mean it really became something funny to dark in the course of its delivery. It wasn't something recontextualized, or commented on, it actually transfigured as I watched it, and that was heavy.

Jay: That's exactly the part I was just thinking of!

Jim: Most analysis/critical thought on Japanese films identifies the "empty space" as some sort of "Japanese-ness," you know the whole line, but for me, it was empty space, which, of course, is not empty at all, but filled with more potential than if you filled it with something.

Jay: It's like seeing theater. For me, the beginning, when a curtain opens and it's just the empty set first showing itself—and you start to adjust to the stuff that's sitting up there. The lights. The room. It's so full of potential. But then almost always it slips from there. It does what it's supposed to and loses that hovering potential for "aliveness" of the first few seconds. I actually think Richard Foreman speaks in these terms in a text where he's trying to describe Jack Smith. But some films, plays, etc., can keep that feeling, which is really hard to articulate. And it's not like you want murkiness, but just some room, some generosity. I think of it in those terms. I think Sherman's interested in all the "extras" in the ordinary. He'll use an object, a phone or a playing card. But he is careful to create theatrical structures that maximize all the potential connotations for that object—intellectual, poetic, political, its physical characteristics—a whole range of associations is purposely activated.

Jim: I remember when I was in college and I'd be asked to write "a string trio" or something for "piano and violin," it really bothered me because within those parameters, you are basically dealing with what you can do rhythmically, harmonically, and melodically, not with sound. Regardless of how much you dealt with sound, it was still tied to the foundation of "this is being produced by a piano," etc., and with that takes a lot of cultural baggage (which of course is one route you can take a lot of advantage of).

Jay: Right. So you're already dealing with preconceived cultural modes. You don't get to step back and really take on the sound and the full range of what's actually right there.

Jim: From that, I got the idea to make these sort of pieces on tape, and do as much to smudge the lines of the instruments' defining characteristics, not with electronic manipulation, because that'd be effectively the same thing, then you're dealing with "electronic sound." But I wondered how could you reclaim the SOUND of piano, violin, trombone, etc.? How can I hear the sound again, like for the first time, and not have any cultural signifiers floating around in it? And in many ways I saw this in Mr. Sherman's work. Is that a fire engine toy, or, what the hell is it? Or in *Secret Horror*, where bedsheets, a can of nuts, even waking up were used in a way that obliterated such an ingrained definition.

Jay: Wow. I was hoping to articulate that I've always felt a deep affinity between your work and this particular kind of performance work we're talking about here. And you said it really clearly. There's a politics to that sort of thinking too. Not allowing for things to be handed to you already submerged by a long and very controlled history, not already having things act automatically like they should—according to cultural codes or aesthetic paradigms. But to really challenge the material and yourself. Very few people do that. Like in Sherman's case, it's amazing. He really builds a new medium, a new form for recuperating these possibilities. And I think you achieve that too.

Jim: Of course, you have to be already loaded with the set of possibilities for those to be confounded. Sometimes, if you're dealing with cultural flotsam and jetsam, you may believe it's inherent, like it existed in you from when you were born. Nonetheless, you have to be reminded of it, so that you know, maybe subconsciously, what rulebook we're all using.

Jay: For Sherman, like any great artist, his form is a delivery vehicle for his experiments and for his needs to communicate. But because it's so personal and idiosyncratic, he doesn't have to contend with the heavily loaded baggage of self-references that comes with a more conventional "medium." In the late 70s and early 80s, when his work was really at its most intense, it reminds me of the highly complex poetry that was concurrently emerging. And it seems this heady experimentation was squarely geared toward phenomenology, coming out of Wittgenstein and early post-structuralist thought. It was dealing with fundamental issues of reality, perception, the extremes of language, etc., even if it was full of everyday detritus. And there does seem to be a shift where maybe that sort of direct engagement is now a bit naïve, or at least overly earnest or unfashionable. And you have to see that everything is really cultural content already. So the unit of analysis, the frame, moves out to try and include this as well. Does that make sense? It's a move Mike actually makes right from the start, designing his early videos so they at least look like "entertainment."

Jim: Yeah, of course. There are definite cultural shifts that are pushed along by new thoughts/philosophies, etc. For example, you can see clearly how much effect Freudian thought had on films in the 40s and 50s (and to another interesting degree, what countries absorbed it in what order). I remember watching *Possessed*, the Van Heflin/Joan Crawford film, with its overtly Freudian framework, and thinking, Wow, wouldn't it just be obvious for people to see things that way; why are they making such a big deal about it? It's very difficult to imagine how people viewed the world generations before you. It reminds you that there have been profound paradigmatic shifts. The "Internet generation" is going to see the world in such a fundamentally different way than we do, and we can see it happening, in retrospect, what it was like to watch Freudian perception take root, or phenomenology, etc. That's where artists come in; they are a little ahead of the curve.

Jay: And things move so fast, it's hard to step back. A lot of the more interesting art lately is beginning to deal with this idea of how culture disseminates, which is such an amorphous and vastly changing entity. People are getting interested in "distribution" as a medium, in specific ways.

Jim: Well, it really struck me in Mike's *How to Curate Your Own Group Exhibition* video, where he talks about "being content providers."

Jay: Yeah, that video has become very prescient. All this pseudo business-speak applied to the art world. Mike's proclamation: "As the information superhighway continues to expand, artists will barely have enough time to sleep, as they become the content providers for the future." Like all his stuff, it's very funny but it's bleak too.

Jim: I think the need for "content" in this age of "constant refresh," 24-hour news, etc., and the inherent need to sell advertising time, has redefined "content" into a continuous slight manipulation of the same information; so, in a way, we have Stuart Sherman performances in the form of headlines on Google news. Just refresh every ten seconds. You get every variation of how to conjugate a verb. But of course the context itself shifts too; what is considered a "development" is reduced to smaller and smaller events, smaller details.

Jay: And there are more and more people working and participating in the culture industry that need things to do. So it's in everyone's interest to keep it all moving along fast, to advertise "the new" even if we know it makes the reality we present increasingly superficial.

Jim: But by the nature of "living" being a blurred picture, it is, by its nature and presentation, still "news," and is taken in that way. So the standards lower. Instead of it viewed as "the same crap, but different," it's a development. The paradigm shift may not have been identified, named, and established on a cultural level yet, and everyone is still using the last rulebook.

Jay: Can I ask you? As an artist who acknowledges this kind of mediated reality shift, where does it put you in terms of creating things?

Jim: Hell, for me, it has made me want to stop.

Jay: Is it hard to find a sector for personal expression and artistic work?

Jim: I think the ability to actually work with the context you place it in has become much too slippery. More and more difficult to actually make that decision for yourself. You can't DECIDE to represent/present something in this light, cause it's going to get snatched, recontextualized, reformatted, no matter what you do. I know some people think that's "great," but I also think it sucks, because there's a whole set of parameters, that for me were really interesting, that you can't play around with anymore.

Jay: Now everyone's a producer as much as a consumer. There's so much "creativity" on the loose. I see this a lot in the gallery world. I'm always so excited to present something I think is amazing, but inevitably the "audience" is primarily eager producers who are looking for things to take from. Our audience is collectors and artists really. It's people who have a vested interest in the art world. But whether they're writers, people who buy art, or artists, they're looking to acquire something they can re-use for themselves. That's the way the system loops. And increasingly, with seeing art, people think they "got it" if they see a tiny video on the Internet, or a jpeg of a gallery installation. Now people trade hard drives full of music, videos, etc. "Getting it" is a matter of data transmission and not a slowly revealing experience. At the same time, taste really becomes a calling card. You build yourself pretty fully through your consumer choices, and especially aesthetic choices, which are so highly coded at this point—beyond any clear articulation.

Jim: Yeah, it's a tough call to make, because to a certain degree I really know you can't make someone like something they don't just plain like, regardless of their peer circle, etc. But within that field, the level of distinction breaks down real real fast. Do you know this book *Art and Physics*, by Leonard Shlain? He was an eye doctor, not an art critic at all. His basic idea in the book is that artists are able to see new modes of perception before it can be defined by, first, science, and then in words. For him—and I'm remembering now, so I may be a little off—words are the last form of communication, as it is a defined representation. But in art, you are able to express things on a nonverbal level, and in this way can see beyond what has been defined.

Jay: So at this point for you, when you want to make something, want to communicate an idea, do you find that there are forms that you can still work in that feel available?

Jim: "Actual experience" is utmost important to me. I am interested in how things "actually" happen. We can abstract-alate all we want, and ideas come from that, but there's a major fallout from the era of artists who took a disingenuous view of "intentionality," that to be interested in what happens, how things actually occur, is to deride abstraction, and it doesn't. It is of course interesting to see things from an externally created perspective, and all of that is fine, and a lot of great things come from it, and I'm interested in it myself, but it is not mutually exclusive to the perspective of intentionality. Because it is that way we can see how someone tackles the questions they have posed, roadblocks they encounter.

Jay: Right. And it's such a safe position. People really save their skin with this "distance." You know, no risk because everything's in quotations. And what does that communicate? Even if you try and it's awkward, awkwardness is fine. It's honest. I think it's a particular challenge to find a personal space, not to sound corny. To find a way to honestly work subjectively with materials to communicate, and deeply, you know? And on those rare occasions when you find that kind of work, it's amazing. You see often with younger artists, as they "develop," they're often just polishing and streamlining their practice so it's legible in the right ways, looking for some small twist to put on something, to extend an existing discourse. It's the currency into the system, which is a social system as much as anything. But just to flip this coin completely, "influence" is also an important aesthetic residue. Sometimes the only way something underground or ephemeral can be kept alive is through the way it affected someone else. So for Sherman's work, he was ill and died in 2001. Basically no documentation has been available of his performances and he's been completely off the art world's map, gone without a trace. His performances were always for small devout audiences, even in the 70s and 80s. So his infamy and legacy has survived primarily through his effect on other artists, like Mike Kelley, Michael Smith, Christian Marclay, who have been influenced by him in their own work, and who have written and described what they thought he was doing.

Jim: That is an important distinction. It's quite often that with artists like this, their first influence is a result of some kind of telephone-game. Sherman's not like Chris Burden or Vito Acconci, where even if you can't see their films, or the performances, there was at least a fair amount of photo and text documentation. But with Sherman it was more through how other people said they were influenced by him, and the way they influenced him. Yet, the funny thing is, it's not like you are really seeing a representation of Sherman's work in other people's work, and you can sense that. Yet, there was something magical about this effectively private thing that had happened.

Jay: And some of this is the nature of the work. With the other performance artists you mentioned, there's a simplicity, a bluntness to their activities, that travels well, through documentation and description. With Sherman, it's the opposite. They're very puzzle-like and multidimensional, partly because his background is poetry and avant-garde theater. People take little bits from him, like using objects in kind of pun-based ways, or his deadpan stage presence, but that's just the tip of the iceberg.

Jim: But in general that hermeticism, I think, is a sort of fork in the road for some people, the idea of "getting it." It seems to be either "I have to learn this person's logic, this person's language" or "I am an observer of this foreign language." I really think that step where you translate your own language into some hybrid with the audience's language is missing Mr. Sherman's work, but as a deliberate decision. It is unlike work that tries to simultaneously deny that step, yet demand you work for it.

Jay: For me, it was an absolute epiphany when I actually first saw tapes of Sherman's *Spectacle* performances (after tracking down his Estate). It just really works for me, perfectly. I do think of Stuart in terms of writing, especially poetry. For me great poetry unlocks language, opens the words themselves to their more full potential and reconnects them in unexpected ways. There's this great essay by the American poet Clark Coolidge, who'd written these very impenetrable and weird short pieces in the early 70s. He gave this talk about reading a science fiction book and in the book these children begin moving objects around, and after a while they'd hit certain configurations that seemed to make no logical sense, that should have been just nothing, but then something really magical would happen, a portal would open or something. That can happen with language, just by putting two things next to each other, it's like "wiring," in a way.

Jim: It is interesting how someone can use a guarded, inexplicable language yet still convey a very distinct and definable feeling. Of course, that's their artistry. They have a unique way to articulate on a nonverbal level, and when things seem to resonate within us, I think we tend to try and express that verbally, as opposed to through our own action. There's an attention to the layer of translation that ties Sherman's, Tati's, and Mike Smith's work together.

Jay: And it's all work that's so highly composed, so perfected. But doesn't appear to be. I think everyone we're talking about is extremely effective on those terms.

Jim: Sherman's work may completely disregard—and I don't mean that in the negative sense—the need to "communicate" to the audience with means. It doesn't reference or utilize what is generally agreed upon as communication, but of course it is, because something is being sent out, and we perceive it. Tati is in many ways the patron saint of this approach. The way his films seem to just "happen," the way that the surface is so still, and yet it isn't motion "underneath" we're looking at, it is all there on the surface, but the source of gravity is deceptive.

Jay: This is something I really find so inspiring in Sherman's *Spectacle* works: their utter integrity and their utterly fragile nature. There's no hint of concern for their being fashionable, or for wanting to appear superior. He's not doing it for anyone else. It's not really for an audience, which, like you say, sounds weird. But it's about really creating the world he wanted to live in for those brief minutes when he was performing. "This is how my head works and how I think things REALLY can work and I'm going to stage it." Here he is very aligned to the playwright Richard Foreman, whose own iconoclastic work could easily be a part of this conversation. It's a real need, to compose and perform these rapid connections. It's like a personal alchemy, a personal language. But you can watch it and it works even if you just see it concretely and formally. It doesn't demand you analyze it for a hidden meaning. For me, that's one thing I like very much. It makes me think of musical structure. I think we've talked about this. You can see it as visual music, as organizations and change over time. And that's a very full way to look at it. You're not missing anything.

Jim: When you first saw Mauricio Kagel's films, especially *Tactile*, did you see any correlation between his work and Sherman, and Christian Marclay, especially Christian's fluxus pieces?

Jay: Most definitely. Exactly along these lines. You knew Kagel's work intimately before having the chance to see Stuart's. How did you find they related?

Jim: When I first saw Kagel's films I remember that same sense of wonderment at watching him work through unforeseen variations. Even though *Antithese* was "large scale," it was really about applying small permutations to a variety of closed-off materials. Kagel's way is, well, it's still colored by the "new music" mentality, to put it crudely. Its manner of presentation and performance still had "new music" stamped all over it, but I was still amazed at the incredible invention in his films. Now that I think of it, *Blue's Blue* is a bit like Mike's work, funnily enough.

Jay: Kagel's movies are so unique. The more plot-based ones are so strange. Everything's tethered to this musicality, but he gives you so much else. I'm thinking of that one that takes place in a hospital, *Hallelujah*.

Jim: *Hallelujah* I can't connect to as much because it is too interested in questions raised by the practices of making music, which I know are what, in a large part, makes his films unique. But for me, it's not, well .... Kagel's films are really exciting, but they lack a certain extra dimension that I find in Mike's and Mr. Sherman's work.

Jay: I can see that too, especially with the concert films. You see it on the performers' faces, that it's shtick a bit. Very good shtick, but you don't get the same directness. You feel that European history seeping in.

Jim: Exactly, and that's part of my problem; the "breaking boundaries" is still a new–music gambit. The reference is clear, loud, and not only seems obligatory, it seems to still feel "needed." Unlike John Zorn's performance film *Fidel* (1979), which really bridges the two in a unique way.

Jay: It's perfectly in-between. There's that new music background, but he also was heavily immersed in the 60s–70s New York performance avant-garde. Which was much more ahistorical and self-directed. There's not that feeling of needing to make all these "nods."

Jim: John's film is distinctly different to me from Mr. Sherman's films, in that they reference a confined space that object are placed in, as opposed to the movement of objects defining space.

Jay: And though he performs himself (like Sherman), he downplays his presence to the extreme. They both make their performances of small-scale object manipulations, but Zorn's is really more centered on extreme possibilities for music—visual manipulations as silent musical compositions. *Fidel* has a most definite "frame." It's literally a tiny white square on a black tabletop, and Zorn proceeds to introduce countless tiny objects, one by one, placing and then removing them. Then he begins these small intense juxtapositions which operate as harmony. It's SO rigorous. There's really not much like it.

Jim: Well, effectively acknowledging the baggage of new-music history is the same as in other people's work, but for me there is something in new-music history which is frontloaded with the concept of "innovation," which I find to be distracting, and a bit, no, completely illusory. There's no sense in Mr. Sherman's work about the "idea" of innovation. I remember in college, I had a professor who had a timeline in his office, and at the end of it, he'd penciled in his name. It's inherent in those systems to look to the validating system of history.

Jay: But for you, coming from that background of new music, are there methods you've found? Critical ways to step out of this? To take what you need but not feel like you're in line?

Jim: It's a major problem, I believe, to wait for others to validate you. It's of course a constant source of frustration to see people "get it wrong," but then you have to question, and it's the most important question: Did I communicate? What DID I want to communicate, and do I want to communicate at all? Well, one way I know, for me, is that during college I chose not to take that route. I remember the same professor telling me maybe I should take time off of school to get these "records" out of the way.

Jay: Otherwise you're working and you're "innovating." Taking little steps and waiting for someone else to say, "Look, this is now a new direction." It takes an external definition for it to make sense.

Jim: That's why many avant-gardists actually continue along the line of "refining their work," but there is an important distinction, I feel. There is a line that's crossed where "refining" becomes something apparent only to the creator in the process of creating, but the end result is effectively the same.

Jay: You see sometimes in the arts, especially with artists that teach, artists will support younger artists working in their wake. They need to foster a timeline where their name is at the beginning, instead of the end. I guess it's a form of insurance.

Jim: I don't understand that way of thinking. OK, it's maybe fine for some people, I guess, but I really just don't understand it. I mean, I'm making my stuff. What do I care about people after me? I mean, I want them to show me something I've never seen before, show something in a new perspective, a new light, a new way to see it.

Jay: It's often said that artists are inherently doing the same thing over and over again, whether they see it themselves or not.

Jim: That's where that line is, I believe. Because, for the audience, they are effectively doing the same thing. I totally understand the flipside of that, because I know when I'm heading down the road of "refining" and losing the possibility of a breakthrough, really, in refining something there are breakthroughs, but the stumble you make by tying your shoes together lands you much farther. It's inherently a different experience to make something, and live through the real-time process of creating something, and the result, which is basically a report to the audience of what you've been up to. In many ways everything is really like the same play with a different cast and set designer, but I think a lot of people are approaching it from the other perspective. That's why Sherman's work is unique; he's taken this idea to a logical other endgame.

Jay: That's interesting. How do you mean?

Jim: Well, what I mean is that in Sherman's work, he has taken so much of "hiddenness" away, it somehow is apparent that this is not "representing" something else, it truly is what you're seeing.

Jay: Oh, yeah. That's great! This is really getting at something. Tony Conrad talks a lot about making endgame works. I like this because it actually does make them hard for other people to "extend" in that art-historical way, if you're already taking things to absurd extremes. And I really agree with you, Sherman's work is not "coded" or secretive at all. It's stripping everything totally away, then reconstructing, but tentatively and just for a moment. He said in an interview that he likes to perform fast because he was worried that if it were slow, viewers would start aestheticizing the objects, focus on the surface qualities or particularities, and he wanted it all to be very provisional. Up and then down. Aligned and then obliterated.

Jim: And when you aestheticize what you're seeing, you fall into the trap of "symbolism." For me, to use a "symbol" means you are establishing a map key, and for me, the whole purpose of making any form of creative work is to take advantage of that medium's unique way to communicate, in a way that you can't verbally. If you are instead using it as a reference to verbal ideas, I don't really see the point. I really question what the point of that is. It's the whole "personal expression" thing. I mean, it's funny, but, you know, I really don't want to know how the artist "feels," I want them to open the world up to me. If I want to know how someone "feels" I'll call my mother or something.

Jay: It should be more about activation than expression. But if it's done right, it is expressive of a need to communicate. But not to editorialize, etc. I really agree with you about that.

Jim: Of course there's "expression" in everything. I don't want to assume that what I do is a genuine expression of that emotion, or idea. If you don't question that, you are just "expressing yourself," and that's quite often is misconstrued as communication. Everything you do is "personal expression," but to work in that mode is like a boomerang. It always comes back to you, you aren't willing to let that thing go, to throw it and let it go out there and live on its own.

Jay: It doesn't have to be this dichotomy of formalism vs. expression or something. To go back to Tony Conrad, who has dealt heavily with what we're talking about—beginning with his Dream Music in the 60s, it was offering this very generous kind of temporary sound architecture. Tony is always clear that the point was to dismantle the composer/player/listener relationship. To create an experience that empowered the listener. He has a great ability to do things that are simple but have intense ramifications. That's a real clarity.

Jim: I think that is a common point amongst most of the artists we've been talking about. It is staggering sometimes to watch/hear/understand the simultaneity of simplicity and complexity in their work. But that complexity comes from their life experience, a lot of it comes from the context they have created; it creates resonances that are richer than any stated intention. Maybe Tony's *Film Feedback* is the masterpiece blueprint for all of these ideas were talking about.

Jay: A tight structure, a lot of room for unforeseen effects and resonances, a funny sense of experimentation, and an ability to take a "form" to an illogical extreme—it's captivating.

CHAPTER 22

WHY 211?

EVAN PARKER

"Memory is gone and the power of thinking is on the wane."
—not Beckett; Josiah Crawley in Trollope's *Last Chronicles of Barset*

Pica pica. I am a magpie … at least that was how I wanted to start the piece before I discovered that Michael Schumacher, an improvisational dancer, works with a group called that. Then I remembered a Broetzmann record, and then a piece by Sylvia Hallett on one of the Freezone CDs on psi! As the number of people involved in improvisation grows, it is increasingly difficult to say anything that hasn't already been said better elsewhere. Or to think of a title that hasn't been used before. I was distraught after my *The Eleventh Hour* had been issued to see that Fred Frith had already called a piece *Eleventh Hour*; the "the" was not much of a fig leaf. And come to that, there's even a group called "The the." I think I will have to go more in the direction of the enigmatic—"Lines Burnt in Light" and so on.

In my fantasy other life, I am a totter—I just tried looking up the definition; nothing there. Maybe it's Cockney slang: the distinction between a totter and a rag-and-bone man may be hard to get right. They are both free-lance collectors of others' unwanted stuff. I enjoy at least in theory the idea of having a large space for sorting, classifying, and storing the amazing things that other people throw away. The photographer Thomas Struth has a beautiful Buescher alto that someone just put out on the street in New York. It may be that a totter is less well organized than a rag-and-bone man, may not even have a horse and cart or, more likely these days, what we call a van. (What do Americans call vans?) I think the main difference is the opportunistic and spontaneous, impulsive nature of totting as against the more systematic and organized nature of the rag-and-bone man. I've seen the term skip-diving (skip=dumpster), which makes it all sound rather chic. Back then Jamie Muir wrote a nice piece for a short-lived magazine called *Microphone* in which he emphasized the difference between a junk shop and an antique dealers, where all the good stuff has been found and identified. The bricolage nature of some group improvisation is part of the aesthetic: like a visitor to a junk shop, the listener will have to sift through and find the gems, while at the same time enjoying the ambience! This was the way the critic Benny Green heard Sonny Rollins during his month at Ronnie Scott's in the late 60s: "pearls on a dung-heap." I think I was after the same point in talking about the duo music with Paul Lytton from the early 70s when discussing the critics' famous "architecture/lack of" complaint I emphasized "shelter rather than monument." The first time it was printed there was a typo which made it read "snelter"—very puzzling.

There is a musician here in Faversham called Henry Dagg. He has his life organised so that storage and the accumulation of stuff are no problem. A former cellist, he has won saw-playing competitions in the U.S. (CD *Music from the Cutting Edge*) and builds extraordinary instruments using the heavy metal and wood-working machinery he has assembled in his former biscuit factory home. There is a forge and all the gear for casting molten metal. He also plays keyboards in a Genesis tribute band—the only such band to have a genuine Mellotron. The wrought-iron fence at the front of his house is in the form of a musical stave and inset at regular intervals are lyres holding tubular bells, each set tuned to a different scale and all the sets forming a cycle that forms an endless loop. When I visited he was hard at work on a Giant Kithara along Harry Partch lines but with an improved tuning head.

As the great Joni says, "Diving down to pick up on ..."... searching for and stumbling on the shiny things to hoard. At this point there should be some treasures to share, some arcana even. My first idea had been to interview Andria Pisu, the brilliant young Sardinian launeddas player. I heard him for the first time this summer in Palau. I even have the first notes for that piece... In Benzon's study, published in 1969, the tradition of launeddas was in crisis—there were three or four distinct schools of playing and each master had only a few students. The instrument was in steep decline and in risk of extinction. Since then there has been a great revival. Why and how did this happen? What made Andria Pisu decide to take up the instrument? How did he learn? I remember reading in Benzon that the established masters were reluctant to share all their secrets with their pupils for fear of losing work to them. This made me think of the late Bismillah

Khan and how the shenai is taught. Seeing BK perform with his circle of students: most just playing the drone but a select one or two allowed to echo some of the master's phrases. This in turn made me think of Kadri Gopalnath, the Carnatic music master of saxophone, and the great courage it took for him to break with the family tradition of nadaswaram. "You see, Sir, I just fell in love with the saxophone." So intense has his love of the instrument been that in parts of South India, kadri is used as an alternative name for the saxophone. That reminds me of sitting at the kitchen table telling my father that I had been "required to terminate my studies" in Botany and would henceforth be pursuing my love affair with the saxophone.

How far back are the lines of transmission of launeddas lore transmitted from one generation to the next recorded? In an intensely oral tradition it may be that the history of the teaching and the taught are very well remembered. There is speculation that the launeddas is a direct relation of the instruments shown on Ancient Greek vases—the reed version of the aulos. The tradition may well extend unbroken into antiquity. The self-congratulatory post-industrial climate in which we live tends to make us undervalue the genius, poetic sensibility, ingenuity, knowledge, and wisdom that underpin such cultural survivals. Put with typical eloquence by Lewis Mumford: "Man has formed a curiously distorted picture of himself by interpreting his early history in terms of his present interests in making machines and conquering nature ... ritual and language and social organization were probably man's most important artifacts, to give form to the human self using only tools that could be constructed out of the resources provided by his own body: dreams, images and sounds," in *The Myth of the Machine* (1967).

That great body of traditional skills and arts seems to speak not just of "know-how" but "know-why" (I hope I coined that myself). It is not even necessary to visit the Great Pyramid at Giza, the stones in the foundations that form the backstage wall in the jazz club in Bamberg will do just as well.

The rhythm patterns in Sardinian music are also the basis of dances. There is evidence that in earlier times dance was also a way of recording esoteric knowledge. In his essay in the book he edited with Joseph Campbell, *In All Her Names*, Charles Muses describes a dance or perhaps, more properly, movement ritual of the women of the Choni people of South China—

the Pace of Yu. In the commentary Nei P'ien by Ko Hung it says, "As you perform the Pace of Yu you will keep forming hexagram number 63." Reading the I Ching as a narrative account of spiritual development, Muses says Hexagram 64 "expresses simply an anti-climactic recycling for those who did not complete the Heroic Journey of hexagram 63." He translates Hu Tao Shih Tzu Yuan Yu—Tiger Way Is (precisely) Your Origin(al State) Return (journey).

Ornette called a record *Dancing in Your Head*, perhaps as a rejoinder to the people who say you can't dance to free jazz. The dance of the nervous system is as important as the dance of the muscular-skeletal system. I saw this YCDTI assertion made and rebutted at Ronnie Scott's the first (only?) time Weather Report (Omar Hakim on drums, I think) played there. At the Old Place, Ronnie's original club in Gerrard Street, there was a small patch of wooden floor about the size of a fireside rug which in his compering Ronnie used to draw attention to and encourage people to dance. I was never sure how serious he was.

Coltrane's profound interest in astrology and the roots of religion connect him in my mind with Muses. As a young man, Muses set out to debunk astrology as being nothing more than superstition. However, his research led him to the opposite conclusion. He also saw the roots of all religion in Shamanism which, *pace* Eliade, he saw as being "neither Archaic nor strictly speaking a technique of ecstasy." There is much here to fire further research. The major published Coltrane material on this so far is the chart of the twelve tones related to the Zodiac, a copy of which was given to Yusef Lateef and reproduced by him in his lexicon of patterns and scales. But there are many other fragments and allusions in titles which need to be collated and edited properly.

There are interesting parallels with Arthur Young's chart assigning physical vectors to the signs of the Zodiac in *The Geometry of Meaning*.

I wanted to ask Andria about the role of launeddas in the social customs: funerals, dances, weddings. Who was his teacher, how is the teaching done? My guess is that notation plays no role at all and that it is all to do with mnemonics and memorization. The Indian system of memorizing ragas by the combination of an exhaustive set of four note patterns conjoined at the dominant. Combining this with additive/subtractive cyclic rhythm patterns, as Kadri, said "It is all mathematics." I think a great strength of free improvisation is that it can introduce the irrational numbers into our rhythmic patterns.

It became clear that the interview with Andria was not going to happen, at least in time for this piece—which is constrained by the circumstances in which it must be written. I woke up early this morning in a hotel room in Ulrichsberg in Austria, where Aloys Fischer has been promoting concerts for years. We—the Schlippenbach Trio—had played a concert on each of the previous eleven days and have two days without concerts before our next gig in Graz. We will drive there after breakfast. I began by flying to Berlin and then by road (Alex does all the driving) Hanover, Tilburg, Lille, Tours, Brugge, Cologne, Munich, Karlsruhe, Bamberg, and Ulrichsberg, six more to go. Although this should be tiring in fact the adrenergia is such that three or four hours sleep are enough. I woke around 5:30 and finished the *Guardian* Crossword from several days back and then tried to go back to sleep. Head full of JZ's reminder on deadlines and a desperate desire not to fail set me thinking about the piece again. I was roused by the sound of a brass band and dressed quickly and went out to see what was going on. It seemed to be some kind of war veterans' special day and after marching the short distance up the hill to the church they stopped playing and went in for a service. I went back to the hotel for breakfast and a while later, the service over, they played some more, disbanded, and came into the hotel for a celebratory meal. The beer started flowing before 9 a.m.!

"Crash now, man! If we survive we're going to live forever." Dudu Pukwana's advice to a driver on a late-night drive home after a gig. The business of driving home after the gig was always largely a matter of saving money. The whole mind-set of the touring musician is how much are you going to take home at the end of it? A night or half a night spent driving might get you to a place where you can stay for nothing or in the case of a London-based musician it would get you home. Either way, money saved. In the late 60s and early 70s it was quite normal to drive to Newcastle, do a gig, and then drive home. It was hard enough just to be a passenger, but some guys specialized in doing driving too. One powerful memory is of a gig in Newcastle or somewhere else far north and then driving back. John Stevens felt tired and climbed into the back of a van without rear seats to lie down. He slept on the bare metal floor with his head on the wheel arch as a pillow. These days people tend to offer a hotel as part of the deal, but sometimes after a gig the spirit of the old days emerges and someone says, "I'm going back now, anyone want to come? There won't be any traffic."

Back then in Germany with Alex von Schlippenbach and Paul Lovens under similar conditions, Alex was so tired he had the idea that Paul should drive for a bit. Paul had maybe had one driving lesson, obviously no license, and had certainly never driven on the autobahn, but he gave it a try. Alex's idea was that he could get a little sleep, and if he was needed Paul could wake him up. I was in the back and not entirely happy with the arrangement. As Alex nodded off the speed started to creep up from the agreed 50 to 80 mph and on, and I was so nervous that I made Paul nervous and after about twenty minutes the experiment was abandoned. Paul has never since had a license, and to this day always sits in the back seat and prefers to take the train wherever possible. Another time back then when German winters were icy and snowy we hit some black ice and went into a skid, turned a full circle, and came to a stop in the inside lane facing ahead again. There was a lorry bearing down on us, but Alex stepped on the accelerator and we got away from it. This is now referred to as "the autobahn pirouette."

In Berlin I had met Rainer Rucker again for the first time in at least ten years. It was a great pleasure to see him and to catch up a little. I had originally met him as part of the team running improvised music concerts in Wiesbaden but he moved to Berlin many years ago and took up as a saxophone repairman with a workshop quite close to Dieter Hahne's record shop in the Behaimstrasse in Charlottenberg. My repairman in London is Willie Garnett, who also plays and runs a rehearsal big band. These are two exceptional generous-spirited human beings and have much more in common than is immediately apparent. I think it would be fair to describe Rainer as cerebral. He introduced me to the writings of Victor Klemperer by giving me his copy of *LTI* (*Lingua Tertii Imperii: Sprache des Dritten Reichs*), assuring me that my German was up to it! Back home now I have the book in front of me and I am determined to work on my German. I met Tomas Schmit for the last time about a year before he died and lamented the poor progress I had made in German considering how many years I had been going there to work. I asked him where to start to improve my reading. Without hesitation he answered, "Kafka." Determined to act on his advice, the same evening I found a paperback of short stories. I have a clear program for the year ahead and a resolution for the annual ritual in Brittany.

During that visit with Tomas we had talked about his contribution to the book of interviews with Dieter Roth that his partner Barbara Wien had edited. Typically, this work of re-examining the accuracy of the published transcriptions from tape had led Tomas into discovering many mistakes in the originals. Led by a clear sympathy for Roth's ethos, he had a nose for where to look. We also talked about his adoption of the word processor. A major step for one so set in his way of making art, which had been mostly done with a typewriter and pen and ink; and then Tomas astonished me by saying he was now also making CDs of his readings of his texts. This encouraged me; as the recent convert to mobile phone, I used the camera/video clip option to take a shot of him while pompously (mock) declaring that he was now "Archiviert fur die Ewigkeit." I wish I had had the chance to ask Tomas what he thought of the book of Rudolf Steiner's blackboard drawings. I felt some affinity of approach even though I knew that Tomas had an aversion to all things Steinerian. Too late now.

Roth's ethos: the so short (anag) phrase that covers a Herculean life's work as the bricolagist's bricolagist. From the *Gesamte Scheisse* to the *Review for Everything*, Roth was keen to include everything in his work. What an incredible and marvelous mountain of pearl-strewn shit he has left behind. I met him on a flight to Heathrow from Rejkavik back then and Fate had put me in the seat next to him to his left. I was keen not to stare but was already fairly sure who he was. As we settled into the flight I read over his shoulder and was then certain. He was reading proofs for some of his writing and noticing my interest, introduced himself with the explanation that although he was better known as an artist, he was these days much more interested in writing. (As Tomas accounts in the interview book: Dieter asked him, "Hast Du was buchiges raus?"... and added the comment "Was buchiges rauszubringen und dann rauszuhaben, war offenbar auch seine grosste kunstlerische lust." And here's another bit that I understand expressing his absolute enthusiam for Roth's writing: "Seine literatur eher zu nichtkonnen, zur jux-seite zu rechnen ... grundfalsch! grundfalsch!!") As we got closer to Heathrow, he also explained that his custom was to spend half of each year in Iceland and the other half of the year traveling; that whereas in Iceland he never drank alcohol, while away from Iceland he drank as much as he could. I joined him for a "quick drink" in the first bar he could find at Heathrow and he set about showing me how it worked. He downed three pints in about three minutes, and I forget what happened after that. We must have exchanged addresses because later we swapped records and books and I even made a contribution to the "*Review for*

Everything"—I couldn't resist the line "We print any shit." He was also open to making work with other artists—a notable series of collaborations with Richard Hamilton. It is still quite a rarity in that world for visual artists to collaborate, but Dieter was keen on it.

Rainer and Willie have been waiting patiently for me to continue with their stories. Rainer had undertaken, about fifteen years back, to restore a C melody saxophone by Alphonse Leduc that I had bought in a ruined state from a shop in Nottingham where it was being used as a window decoration (complete with a flower pot in the bell). I was on tour with Kenny Wheeler Large Ensemble and the assistant recognized me. In consultation with his boss and on the principle that if I was interested in it it must be valuable, they arrived at a fairly steep price. The project had gone into abeyance as Rainer had given up repair work, and the parts were stored in boxes to await a revival of his fortunes. This visit Rainer told me the place had been broken into and the boxes, along with all his tools, stolen, and that although working on instruments remained the love of his life, he now wrote software for a living. Willie I see as often as I think I can get away with it without becoming known as a "time waster." Encouraged by what Ned Rothenberg told me about Sonny Rollins—he goes to a repair man every week if he can—I visit often just to have Willie place his healing hands on the horns. In the scale of things, Willie's healing hands are more like a Rolf massage than Reiki. He is not terribly interested in cosmetics but he can balance the action and make sure everything is closing with the best of them. He has an enormous heart, with time for everyone, including the middle-class Putney mothers who seem to treat him as a free service covered by their Council Tax to keep their kids' clarinets and flutes in order. The long and the short of it is that Rainer could not afford to go on with that work in Berlin, a city renowned among musicians for its (relatively) cheap rents, and Willie continues to defy the laws of economics, happily plying his trade in London, the most overpriced and expensive city in the world. Discuss.

In the space outlined by Kafka's "You will not do anything without others" and Simone Weil's "Money is a lie. Too general a sign" is where I hope I live.

> What we are after is a world of expanded intelligence expressed with poetic force and clarity. —Kenneth White, "On the Atlantic Edge" (2006)

Victims of Bush and Blair might like to ponder the following:

Q: To what extent are the citizens of a government responsible for its mistakes?

A: Your question as to the politics of the so-called democracies is a good one. They are now so rigged with hidden agreements between corrupt politicians and criminal transnational corporations that no amount of voting can cure it. "Democracies" inevitably become police states in which the people have no power over their leaders whatsoever. (Musaios in *Access-The Lion Path for the Twenty-First Century*) and then:

> As democracy is perfected, the office of President represents, more and more closely, the inner soul of the people. On some great and glorious day the plain folks of the land will reach their hearts' desire at last, and the White House will be adorned by an outright moron. (Written by H.L. Mencken in 1920.)

In the commentary attached to the blackboard drawing called *What Science Describes* Steiner is quoted: "Science today describes a world in which we would all become neurasthenics and hysterics. The good thing is ... that this is not our real world and that our real world also possesses other forces than those described."

> His principal concern of course is to arouse and maintain a reputation for profundity and wit. This done by the simple mechanical formula of antithesis; if you like winkles he proves that cockles are inveterately better; if you admire Ruskin he tears him to ribbons. If you want to learn how to swim—as it is safer, he shows it is more dangerous to know how to swim and so on. I know his whole box of tricks. I myself am now playing the clever young man by writing out this analysis just as if I were not one myself. (From W.N.P. Barbellion's *The Journal of a Disappointed Man* July 3, 1915.)

Geschwindigkeit ist kein hexerei. More or less: "Speed is not magic." The late Buschi Niebergall was keen to teach me to slow down, and this expression was one way he used. He also played a very long note on the E string of his bass and asked me to listen to the speed. I suppose something along the same lines as Stockhausen's *How Time Passes*. We were in Bremen for the recording of Broetzmann's piece *Machine Gun*. My keenest memory is of Han Bennink being trapped behind an array of curtains and mattresses in an impromptu drum booth, the only way the engineer could get any kind of balance. Every so often he would poke his head out and express some irritation at being damped down.

While thinking about this—a great band that Broetzmann put together (after the Machine Gun band) played for several days in Berlin at a club called Litfass. I think it must have been early November 1969. It had Broetz and me on saxophones, Paul Rutherford on trombone, Fred van Hove on a strange electric organ, Derek Bailey on guitar, Buschi Niebergall on bass, and Han Bennink on drums. One that got away—as far as I know there are no recordings.

> In a very cheerful mood. Pleased with myself and everybody till a seagull soared overhead in Kensington Gardens and aroused my vast capacities for envy—I wish I could fly. (Ibid, May 10, 1914)

In the summer, after a gig in Exeter, I traveled back to London with Catherine and Phil Wachsmann. We stopped for tea at his sister's place in Wiltshire. She and her husband are bird watchers (or "birders," as Han Bennink describes himself in a recent interview). They have martins nesting in the eaves of their house and have fixed a webcam in the nest so that they can watch the nestlings hatching and being fed on their computer. Phil's brother-in-law also goes hang gliding, the closest he can get to flying.

> The improvised solo coming out of one musician, with others supporting him, is a dead end… In front of us we have many years of the collective improvised effort, the intuitive and adult collaboration between peers." (Warne Marsh, *An Unsung Cat*)

On tour with George Lewis, Barry Guy, and Paul Lytton we arrived at the Apex club in Goettingen in time for the gig, but too late to check into the hotel before playing. After the gig, the promoter left two keys and a map of the way to the hotel. We had not planned to share rooms but this was late on a cold night in winter, and the idea of waking the proprietor to ask for extra rooms was too intimidating. We reluctantly accepted the situation, and since both George and I were known to snore heavily we agreed to share, leaving Paul and Barry sharing across the corridor. George had the idea to try to record our snoring and wanted to fall asleep with his finger on the pause button hoping that the hand would fall away from the machine and it would go into record. Paul and Barry were kept awake for hours, first by the unsuccessful attempts provoking very loud laughter and later by the mighty combined weight of our snoring—which went unrecorded but became known as the Snoratorio—a wilful distortion of a John Cage title.

In the same vein as Tomas' question "Did Kafka write poetry?": did Warne Marsh ever play solo? It seems likely. Are there any known recordings?

"It's a beach scene." said the famous fixer Nat Peck, when I asked for a bit more information on what my involvement in Michel Legrand's music for the Louis Malle film *Atlantic City* might be about... I was tired by this time of being used to represent various types of psychosis. One MD referred to us as "the paranoia boys." You may know the film—Burt Lancaster aged small-time gangster and Susan Sarandon the love interest. Many people think it is one of Malle's best films. Anyway, I was on the road somewhere in Italy when a call came through that Nat Peck needed to speak to me about doing these sessions. Of course I knew of Legrand, not just as a composer of hits but also as the French guy who had made a record with Miles and Coltrane as soloists. The whole project had to be completed in a hurry because of the potential tax advantages to a consortium of Canadian dentists who were putting up the money. The spirit must have been close to an improvisation all the way, and by the time Legrand came to put the music on, it had to be quick. Improvisation is always at an advantage under such circumstances as are its polar opposite, the war-horse classics. Legrand's solution was to use both. An assembly of London-based free players, Barry Guy, Tony Coe, Howard Riley, Paul Lytton, and me, with his old chum Roger Kellaway added at the last minute as an extra keyboard player for a small part of the score, and an orchestra of the usual suspects—straight players moonlighting from their orchestra gigs—doing bits of Bellini's *Norma*. Why such attention to detail, you ask? Where the hell is this leading? Well, in those days—early 70s—Kenny Wheeler was working hard as a session player. Great reader, great soloist, therefore much in demand for all kinds of stuff. The pattern was that studios were booked in three periods a day, 10 a.m.–1 p.m., 2–5 p.m., and 7–10 p.m., and the top players were doing two and sometimes three sessions every day. Well, Kenny sometimes had a morning session and an evening session on the same day but nothing to do in the afternoon. His custom was, rather than go home and back, wasting time on the tube, to go to the cinema nearest to the studio and sleep there—obviously, the particular film was of no great importance.

Anyway, several people had gone to see *Atlantic City* after I mentioned my involvement and came back reporting that there wasn't a note of me on the track. Kenny went to the cinema for a sleep and later that week asked me on the phone if I had been on the music for "a film with Burt Lancaster. I thought I heard you, and was that Tony Coe? and Barry Guy? Howard Riley and Paul Lytton?"

Talking about sleep and music, here is another good story on a related subject. I persuaded Ken to come to a concert by the London Sinfonietta playing Messiaen's long work *From the Canyon to the Stars*. This time he could get to sleep and fell into quite a deep slumber after about twenty minutes of the first half of the piece. At the interval, we filed out to the bar and Ken disappeared. I thought he had gone to the toilet but he had gone home. On the phone the next day I asked what happened and he said, "All those sixth chords! I just couldn't stay awake."

"Laws are made to guard the rights of the people, not to feed lawyers," said Bacon, but then he was stripped of his title, wasn't he?

In the late 60s when I had only known John Stevens for a year or so we were encouraged by Armorel Weston (Veryon's sister) that people in Copenhagen were crazy about free jazz. We decided to go and live there. In fact, John ended up playing in an r&b band and I was cleaning house for some well-off academics (whose house was already spotless). Apart from the playing that we organized for ourselves, mostly in the basement of the student house where we were the guests from hell, the main consolation was the concerts that we heard while there. A most memorable evening was the trio of Sonny Rollins with Jymie Merrit and Max Roach. That late-60s period of Sonny after he had come back from the Bridge was just sensational. John and I got in for nothing and listened from the wings. When their set finished, Sonny left the stage from the other side and I went round the back from my side to say thanks and saw the titanic Mr. Rollins walking towards me smiling broadly … oh no. Those exercises are clearly described in Larry Teal's *The Art of Saxophone*: "draw the corners of the mouth back as far they will go in a tense 'smile,' hold the position, then draw the lips together to form a tight O, hold the position, and repeat fifty times."

> Human lives are essentially not to be summed up, but to be known, as they are lived, in many partial and inarticulate ways. —Iris Murdoch

"Please don't judge us by what you see there."

Final remarks in a conversation with an American lady on the Boeing to New York in 1962. Flying for the first time in my life, I had told her I was only going to be in America for two weeks and I didn't think there would be time to leave Manhattan.

The late Numar Libin, founder of Nimbus, told me that he had lived in the same apartment block as Sidney Bechet in Paris in the 30s, and every day after Bechet had finished his scales and arpeggios, he would end his practice sessions with playing strange sounds, like birds and animal cries. Numar asked him about it one day and Bechet told him, "Sometimes I think what we call music is not the real music."

A lot has happened since then.

Taken from a work in progress with the working title *211 Maxims and other thoughts from a life in improvised music.*

CHAPTER 23

NOCTURNE MEDITATION
THE NECKLACE ETERNITY

ZEENA PARKINS

I have been extremely fortunate to be a part of a virtual costume ball round-table discussion of my work with a highly unusual collection of artists and scientists: Sonia Delaunay, Kali, David Attenborough, Isabelle Eberhardt, and Joseph Cornell:

SONIA DELAUNAY (1885–1979)

Russian-born painter and designer. Her hand-painted fabrics revolutionized the design of textiles. Also produced paintings and murals, as well as designs for theater, ceramics, mosaics, and stained glass.

I love your choice of garment when you play. You display great visual depth through clothing. So if you were restricted to one compulsory uniform, which must be worn every time you play, could you describe it in terms of fabric, layers, hairstyles, influence, accessories, and details?

Sewing and creating clothes and costumes has been an on-again, off-again obsession for many years. I have been intrigued with fashion, garment design, and dress-up, in various forms, for most of my life. I first started sewing when I worked for the Janus Circus, a project directed by Christopher Wangro, who I met at Bard College. I was seamstress/designer, as well as dancing bear, tv set, and grant writer/bookkeeper. We all did everything. It was a kind of theater collective. I wasn't responsible for every costume but quite a few: pants and cummerbunds for the stilt walkers and of course the bear outfit. Finding fabrics, touching materials, the textures, patterns/colors, a very sensual experience.

Transforming the sculptural body, chameleonlike, inhabiting another body or place, becomes an expression related to music/sound making, in performance, composition, and installation. Extending a sense of humor, a sense of play. Elegant surface and congested texture translated to movement and musical gesture. A kind of dance.

When I moved to NYC I would often sew my own clothes simply because I was too broke to go out and buy anything. A great place to listen to music, spacing out in front of the sewing machine, turning a piece of fabric into a 3D object that would drape onto and transform my body. I lived with a hugely talented costume designer/performer, Liz Prince, for six years. From Liz, I learned about sewing, fabrics, and a way of translating imagination into a compositional place. She could make a dress out of anything: metal, cloth, paper, cellophane, keys, dollar bills, scrub brushes. Not unlike musique concrete: taking all matter of material seriously and equally without a hierarchy of importance. Not unlike my own choice of materials as a composer: acoustic/electronic instruments, field recordings, foley.

Then I lived next door to Ellen Berkenblit, a brilliant painter who makes menacing, colorful, moody, humorous work and also, at the time, designed and fabricated exquisite garments. Her sense of color and texture is lush and delicate. For fifteen years I lived in the Lower East Side and consistently heard (among lots of other things) the sound of a sewing machine in very close proximity, mostly from just a room away. And it was extremely satisfying.

The uniform, if used for performance, would be like a second skin, the part of me visible not invisible. I would need flexibility within it, as movement and gesture are an important part of performance. My body would be extended, reconfigured, reconsidered in much the same way that I have thought about recontextualizing, reframing, and extending the harp, an extension of an idea. It could be layered like petals of a flower or shell of an insect and textured like the skin of a forest creature. Perhaps with a sign marking cultural time and place. The eye of the figure: fragments and threadings that map an expanded expansion.

"Material is a means of communication," Anni Albers says.

Kali

I am Kali, goddess of Hindu, the apotheosis of Nature, frightening as I am inevitable; like death, disease, demise, none can escape me. Kali represents justified anger and the reigning goddess of traumatic transitions.

What provokes you the most?

A list that is in constant motion: Jean Genet: *Un Chant d'Amour*, Xenakis, the 104th thing, Kenneth Anger, Michael Snow's Back and Forth, Paul Celan: "harps, Carpathian notnot," Xenakis, Lewis Mumford, Bucky Fuller, Falling Water, Detroit/Highland Park, Seeing Is Forgetting the Name of the Thing That One Sees, Unica Zurhn, Monk/Mingus/Sun Ra, Maya Deren: *At Land/Ritual in Transfigured Time*, Jonas Mekas: *Lost, Lost, Lost*, Diego Rivera's mural at the DIA, Athabascar Glacier, Masada at Mogador, Boulez rehearsing Messian's *Chronachromie* at Carnegie Hall, playing a Gleeman pentaphonic clear, Schoenberg *Op23*, James Turrell: *Pleiades and Danae*, Peter Weir: *Picnic at Hanging Rock*.

When you start to write a song, how much of your emotion take part or behind it? Or it should be more political or intellectual?

At the beginning things seem to arrive when needed with new perceptions. Preparing for a new project takes a long time and it can be quite fuzzy at the beginning. As I'm writing, the thing itself, whether it's a song or a string quartet or an installation, but the thing itself becomes more evident. Clarity emerges and the piece begins to inform me. The germ to start is mostly a challenge to try something that I haven't done before. A chance to deploy a new system, try a new color.

Which emotion drive you most when you're playing, anger? Sadness? Happiness?

The state of performing: it's not emotion that drives me directly, it's a component, but it is the desire to connect and disconnect at once, where there can be a magical split of a conscious and unconscious place. To steer and to let go. It's a matter of discipline. As a performer, it's rich terrain to locate and to inhabit (a trance with the lights on). Ordinary things like technique/form /notes on a page and emotions meld together and then peel away into another realm of concentration. It is a question of immediacy, extreme focus, and willingness or desire to give oneself over. A present absence.

David Attenbourough (1926–)

He was a pioneer in guiding the BBC into inventing the nature documentary. His tone, his faith, his hope in nature has inspired millions of tv watchers. After decades of work he is now working on his most ambitious project, the origin of music, which of course came from the animals before any humans had appeared.

How much of nature is there in your music; is any of your phrasing, scaling, or rhythms and such, consciously drawn from nature?

Directly in the case of working on the reconstructions of *La Mer* by Debussy. (There have been two so far: one at the Whitney Museum at Philip Morris and one at Tonic. A third incarnation of this piece will be presented by graduate students and faculty at Princeton University, in Winter 2008.)

In *La Mer* I am writing beyond or into a different state. It is not an interpretation or an arrangement but a rebuilding or extended transcription. Debussy writes: "The sound of the sea, the curve of a horizon, wind in leaves, the cry of a bird, leave manifold impressions in us. And suddenly, without our wishing it at all, one of these memories spills from us and finds expression in musical language." This, filtered through my urban sensibility, was the starting point for my *La Mer*.

Growing up in inner-city Detroit, from which the ocean was a brief summer refuge, my initial attraction to Debussy's *La Mer* was to manifest a kind of process and musical action that would adhere to and pull away from the Sea. Then of course there is the City, which is a living organism and nature all its own, and as a daughter of a city planner the city organ held significant sway on me. In the end the piece finds a balance between something concrete and something unexpected and uncontrollable.

There seems to be evidence that not only animals but also humans were communicating in music long before the invention of language, can you relate to that in your everyday life?

There certainly are effective nonverbal ways that living creatures have to communicate ideas, desires, instructions, feelings, meanings. Audible and inaudible sounds, perhaps even music, play a huge role in sending messages. As I spend many hours a day playing, not engaged in the world of words, I suppose yes, I can certainly relate to that in my daily life. And quite profoundly with some of my collaborations; in many instances very few words are needed and therefore are actually spoken. Ideas are expressed through process and action. Not to be evasive or elusive, but sometimes words are simply inadequate.

ISABELLE EBERHARDT (1877–1904)

Traveler/explorer/cross dresser/journalist/author.

Eberhardt and I were lucky enough to find the time to meet and speak in person.

What compelled you to have a dialogue with me and create this music? Is it a conceptual reading of my life?

No, not that. Zorn asked me to do something for his new label. It came from an offer, a request, simple as that, and it created an opportunity for me to explore something I had never done before.

Eyes open searching for a topic. I looked around, as Agnes Martin says, "for inspiration." I was making music for choreographer Jennifer Monson. We were working on her piece, *Blood on the Saddle*, for Danspace Project at St. Mark's Church. Jennifer handed me a biography of Isabelle Eberhardt, I read it and was immediately hooked. Then I discovered the collection of short stories, *The Oblivion Seekers*, translated by Paul Bowles.

It was clear that this is the world that I would inhabit for this new piece. It was a beginning. I thought about/read/listened for about a year before I actually wrote down any music. A kind of research: collecting/gathering information/thoughts and then processing it, responding to it. Organizing and writing the piece in my head over and over, trying different things, drawing pictures, working on form. This was also the manner in which I wrote the subsequent pieces that became a trilogy of recordings for my group the Gangster Band (*Mouth/Maul/Betrayer* and *Pan-Acousticon* being the other two works).

At the time, I really lacked the skills to just sit down and write a piece. I never studied composition formally. I developed a way to trick myself, though; I wrote a screenplay for Isabelle. I decided on orchestration: strings/samples/percussion/piano. Out of a murky beginning, Isabelle began to take shape.

Your story was compelling: how you lived your life, the choices you made or didn't make. I don't think I ever noticed this when I read *The Oblivion Seekers* the first time, but right at the beginning, there is a quote:

"No one ever lived more from day to day than I, or was more dependent upon chance. It is the inescapable chain of events that has brought me to this point, rather than I who has caused these things to happen."

You were so open to the events as they unfolded, and you were willing to react to them and be present in them and go with them. Of course you didn't have responsibilities of children and family. You were a very young woman, who eventually was to die a tragic death. You had the luxury to explore another kind of approach to living a life: a woman dressed as a man, convert to Islam, living in northern Algeria, an explorer working as a journalist, writing short stories, with a healthy sexual appetite.

Now I realize there really was some kind of connection between us. Although, there was so much more to it: your life was full of contradictions, you were a radical. I don't consider myself radical, but I see how you actually did choose to express your life and be present in the moment.

Yes, I totally saw the connection between the two of us! I underlined that exact line and thought—oh that's Zeena so it's interesting that you realize that now—fourteen years later. So I want to get back to the screenplay that you wrote for me. And why you felt that you needed to write a screenplay in order to compose music and how that anchored you to my story, because obviously it was immersing yourself into my story that you then translated so brilliantly into an opera—it's like this opera.

I needed a structure, a form. I needed a way in, but more than anything else, I needed the images. I am totally driven by images and how sound connects to image and space. Space in either an architectural, natural, or emotional landscape.

So what did you see/in this imaginary north Africa that you discovered throughout your research of my life and writings and the indigenous musics...

The desert captivated me: the heat, the illusion and reality of emptiness, the dust and the light. This compelled me as a composer. It was very much in the realm of imagination. The short stories, your life history and music from Algeria, and even Turkey. I have never been to any of these places. In the end, it was a very fanciful kind of research that I did before actually writing the piece. I would set up rules and break rules. I was not creating a manifesto with the screenplay, it simply set up a situation where I had distinct images and scenes and sense of space and place, and that drove me more than anything else. Narrative was never intended to be the main focus. The screenplay served as a kind of stimulant.

What are those images?

They are both physical and emotional ones that pulled and tugged at me. I invented ways that I could access and express an understanding of what those images were in this collection of pieces called *Isabelle*. The short stories were also quite potent triggers.

OK ... so this piece *Outside*, which is about a vagrant who gets ill and just walks out of the hospital to die in the open land with the sky. That was such a big theme in my work and my life...

You walked out the hospital too, just before you died, you were in the hospital for malaria and your husband got you out and you lived in a hut by the dry river bed—and that's where you died. There was a flash flood. You had been in the hospital and walked out.

Yes, exactly—but this whole notion about being out on the land: the vagrant is the freest person because they are completely outside of the system and they just do what they want to do—and in a way that is how I lived my life and I want you to talk about this in terms of music and being outside .... of making music the way that you make music...

Let me start by telling you about Sara Parkins, violinist, and Maggie Parkins, cellist (both of the Eclipse Quartet). I used Sara and Maggie for the first time in *Ursa's Door*, which was another score I made for choreographer Jennifer Monson. They were not improvisers, they were classical musicians, but they were extremely open-minded and wanted to participate in different kinds of music. This made them perfect musicians for me to work with. I was very lucky. As I listen to this section, now, I am remembering that the violin and piano had set parts but not the cello. I gave Maggie pitch areas but then especially early on when I wanted to elicit improvisatory parts, I would do a kind of conduction in front of Maggie and use my hands to conduct the shapes, gestures, densities, and tempos of the sounds I wanted her to make. It was such a personal expression and a very private action, as I think of it now. I was morphing together a dance, a Butch Morris Conduction and information or details that perhaps a director would give an actress when they are going to work on a character in a scene. We would talk about pitch areas and playing techniques as well as the atmosphere of the particular piece. I was making a part for her with her, live spontaneously, by giving her shapes and gestures of what I wanted the part to be. She was absolutely perfect in deciphering this kind of information, and we have used variations of this technique off and on through the years. Of course, now they are great improvisers and I have much more experience as a composer, so it's not necessary in the same way that it was fourteen years ago. This has nothing to do with traditional music notation, and at least with Sara and Margaret, I found it to be a very successful way to get certain kinds of parts down on tape or to get them to connect to their instruments more as inventors or explorers, rather than interpreters. Until recently I probably would have been very embarrassed to even admit this to you. Perhaps I thought it made me less of a composer or that I was masquerading as someone with less specific intent, but now I realize it's fine. In fact, there was so much specificity and it was clear that the results were perfect. At the time, I could not have written down anything that would have been more precise than what Maggie played responding to my descriptive and visual cues. Somehow I was able to create a situation in *Isabelle* where I gave myself permission to write a piece, in whatever way possible. It wasn't easy because I didn't have technique as a writer at that point to help me, so I had to invent as I went along. Fourteen years later my skills are quite developed; however, I will say that, for me, *Isabelle* works, even if the composition problems could have been solved with different solutions. I am still very proud of this piece. It was a first, and I wouldn't want to change anything in it.

Joseph Cornell (1903–1972)

Sculptor/painter/filmmaker/assemblage artist.

What is the difference between sexuality and sensuality?

One is inside atmosphere and the other one is glowing atmosphere.

What was the worst response you've received to a gift given?

It was glanced at, ever so briefly, and tossed away.

Why are some people so inadequate?

Because they are completely unconscious.

What is in the princess's jewel casket?

A clear plasticine harp designed by Don Buchla, which has LED lights for stings and motion sensors and triggers.

Tell me a word that means two opposite things at once.

Ruffle.

Tell me about the perfect gender.

An unidentifiable gender: male and female combined.

Where does all the clutter lead?

Philip K. Dick had an idea for this and invented a word for it, something called "kipple." No matter how much you clean it up, it continues to re-appear again and again. Unwanted papers get discarded and magically reproduce themselves. In a tiny NYC apartment nothing could be more infuriating. It's a kind of live-in ghost.

True identities/real-life collaborators of Zeena:

Sonia Daluncay: Mandy Macintosh/filmmaker, visual artist
Kali: Ikue Mori/composer, filmmaker
David Attenbourough: Björk/singer, songwriter
Isabelle Eberhardt: Cynthia Madansky/filmmaker, visual artist
Joseph Cornell: Daria Martin/filmmaker, visual artist

CHAPTER 24

NINE PREREQUISITES FOR INSPIRATION

MAJA SOLVEIG KJELSTRUP RATKJE

"Life belongs to the living, and those who live must be prepared for change."
—J.W. von Goethe (1749–1832)

This text is based on notes written for an interdisciplinary seminar at NTNU in Trondheim, Norway, for which I contributed to a talk on inspiration. I was most inclined to say something on the subject of inspiration in general, rather than talk about my own more or less inspired work. If inspiration is something universal, this should be possible. That could be an inspiring challenge, I thought.

As creative people in all fields will experience, there is no limit to what can give inspiration: it can be anything from works of art to ordinary everyday life. Another point is that what inspires is often both irrational and illogical; it frequently develops from an indirect form with no evident connection between the inspiring impulse and the end product. One is not always even aware of having been inspired by something until the work is finished, and one often ends up with something quite different to what appeared to be the original idea. This was indeed the case for the speech I was to give. The solution I arrived at was to approach the issue from a slightly different angle to that from which I started. The question I asked myself was: What are the conditions necessary for me to be inspired? From this line of inquiry I came up with *Nine Prerequisites for Inspiration*, in which I believe many will be able to recognize things from their own experience, whatever their field of activity.

Freedom

Freedom is the most important prerequisite for inspiration. By that I mean freedom of expression and of movement, and freedom to think for oneself. And people must have the right to use their own freedom as they wish, to be on top of it, to own their freedom. This postulates a democratic society in which power belongs to the people. This is not to say that lack of freedom cannot inspire: most artists have felt the sudden release of inspiration following an oppressive period in their life. Suppression has provided a kind of political inspiration to artists like Shostakovich, Gubaidulina, Kandinsky, Oscar Wilde, etc. Olivier Messiaen wrote one of his most beautiful works and one of my favorite pieces ever, *Quatuor pour la fin du temps*, in a concentration camp. But I think it is important to underline the fact that in cases like these inspiration arises not because of but in spite of oppression. I would argue that the fragility and irrationality of inspiration demands individual freedom.

Space and Time

Inspiration is not a constant quantity, on hand to be harvested in abundance. To survive the brutality of reality it needs to be cultivated and cared for, like other fragile plants. To make space and time for inspiration is to give it a chance. Ideally, with all the time in the world, one can enter this magical space, spend some time there, and see what happens. But one has to avoid being too eager to get results. Forced inspiration does not lead to any creative fulfilment.

Childlike Curiosity and the Ability to Think Divergently

A generally curious attitude to life is essential for an inspired existence. There is no contradiction between retaining a childlike or childish curiosity whilst simultaneously acquiring and cultivating knowledge. Curiosity is inspiration's best friend. One has to bring it along, both when searching for certain knowledge and when encountering the unforeseen—such as placing familiar objects in new contexts. Drop the well-known patterns tied up with unnecessary politeness and prejudice. It can be a good idea to simply start breaking some rules or routines—what about going to a concert or buying a ticket for something you know absolutely nothing about?

Inspiration comes most easily to those who unconsciously and naturally combine curiosity with divergent thinking. Inspiration thrives in the encounter between childlike playfulness and adult knowledge; knowledge laid down by way of experience in so-called cognitive schemes. Someone who can easily and playfully move around between these banks of knowledge will be able to discover new connections and possibilities. This is what happens in an inspired moment. Things originally arranged into strict mental schemes acquire new functions when new connections are made, giving previously unsuspected possibilities and results. $E=mc^2$. If you are prepared to see life in a new way in terms of ideas, inspiration will lend magic to the new connections—and new knowledge is laid down. It is important to be the owner not only of your own freedom, but also of your own knowledge.

Flow and Inner Motivation

This is the most abstract and difficult paragraph to say something sensible about. If I start by saying that inspiration appears in different dimensions, I am referring to the multi-layered functions of the mind, how nothing in life is ever experienced linearly, how it never can be.

A very characteristic and often very cliché-filled way of describing how inspiration works is by comparing it to being "struck by a flash" or having an "illuminated moment." It is often characterized as a brief sense of recognition in relation to something that has not yet taken shape, whether it be a specific idea for an entire work or for a component part of something. The feeling is abstract and yet very specific. Another way to describe how inspiration functions is to show the existence of a very intimate dimension in which there is room to get involved in a more active dialogue with inspiration. This dimension exists in what we can call the gestation period between an idea arising, in the form of something amorphous or abstract, and its delivery into the world as a work or a chosen framework—as for instance a framework for improvisation. It has, unlike the "illuminated moment," a time span that allows us to carry on a dialogue with inspiration and alternately store ideas in the subconscious for them to grow beyond our prejudiced control. A third, though by no means final approach is to look at inspiration on a more global, general level, where several different kinds of influence affect the creative process over a longer period. The inspiration working here is of a more random kind and of a vaguer character. It is not easily traceable either when it happens or in retrospect.

All these dimensions exist in parallel, infiltrating each other and affecting the final result. Like children, all ideas are unique and require different upbringings, and equivalently different methods. The trick is to let your ideas flow freely between these levels, and be able to limit yourself or go in deeper where necessary. Choices should, as far as possible, be made on the firm basis of an inner motivation, which means one must be fully conscious of the danger of letting the creative flow be directed by outer demands, others' expectations, hopes of success, and other motivations from the outside which we are often all too willing to meet and give way to. Inner motivation ensures continued contact with the original idea, even after the necessary choices have been made.

Maximalism and Anarchy

As I mentioned before, it is impossible to predict exactly what may provide inspiration. This includes a wonderful feeling of freedom—for those who dare: at the starting point, everything is permitted—and anything may be relevant, so don't clear your attic out—either mentally or physically! Collect items you fancy and that for different reasons attract your attention. Remember also to collect and study things that seem for the moment to be meaningless or irrelevant. The twists and turns of the creative process may lead you back to an important encounter with something that at first seemed quite neutral, or even something that made you feel repelled or exasperated. In his *Incomplete Manifesto for Growth* the designer Bruce Mau writes that one should not tidy one's desk: "You never know what can come in useful." Of course this also applies, in a metaphorical sense, to the mind. When we speak of inspiration it is usually in terms of the dimension in which inspiration gives rise to an idea as if in a moment of enlightenment. To prevent this moment from suffocating amongst our own and other people's limitations and prejudices we have to strive to attain an inner anarchy.

Motivating forces from outside are a constant threat that may easily lead to the artist choosing to limit his or her options prematurely, leading to a subsequent restriction of artistic freedom. But at the point where the work begins to move in a clear direction, where some parameters must be defined, or for instance in the context of improvisation where a definite, limiting choice has to be made, the artist is granted the ability to mentally "clear the desk" in one accomplished, virtuoso swipe. The onward flow is a continuous process of storing information, repeating what you already have in a series of new contexts, getting new impulses, storing the new information, etc. In this way the creative dialectic that arises in the wake of an inspired moment can be exploited.

Tools

It is not easy to say what comes first—is it the search for a method of dealing with an idea that creates the tool or is it the tool that determines the method? In many cases it is both, perhaps even both at the same time. Nevertheless, everyone who works at translating abstract ideas into reality undoubtedly needs to get hold of tools that can help in best possible ways. There is no fixed recipe for this, but artists and other creative people are bound to develop flexible, adjustable tools of their own to suit their individual needs. Occasionally tools of this kind are incorporated into an academic method or become objects of research, even in classroom situations. Examples of well-known tools in the history of music are the schools of Bach, Palestrina, and Messiaen.

Collaboration

The question of how to deal with inspiration, how to tackle an idea, has as many answers as there are ideas. By including curiosity and openness in your own choices, you are better equipped to be able to learn when encountering other people's choices. The choices of others may be a new and invaluable source of inspiration in a creative process. By collaborating with people who operate in other fields one is constantly learning how to see the world in new ways. Creative people need to be in touch not only with themselves but also with the world and with what is happening around them in order to have anything to say at all. In 1999 I wrote a Manifesto, where, among many other things, I stated: "Music has to be in rhythm with the times. Composers and performers have a duty to keep themselves up-to-date in every way possible, and not just inside their own professional field." It is not just a matter of being inspired, but also of giving inspiration.

An individual's evaluation of quality will always be subjective, but it must not be repressed to the extent that the sum total of choices made brings the work down to an impersonal, average level or a lowest common denominator. When it comes to collaboration, the sum of the parts is not a logical sum such as 1 + 1 = 2. What if 1 + 1 = a horse or a smell? Everything is possible. A person working alone tends to create his or her own arguments for and against the choices made. When meeting others, given that the project in question involves close collaboration, it may be hard to appreciate your collaborators' choices, especially if you have been confronted with the same choices but decided on another solution. For that reason artists often find it easier to appreciate forms of expression that are remote from their own decision-making than those that lie close to their own specialized fields. If openness in the encounter with closely related fields of activity poses a greater challenge, it isn't less valuable in terms of learning from it.

Ambivalence

Never be cocksure. Everything has more to it than meets the eye. That explains why there are always discussions and conflicting attitudes to what is relevant in art, or for the "Work." There is a whole academic tradition based on this, more or less relevant to those who are actually engaged in creating something. In artistic collaboration processes there is often disagreement about both methods and aims. This is a good thing. But regardless of what creative choices are made, it is important to keep as much as possible of the fragile ambivalence from the starting point of an idea still present throughout the work. One-dimensional art is seldom very rewarding. But beware of letting the ambivalence block every source of creative energy. After all, you have to start somewhere.

Patience

Inspiration cannot be coerced, nor can it be ensured by means of routines and tools alone. In the long run only one thing counts: patience. And from time to time the best thing you can do is simply to put the whole thing aside and relax. Did you say a bath, Archimedes?

CHAPTER
25

GLITCH

MARINA ROSENFELD

John Cage: Marina … umm, are you comfortable with doing this interview now? Yes? Shall I state the date? January 1, 2007, my goodness. OK, let me start by saying that I … I love your work.

MR: Really? But you wrote in *Silence* …

JC: I'm trying to re-evaluate. I've been a bit … confused …

MR: Don't be so hard on yourself. Yvonne Rainer wrote that the essence of your project was a "web of undifferentiated events set in motion by and referring back to the original flamboyant artist-gesture, in this case the abandonment of personal taste." It's a little harsh, but let's not be squeamish. Anyway, from the vantage of a couple of decades, I can appreciate the music, the somber, slightly genteel spectacle of clarinets and cellos and tubas intent in conversation with more recent inventions. I love that. I owe you that …

JC: Thank you. I … wish I could have … I see now that I … You know, when I entered the anechoic chamber and …

MR: Oh my god, please, that whole language of scientific justification bores me to tears—the anechoic chamber, the oscilloscope, the whole justifying discourse of the laboratory …

JC: You seem a little pissed off.

MR: No, no, I'm not, not really. Let's start somewhere else …

JC: Well, how would you like to talk about your work? We could begin with your instrument, this sort of hybrid you've adopted, the original dub plates you make in series, the live mixtures, your hands ...

MR: My dub plates are a form of notation—musical housing. I compose with/for/through them. They are interpretations—deteriorations, transformations, generations—of interpretations, way before they even sound. They are, in the ultimate sense, both representational and completely abstract.

JC: I'm not comfortable with the representation part.

MR: You're not supposed to be. That Rainer bit I just quoted was in an essay she called "a revisionist narrativization of myself as subject." I am writing about myself right this minute and calling it a conversation, but what I really wish I could do is revise the conversations I had a long time ago. I spent so long worrying about how to make a sound that wouldn't arrive dead ...

JC: I wouldn't change a thing I ever said ...

MR: Even when you called Glenn Branca a fascist?

JC: Even now, I don't ... I can't ... I don't like large groups of loud people ...

MR: Let's leave my family out of this. But you're right to be wary: crowds unleash energies of all kinds as, unfortunately, we've seen. It's kind of dumb to pick a side on this one. The modern divorce of music from music-making, that is, collective social situations, epitomized for Adorno even in 1927 by the use of headphones, was already apparent in the evolution of the piano "from a musical instrument into a piece of bourgeois furniture" in the nineteenth century. Next in this trajectory was the gramophone, its output destined for private consumption, i.e., the home; he called its domain "the pregnant stillness of individuals." (But isn't this exactly what we're not? When I listen I'm never quite alone.) He also razzed people listening to headphones as "petit bourgeois girls, most of them underage." Well, girls are the ultimate headphone wearers—aloof, but also aware, skeptical, porous. Music on headphones is the outside coming in. And the outside—

the crowd—is only getting bigger, and louder …

Can you tell I've been reading Adorno?

JC: Yes. Is it helping you sort anything out?

MR: Not really. But I like to gaze across the divide. Let's say that when I get a whole orchestra to play electric guitars with nail polish bottles as musical implements …

JC: Are you talking about the *Sheer Frost Orchestra* now?

MR: Yes. Let's say I'm making a covert reference to painting: there's a little brush inside each bottle, surrounded by pigment, agitating space over the instrument's strings. At the time, the cross-disciplinary gesture seemed to be a way of confronting the intense gendered-ness of the guitar, though, of course, what everyone liked about it was the sexual reference that remained. Power wrapped up and contained in a very tight package. Painters love to sentimentalize musicians as social animals, doers, emotional beings. But they make much more money than we do.

The visual—when you are interested in it and you make music, you're now supposed to be a sound artist. The sounds you make are suddenly categorically metaphorical. OK, I hereby reject the entire category (I've already done this for a couple of years, actually) and embrace music, which is only as ephemeral as smell or touch—that is, not really at all. Music is primarily material, and records are primarily filmic—two-dimensional surfaces, screens. As I said, tracks engraved onto dub plates are themselves a form of graphical notation. The invariable shape of a record player, the circle in the square, telegraphs the configuration of notehead and staff, have you noticed that?

JC: No … I don't think I have.

MR: It's ironic. The idea of the note is very powerful, once engrained. Surprisingly flexible too. Let's say improvised music (electronic music, all music really) is essentially a flow of signals, and, thus, essentially describes thought, or the architecture of thought, another intermittently invisible entity that we can now visualize again, just like Spinoza did in the 1600s—

it's material, that is, godlike—god for atheists.

JC: Is the turntable valuable to you for its visual properties?

MR: Not necessarily. The turntable doesn't mean all that much to me, although it is my instrument of choice as an improviser. I like how it feels and what it means and doesn't mean. Its relative and cyclical obsolescence and/or resurgence make it almost ideally marginal. In its implicit conversation with the computer, its more socially adept cousin, it is almost perfectly beside the point; separated from commercially manufactured LPs (because I don't play those, I make my own dub plates—one-offs, one or two at a time), it refers only tangentially to musical history. (I would define that tangent as somewhat comical.) It's a transforming machine, an alchemist, an agent of both repetition and change, but it doesn't do more than play what's already there.

Adorno already had it right in 1927 when he said the only interesting aspect of the gramophone, the point at which it "interferes"—and this is the only thing I want from it—is when its spring wears out and its "sound droops in chromatic weakness," a wonderful possibility that I think I've tactilely aspired to in the wake of every thinned-out Robert Wyatt vocal or timbral Morton Feldman-ism I've ever heard.

JC: (silence) ... Is there anything you'd like to add?

MR: Did you know that "glitch" comes from the Yiddish "glitshn," meaning slip? Has anyone written about that?

JC: Not that I know of.

MR: Someone should ...

JC: OK, thanks, Marina.

MR: You're welcome.

—*New York, 2007*

Bibliography

Theodor W. Adorno, "The Curve of the Needle" ("Nadelkurven"). (Originally pub. 1928, translated by Thomas Y. Levin, MIT Press: 1990.)

Yvonne Rainer, "Looking Myself in the Mouth," October, Vol. 17, *The New Talkies* (Summer 1981), pp. 65–76.

CHAPTER
26

THE CHALLENGE OF "WORLD" MUSIC FOR THE CREATIVE MUSICIAN

NED ROTHENBERG

It's a cliché already but true: the world has shrunk; in many ways it's all "one" music now. The outward-looking creative musician must reckon not only with the music of his or her own culture but with a huge wealth of musical traditions that far outstrips what was available only a few decades ago. The reason that we may find this truthful cliché a bit distasteful is that so much musical "ethnic fusion" is a ploy to capitalize on exoticism, to skim the most obviously sexy veneers of music from distant lands and once again dumb down the music to a mass audience. But that's just the continuing status quo, no use killing oneself about it. An honest and open musician knows that deep music requires deep listening and that this concentrated focus is both a joy and an essential part of musical practice. With any newly encountered musical tradition, when one develops a love for particular materials and approaches them with respect and sincerity, the depth that new understanding can give one's own music can be bottomless.

Of course creative musicians are "fans" of music, but we all must admit to having an agenda in a good deal of our listening. If we have expansive goals to create a wide range of music, we prowl omnivorously in the musical forest looking for inspirational input.[1] This is absorbed in various ways, which can be exceedingly difficult to describe. That is why music writers who strive to line up neat lists of musical influences (usually confined inside specific genres or like instrumentalists) for a given artist almost always miss the boat. For musicians it is actually more interesting to consider influences that are refracted and highly complex—say, Charlie Parker's interest in Stravinsky or John Coltrane's relationship with Ravi Shankar.

1. I have often noticed, conversely, that players who mine a narrow musical seam listen to a narrow range of music or do not listen at all.

In this essay I'll deal with two different but equally valid approaches to world music and look at how my personal path has been to gradually create of a hybrid between the two. I want to stress that these are *musicians'* approaches, not ethnomusicologists'. The focus is primarily on the music itself, not its anthropologic role in its mother culture. One path is intensive study of a specific tradition—in my case, the Japanese shakuhachi (end-blown bamboo flute) and its *honkyoku*, the Zen-based solo music. The other is a kind of intensive but nonscholarly immersion in the art of a particular musician or culture, which creates a visceral resonance between that music and one's own practice. I'll draw on examples of my own creative efforts and attempt to illustrate some of the pitfalls and obstacles one may encounter on the path to integrating a wider range of world music into one's own expressive voice.

* * *

First we have intensive, straightforward study. This can be likened to any normal investigations—if one is approaching western classical music one studies harmony, counterpoint, etc. If one is looking into bebop, transcription of solos and study of chord changes is a normal route. Seen from these vantages points, the shakuhachi presents a tradition equally evolved but wholly other.

I began to study shakuhachi when I was already a practicing professional. I was acutely aware, however, that I had thus far followed a musical path of least resistance. My music was wordy, just like me, chock-full of material and motion. Hearing the shakuhachi honkyoku music of practitioners like Watazumi-do, Yamaguchi Goro, and Yokoyama Katsuya, I became aware of a kind of negative musical space that had yet to find a place in my music. I felt I needed to study and pursue an understanding of this foreign musical world. When I began to play the instrument as a student of Ralph Samuelson, I was not sure that I would ever perform on it. Until the late 18th century shakuhachi was not used in performance, rather it was solely an instrument of meditation. Along these lines, my original goal was a personal inner spiritual and esthetic development rather than another weapon for my stage arsenal.

Watazumi-do, the monk whose shakuhachi recordings were the first that I listened to extensively, spoke of his performances as "breath meditation" rather than music. The expression inherent in the notes is not only in reference to their pitch but, equally important, their tone color and the character of blowing that produces them. For example, on a flute of standard length, E♭ is most commonly played as "Tsu-meri," a soft, covered sound which can either anticipate movement to a stronger tone or end a phrase with a kind of understated question mark. Watazumi's "Do-kyoku" music uses another E♭ in the second octave called "I-kari" and the pitch is the only thing it has in common with "Tsu-meri." It is played with explosive breath, a different head position and fingering, and its sonic role is one of dramatic release. The two notes are also approached from an entirely different set of phrases. So what is often considered timbral nuance in western music—volume and articulation—becomes a dramatic differentiation, which can even be the motific focus of a piece.[2] Suddenly pitch and timbre become indivisible.

This may seem a small item, but to respond to it I was forced to re-evaluate the most basic assumptions of my western musical training as a woodwind player. Wind instruction here starts from an orchestral model. We try to play a unified tone color from the top to the bottom of our instrument and then add articulation and dynamics as the score dictates. This way the orchestral composer can orchestrate with confidence—a loud oboe note will sound like a soft one and blend in predictable ways with the flute. Pitch functions in a melodic and harmonic nexus while tone color adds an emotive shading independently.

2. In fact quite a few of my original shakuhachi works feature phrases which use adjacent contrasting "notes" of like pitch to feature this special characteristic of the instrument.

However, the fact is that all reed instruments have nonlinear aspects very much like the shakuhachi. Not all pitches can be played equally loud and soft; there are strange things like clarinet throat-registers, sluggish low notes on saxophones, and alternate trill fingerings with sounds deemed acceptable for only an instant because they don't match with the "normal" desired timbres. And once one begins to investigate microtones and multiphonics, the western keyboard-based models (play the same sound up and down like a piano) are even more unapproachable. It was this shakuhachi-derived re-evaluation which enabled me to embrace all these nonlinear aspects as ripe material for musical creation rather than imperfections. I think this kind of intimate relationship with timbre is one of the defining elements of my music.

* * *

I will return to my particular path with shakuhachi and world music, but I want to make some related observations here about the development of the creative composer/performer. I strongly feel that it is necessary for every creative artist to pass through periods of self-examination in relationship to the training they received in their youth. At the time of this education the goal of a certain kind of technical proficiency is taken as a given. A part of musical maturity is a fuller awareness of the relativism of that goal in relationship to the wider expanse of sonic creation in a broad worldview. Just as European history alone cannot fill in a total historic picture of how we came to be where we are, European music practices alone cannot encompass the wider limits of the worldwide musical expanse.

As described above and below, shakuhachi was a key element in my particular path through a period of self-reflection, but it can happen in many ways. Indeed, it is different for every creative artist, and is part of what makes one distinctive as an individual. For me, working as a beginner in Japanese music after I had reached a level of proficiency in my "home" musical schools of classical music and jazz, had what I now feel to be some objective advantages. I had no subjective "ax to grind" in relationship to foreign musical concepts that were new to me.

Let me contrast this to another re-evaluative force to show what I mean. An innovative figure like Ornette Coleman certainly caused a large amount of self-examination in the improvising musicians that followed him. He created great polarization because he questioned western harmonic laws from within. Many groups of musicians had positive or negative responses based on the educational baggage they carried. Those who could get by this baggage and respond honestly to the challenge presented by Ornette grew in response to his music. But many deceived themselves with a shallow, politically based response. Two of the most obvious were "that ain't music he's playing, he is breaking all the rules I hold dear" or the opposite: "after hearing Ornette I was released from having to know anything about standard harmony." (In the second case, people didn't often admit their reaction in such a way, but it was their de facto response.) My point is that in both cases the musician ends up weaker rather than stronger as a result of the challenge.

These self-evaluative "mirrors" can come in all sorts of ways. In my case, two of the largest forces were shakuhachi and the new soundworld of electronic music. One tradition was very old, one very new. But both introduced an aesthetic and soundworld outside that which my musical education prescribed. Other composers find these "mirrors" in surprising places; for some it could be a piece of literature or cinema, rather than music at all.

* * *

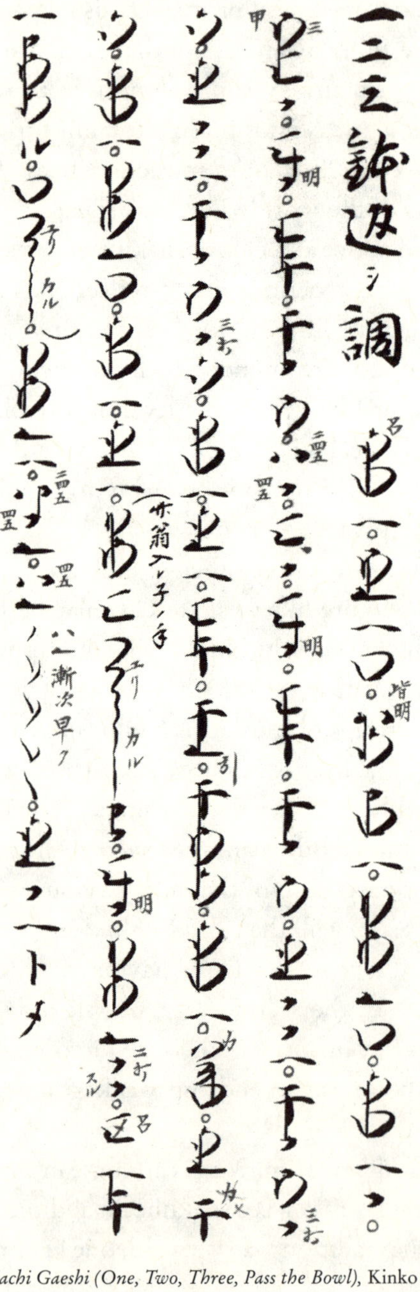

Hi Fu Mi Hachi Gaeshi (One, Two, Three, Pass the Bowl), Kinko Honkyoku.

Let me return to my personal experience as a composer/performer on woodwinds and my study of shakuhachi. Here I will go into a brief technical description which may be difficult for nonmusicians. However, I think it can be highly illustrative of how the devil lies in the details.

The most straightforward but highly involved endeavor was learning to read traditional Kinko-school honkyoku[3] on the alto saxophone. All the Kinko pieces are primarily combinations of the same phrases; in addition, each piece has one or two lines that are unique to it. I created mini-transcriptions of these phrases so that I could "read" the pieces from the original shakuhachi notation, sounding in the same key as the standard 1.8 flute[4] but one octave lower. You can hear the results in my recording of *Sokaku Reibo (The Cranes in Their Nest)* on *The Crux* (Leo Records LR 187). A few of the more uncommon phrases simply could not be rendered on the sax so I omitted the pieces that contain them.

3. The Kinko School traces its lineage back to Kurosawa Kinko (1710–1770). I studied this music with Ralph Samuelson and later with his teacher, the "living national treasure" Yamaguchi Goro.

4. "Shakuhachi" literally means 1.8 "shaku," a traditional Japanese unit of measurement. The 1.8 flute has a low note of D above middle C. I also play a 2.4 shaku flute, which has a low note of A below middle C. Notes are named in relationship to their fingerings on the instrument, not their absolute pitch. So the low note of both flutes is called Ro, written as ロ. The note a half-step higher would be Tsu-meri ツ メ リ sounding E♭ on the 1.8 and B♭ on the 2.4.

I will describe the process of approaching a key phrase to give the reader a taste of what was involved. It is the opening line of a number of pieces and involves notes with profoundly different character.

TSU-meri RO is written as . A "meri" note is a note played with the head tipped down and the finger hole half covered; it sounds a half- or whole step lower than a "kari" note, which is played with the head upright. Thus, the meri note has a muted sound, while the kari note is loud and has a fuller overtone component. In Kinko-school honkyoku, "Tsu" is always meri unless written otherwise.

So this phrase consists of the two notes E♭ and D.

However, there are myriad tiny nuances involved. When studying shakuhachi one has to learn and memorize the ornamentations that go with different phrases. In western notation this phrase in the second octave would look something like:

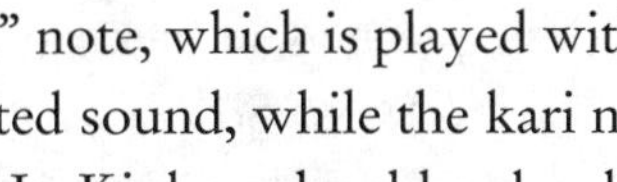

First off, notes on shakuhachi are never tongued. It might seem like a small thing, but it is major! Tsu-meri in this phrase is attacked with a finger hit of great subtlety: if you notice it it's too pronounced; it should have an almost subliminal presence. We would have to notate this in grace notes, as diagrammed above. However, the tendency would be to make far too much of it. Furthermore, many modern shakuhachi players tune their notes to the western scale, but I prefer those who play the Tsu-meri just slightly flat—less than a quartertone, however, so once again our notation doesn't capture it. In turn, the movement to the D is not simple. First the head is bent further down and the hole is further shaded, creating a note call "Tsu dai meri" (E "Big" flat—pitch = D), which is even more soft and covered sounding. Then the fingers and head quickly slide up for an instant before the fingers crash down on RO—the D played with all holes closed that is strong, played with the head up. I can try to show this with the gliss lines in the diagram above, but again it fails to capture the real sonic movement involved. Nor does it really capture the rhythm. The phrase is quite slow, having a duration determined by the length of one's breath. While the two soft notes are approximately equal, their relative lengths differ according to the place of the phrase in the piece, the style of the player, the mood in the room at the time, numerous factors that to me are almost mystical. The Japanese notation has a line connecting the first two notes, showing they move quicker in relation to the third one, but nothing else. The western notation implies a relative equality that may not be the case. For all of these reasons, it never occurred to me to actually transcribe the traditional notation into western tablature.[5] Rather, since I had learned all the ornamentations already on shakuhachi, I translated them to saxophone and memorized them.[6]

5. I have seen some of these pieces transcribed for western flute and I find the results almost comical.

6. This of course is very similar to the way baroque composers left the ornamentations off of their scores. Further, it is in the playing of these small ornamentations that some of the most telling distinctions between players of both types of music can be found.

So picking up my E♭ alto saxophone, I first make the transposition down a minor third, and the phrase becomes:

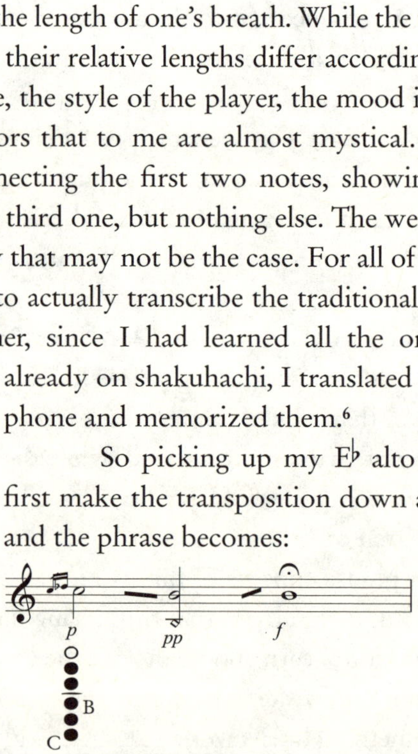

The saxophone has many more holes than the shakuhachi's five, and so I have a host of choices. I am most concerned to convey the phantom quality of the finger articulation and a dramatic timbral change between the two B's. In fact I found two or three ways to play this phrase and use different ones depending on where it occurs in the piece. The most common is illustrated above: to play the C by closing a number of extra holes below the normal fingering; the sound becomes covered and the pitch matches the slightly flat Tsu-meri. I "attack" the note not with my tongue but by flicking a side key normally used to play high notes in the upper octave. I can then slowly close the top-left hand B key until I am fingering the B an octave below the one written but sounding only the first harmonic very softly, thus getting a very covered sound without extra overtones.[7] Then I slide up the left-hand B key creating a slight upward gliss and with another key flick from my right hand land on a loud, normal B. Nothing is tongued. Quite a lot for such a simple phrase, and once again largely impossible to notate.

7. It is a normal exercise for saxophonists to practice playing overtones off the low notes of their instrument controlling it like a brass instrument. This was promoted by the great saxophone teacher Joseph Allard as a way to develop tone color and resonance.

Why do I feel the avoidance of tonguing is such a big deal? First off, when studying any wind instrument in the United States and Europe tonguing is presented as synonymous with articulation. Certainly it presents a wonderfully wide palate of sounds from legato to staccato, slapping, double and flutter effects, and so on. But for a western-trained wind player to avoid the tongue brings up a technical aspect of the kind of self-examination of one's training that I described above. Not use the tongue? It's as if you had to dance without moving your feet! In fact, with this limitation many new possibilities arise. What I call "finger-articulation" is viewed in western classical and jazz music purely as ornamentation. But the shakuhachi is just one of many instruments which eschew the tongue. The expression of articulation is given through the fingers—ornamentation and articulation becomes the same thing! And of course on instruments that use all ten fingers, we have a host of such articulative possibilities. With Indian bansuri, Sardinian launeddas,[8] Indonesian suleng, Irish and Scottish bagpipes, and many other woodwinds, you can hear that notes are attacked largely with the fingers. Some traditions, like Hungarian/Romanian taragato and Balkan/klezmer clarinet, mix finger and tongue attacks in fascinating fashion. For western scoring methodology, this technique creates major problems because such articulation cannot be written as a symbol over or under a note, rather it is

8. The Launeddas are a kind of bagpipe without a bag, which utilize circular-breathing to create an outdoor music for dancing.

part of the notes themselves. One ends up with a multitude of confusing grace notes. There is a famous story of John Coltrane being shown a transcription of one of his solos: he pronounced it unplayable. I am sure that if one showed the Bulgarian clarinetist Ivo Papasov an exact transcription of one of his melodies he would laugh and have a similar response.

This brings up what can be viewed either as a liberating effect of shakuhachi on my solo oeuvre or a cop-out on my part. The small description above gives a good idea not only of the way I transcribe shakuhachi music but also of the kind of movements that I create and use in my own solo compositions and improvisations. I am constantly asked after concerts if they can be notated. I have some musical scratch-pad techniques for helping to remember passages I devise, but the simple answer to the question is no. I was freed from feeling the obligation to render my music in this fashion partly by seeing how poorly western notation captures the movements of shakuhachi honkyoku[9] and partly by stories like the Coltrane one. For me, super-detailed notation is a tedium which only results in a representation on paper, not a sonic result. However, those of us who have studied in conservatories know there can be a kind of tyranny of the score. It is not *music* if it can't be written down. This is partly the old "high and low" cultural argument. Obviously, it would be an arcane exercise to try and render something like Robert Johnson's masterful guitar playing in staff notation. The response of the academic establishment is then to dismiss such things as "folk" forms. But it is exactly my interest as a composer-performer to create materials that have a feel of nonclassical idiomatic playing. Screw this "high and low" divide! I became more than comfortable with the conviction that it is my job to create my music, not to notate it. My questioners sometimes protest, "But then how can these materials be used by other players and composers?" Of course players can come study with me; they can also try to figure out what I am doing from recordings. Regrettably, I have no solution to offer composers.

9. This is also why I write all my own through-composed shakuhachi music in Japanese notation.

The shakuhachi also helped give me a very grounded viewpoint in relation to microtonality. Most composers who self-consciously deal with it choose to compose for string or percussion instruments. This is because they can be tuned precisely to follow originally devised tuning systems, as in the work of Harry Partch, James Tenney, and La Monte Young. Most important, the timbre of the instrument is not greatly effected by moving its pitch. But with wind instruments, microtonality is a more fluid affair. This is very dramatic with the shakuhachi, since it has only five holes; there is a constant interrelationship between pitch and tone color. It applies as well to western woodwind instruments. They are designed with "sweet spots" so the purest tone color occurs when the instrument is played in tune with the piano. As soon as we go outside the twelve notes to an octave box, we have issues of timbre as well as pitch. So microtonal melodies have inherent nonlinear timbral aspects. The challenge is to make this a source of added expressivity, not a liability. The phrases of traditional shakuhachi music showed me how to view an alternate fingering on sax not as a "flat F," for instance, but as a new and different note, which could perhaps grow into a multiphonic and then back to another well-tempered note with more overtone information. The key is to *hear* the movement and be able to sing with it. Woodwind multiphonics are by their nature microtonal, so this type of hearing is required to use them in a musical fashion. In this way, studying the shakuhachi was a perfect complement to the investigations I was making concurrently with extended woodwind techniques.

* * *

One will find, however, that where there is opportunity for growth there is also danger. All great musical traditions have profound masters whose work is both inspirational and daunting. I once asked a highly skilled European improvising drummer why he almost never used pulse. His stated reason went something like, "After hearing Tony Williams, I could not imagine a new way to approach time." In this case a player of genius, through no fault of his own, closes a door rather than opens it. This is because the former player lost track of his own musical voice when confronted with something overwhelming.

So it can go with a foreign tradition. Eventually I did play the shakuhachi in public. In fact, the first time was when the editor of this book coaxed me into the recording studio to play on his record *The Big Gundown*. I received encouragement as well from my teacher Ralph Samuelson. Then I went to Japan and studied shakuhachi with two of the absolute premier masters, Yokoyama Katsuya[10]

10. Yokoyama was a student of Watazumi-do and played Watazumi's school of solo music, called Do-kyoku. Yokoyama became prominent as a featured soloist in the works of Takamitsu Toru, most notably his piece *November Steps*.

and Yamaguchi Goro. Both had numerous aspects of their mastery which are to this day unapproachable for me. If I was to find a personal voice on the instrument I knew clearly that it could never approach Yokoyama-sensei in terms of power and explosiveness. I could practice forever; I would never have that much sonic horsepower. Yamaguchi-sensei played with elegance and delicacy that were equally unattainable. It could be all too easy to lose myself chasing a level of mastery for its own sake. Let me say that I have no problem with western musicians who take on the goal of becoming advanced practitioners of foreign traditions. Studying raga or African drumming as ends in themselves is fine. But the composer/performer who studies with the aim of expanding her creative voice must keep her eye on the prize, which is not to compete with one's master but to integrate the master's teaching into one's personal musical reservoir.

Finally, one finds integration not only by questioning one's background but using one's "outsiderness" as strength. When traditional shakuhachi players try to improvise, their vocabulary is largely drawn from the phrases of their school's solo repertoire. I have found that I naturally hear things on the instrument that would never occur to a native player. At the same time, I have no need to make the instrument jump through hoops, to play western-sounding music on it.[11] I find my background as a western creative improviser allows me to create material which sounds "traditional" because it utilizes the timbral and microtonal nuance described above, but has no sources in any of the repertoire I have studied. I believe this has happened partly because of the other approach to world music that I will now describe.

11. There is a whole school of western-influenced shakuhachi playing called Tozan and numerous performers who try to play jazz and pop music on it. Most of it is a musical case of trying to put a square peg through a round hole, but players like Yamamoto Hozan and his student John Kaizan Neptune have taken this to high levels of virtuosity. Suffice it to say, most of it is not to my taste.

* * *

This other "method" is profoundly nonmethodical. It is to approach a foreign music not as a student in the standard sense but through voracious, visceral immersion. As youths, all musicians have periods of intense listening to their forbears. Young musicians of today can choose their favorites from around the planet. For artists of my generation, exposure to the native music of Africa, India, and Eastern Europe came at a later stage of our development. By the time I encountered Indonesian Gamelan, I had already worn my Sonny Rollins LPs smooth as a teenager in the early 70s, taking his solos off the records in what is a very traditional kind of jazz study. After arriving in NYC in 1978 I became friends with a certain John Zorn, already mentioned above. Around 1981 John and a number of other friends—Anthony Coleman, Anton Fier, and Tim Berne—began working at a record shop called the Soho Music Gallery. This was at the same time as an explosion of world-music recordings, and the shop amassed a terrific selection of these releases from the Barenreiter Unesco, Ocora, Phillips, and Nonesuch labels. For me, hearing the Ocora three-LP set of music from Chad[12] for the first time was an equally revelatory experience as when I first heard Sonny Rollins or Coltrane ten years before. And my response was the same, to wear out the records by playing them over and over. However, there was a key difference. There were no solos to memorize, rather it was music of utter mystery to me. And while I did study African music in a more analytical way ten to fifteen years later, at the time that I first heard these recordings I purposely did *not want to understand* the music from a technical viewpoint. I felt strongly that there was no way I was going to find what moved me so much through analysis and transcription. Could marijuana have contributed to this conviction? Absolutely! I would devour the records one by one, no iPod shuffle mode in those days.[13] In addition to the Chad collection, a Phillips Unesco disc of Inuit Women's songs, the Ocora box of music from Burma, the Everest Watazumi LP, and the "hit" of the time, Unesco's *Music of the Ba-Benzélé Pygmies*,[14] all received similar treatment.

Concurrently with this immersion I had one of the most productive phases of my development as a composer/performer. I made huge strides toward finding my voice in solo woodwind music and as an improviser. Although it never occurred to me to draw directly from any of this foreign music, the simple act of *intensive*, focused listening allowed me to *emotionally* digest it, so the influence on the work I was creating at the time was undeniable. To this day I cannot break that response down technically, the way I have described with the shakuhachi above. But as with the shakuhachi, it did have much to

12. A notable thing about the Chad box is I had heard some of this music a few years before. Federico Fellini used it in his movie *Satyricon*. I remembered thinking that Nino Rota, who was credited for the score, had come up with something amazingly otherworldly. In fact, large portions of the soundtrack are lifted from the Chadian Toupouri Orchestra tracks on this release.

13. I have to guess that the smorgasbord approach to music created by the iPod and downloading technology will have a profound effect on the way young musicians today are influenced by their forbears.

14. Herbie Hancock used a snippet of a pygmy girl singing while blowing a one-note flute to begin his hit record *Headhunters*.

do with a subtle but powerful re-evaluation of the role that music played in my life.[15] When I picked up my instrument to practice, the world seemed like an open place. I felt I could try anything. I was unburdened by years of study pursuing "correct" technique. I think using these very indirect models gave a freshness that could never come from within the traditions in which I was schooled. A saxophonist who immerses himself in Coltrane feels like there are huge mountains to climb when he next picks up his instrument. He is painfully aware of what he cannot do. I had looked up these mountains, scaled a few of them, fallen off of many. Now I had quite a different sensation: there was a strange and wonderful landscape in front of me, and picking up my instrument, I could explore it as part of a grand adventure. The world music I had been listening to was acting as a catalytic muse in quite a magical way.

15. The pygmy music had a particular lesson to teach in this regard. These virtuosos were not professional performers but simply family members enjoying an evening together. It was a look into a lost oasis where music could play the most basic role in family and tribal life.

As Lou Harrison has said, one can only prepare oneself to deal with the muse; she will show up when she pleases. I believe that this kind of open listening to an art form of mystery can at least offer her an invitation.

* * *

The danger of this nonmethodical "method" is simple and profound. Don't fool yourself! In the example of Ornette Coleman above, some very superficial, poorly made music was created in response to the new freedoms that he championed. Likewise, all sorts of drivel has been produced with the claim that it is "inspired" by the "personal discovery" of foreign musical traditions. I think this happens when musicians do not go deeply into their musical responses and apply honest self-assessment. I have confined a large amount of my own composed and recorded material to the trash with the evaluation that it is superficially imitative of some other music, the ideas not sufficiently worked out to make them my own.

Interestingly enough, another problem occurs when the two approaches I have described become mixed. This is the musical version of "a little knowledge is a dangerous thing." I refer to students who study some basic foreign techniques, have what they consider to be a magic moment, and think this equips them as creative artists exhibiting their new profound "influence." My friend and colleague the Tuvan singer Sainkho

Namchylak has given workshops in throat-singing and shamanistic vocal techniques. While we were on tour together she showed me a number of thank-you letters that she had received from students who after a two or three-day workshop had begun their own performing "careers" or, more to Sainkho's horror, were giving their own workshops![16] Unfortunately, because everyone has a voice, more people can fool themselves into believing they are vocal "artists" than happens with instrumentalists. However, this all goes back to the statement I made in my opening: some people will always try to take a short cut to creativity and just skim the top off of materials which require intense and deep investigation. One can only really police oneself.[17]

16. In the case of vocal music, bad instruction cannot only create bad musicians, it can be physically dangerous.

17. This brings up the much more subjective discussion of creative honesty. I think my feelings about that are implied in this article; perhaps I'll take them further on another occasion.

* * *

Of course, you never finish your education; any creative artist is also a lifelong student. For me, as time went on, there was more mixing between the analytic and visceral approaches. I learned rudiments of African drumming, basic theory of raga, and some rhythms from Eastern Europe. I am expert in none of these fields, but enough general knowledge has built up so my outlook has become a hybrid. Then came the opportunity to work with musicians of other cultures. This was the added challenge that brought my understanding of these paths into focus. I came to realize that for collaborations to be successful across traditional boundaries, the artists on both sides had to have come through self-evaluative bridges to find the kind of creative openness necessary for real communication.

The two most extensive associations were with Sainkho Namchylak in the 1990s (documented on the Leo CD *Amulet*[18]) and an ongoing collaboration with tabla master Samir Chatterjee in my group Sync. In both cases this was a "meeting in the middle." Sainkho was working with a range of European creative improvisers already when I met her. She was schooled in many indigenous traditions of Siberia and had participated in large Soviet groups that gave a showcase of ethnic music from all over the country. However, she had a need to experiment and realized that at her creative core she was not comfortable fitting into the model

18. This CD is out of print but available for download at http://www.leorecords.com/?m=select&id=CD_LR_231.

of a traditional singer. For a woman to investigate throat-singing and shamanistic ritual singing was itself outside the norm, as both are normally the domain of men. So while she was certainly from "another place" than me, we had similar expansive goals. From the first time we played together,[19] in 1991, Sainkho felt that I was somehow more attuned to the East than were others she was working with at the time. We went on to play five years of duo concerts. She taught me a few Tuvan and Sayani songs, but mostly we created structured improvisations together. I tried to listen to her in the same way as I had to the Inuit women years before: not to deconstruct what she was doing technically, but to react honestly and viscerally to it. At the same time, the materials I developed from my shakuhachi work had a natural connection with her soundworld.

19. I was sharing a concert outside Stuttgart, playing solo, with Sainkho and trombonist Connie Bauer doing the other half as a duo. After their set, they invited me to join them.

I have occasionally tried to connect with people of both nonwestern and nonimprovising backgrounds who wanted to try something together largely because there was an employment opportunity, but who had little interest in going outside their comfort zone. In all cases, the results have been timid and unsuccessful. Samirji, on the other hand, has come to live in NYC, looking for opportunities to collaborate with all sorts of musicians. He brings with him high-level practical and theoretical expertise in North Indian classical music, but unlike most of his colleagues in that tradition (and they don't call it "classical" for nothing), he has a keen interest to learn as well as teach.

It never occurred to me to try and confront the raga/taal forms of North Indian music directly when working with Samirji. It made much more sense for me to write the music I was hearing using the most basic elements of rhythmic subdivision, two's and three's. I could show Samir my melodies and bass lines along with these and then ask him to fit them into a rhythmic framework in which he would feel comfortable improvising. Thus, he applies his system of taal as he finds it appropriate. So just as Duke Ellington could present any of his wonderfully individual musicians with material which they would immediately make their own, I found I could easily let Samir transform my compositional instructions to fit his musical worldview. He makes his own scores of my pieces, which include the form of the pieces together with his syllabic rendering of my phrases. For instance, I may write a piece in 15/8, giving him a grouping of what we would call a bar of 6/4 and a bar of 3/8. He might call this 7 1/2 and play it accordingly. He could also choose to play it in groups of five based on Jhaptaal,[20] a ten-beat cycle, which thus superimposes a thirty-beat unit where the downbeats of both groupings come together.

20. For those interested in studying the rhythmic aspects of tabla in depth, Samir has written a definitive text, *A Study of Tabla*, published by Chhandayan. See http://www.tabla.org/.

Our "home" musical traditions can give nonwestern musicians the same kind of inspiration that their music creates in us. I gave Sainkho the Rhino box set of Aretha Franklin, and to her, Aretha's version of Sam Cooke's *A Change Is Gonna' Come* had a resonance both musical and poetic. It reminded me of the first time I heard the epic songs of Tsuruta Kinshi.[21] Soul and the Blues come in so many ways. The most virtuosic performances often impress Indian musicians. But a tabla player like Badal Roy has been able to interact very successfully with jazz musicians because he can fully grasp that most basic of rhythmic patterns, 4/4 with a backbeat. It is obvious that salsa music has roots in Africa. Now, groups like Orchestra Baobab are in turn inspired by salsa, and a new synthesis emerges. Happily, examples like this will go on and on in all directions.

21. Tsuruta Kinshi (1911–1995) was a performer of Satsuma Biwa. The Biwa is a 4-string lute played with a large plectrum. This tradition uses it to accompany extended intoned vocal recitations of epic poetry. I believe Tsuruta-sensei was one of the greatest artists of the 20th century.

Finally, it should be clear that I don't mean in any way to deride the importance of a "traditional" musical education, whatever tradition that may be. One needs solid ground from which to leap. From there, challenge and growth are all about openness and re-evaluation. The goal is to develop the tools not only to execute what one has learned but to step outside one's comfort zone and have the courage to reach across the divide to another culture while having confidence in the ground under one's feet.

Related Discography

Shakuhachi

Watazumido-Shuso

The Mysterious Sounds of the Bamboo Flute (Everest LP 3289)

This has been re-issued but strangely with much inferior sound on Legacy SW1a, available at: http://www.shakuhachi.com/R-Shaku-Watazumido.html.

Katsuya Yokoyama

The Art of the Shakuhachi (Ocora OCRC 560114)

Japon 1: Kinshi Tsuruta/Katsuya Yokoyama. (Ocora LP 558518, now reissued as OCD 580059)

Tsuruta and Yokoyama recorded this in 1976 in Paris while performing the famous concerto that Toru Takemistsu wrote for them, *November Steps.* There was a second LP released of these sessions on Chant Du Monde label. Good luck finding it!

Katsuya Yokoyama Plays Shakuhachi-1 (Ongaku no Tomo Sha Corp., Japan-OCD-091, 1989) and *Katsuya Yokoyama Plays Shakuhachi-2* (OCD-0912)

Koten Honkyoku Vols. 1 and 2

Available at: http://www.shakuhachi.com/R-Shaku-Yokoyama.html.

Discography: http://www.komuso.com/people/Yokoyama_Katsuya.html.

Goro Yamaguchi

A Bell Ringing in the Empty Sky (Nonesuch 130364)

This was the stunning introduction to shakuhachi for many western listeners. Yamaguchi (1933–1999) was a "living national treasure" in Japan, an iemoto (highest-level teacher) of the Kinko School.

Great Masters of the Shakuhachi Flute (Auvidis under license of Japan Victor H.M.V.-A 6139)

Discography: http://www.komuso.com/people/Yamaguchi_Goro.html.

Other Recordings Mentioned in This Essay

Anthologie De La Musique Du Tchad (Ocora LP 36–38 recorded April–May 1966)
This has not yet been released on CD as far as I know.

Birmanie (Burma) Musique d'art (Ocora LP 555–558. Now on CD: C 559019/020)

Unesco collection of African Music #3, *The Music of the Ba-Benzélé Pygmys* (Barenreiter-Musicaphon BM 30 L 2303 LP. CD reissue: Rounder Select 5107)

The Unesco and Phillips recordings of *Inuit Women's games and songs* were re-released as Auvidis-Unesco, D 8032. However, this may also be out of print. Selections can be downloaded at http://www.ubu.com/ethno/soundings/inuit.html A marvelous out-of-print LP is *Inuit Throat and Harp Songs*, MH001 on the Canadian Music Heritage collection.

CHAPTER 27

RUMINATIONS ON SECRET CHIEFS 3

TREY SPRUANCE

Though we take this as a *good* sign, our recent lapse into a disregarding attitude toward the sophistication of our own musical mechanisms has been seen by some to be a lamentable development. Truth told, these days what we really care most about is whether or not children will dance around insanely to our lavish and overblown productions. There are definitely plenty of interesting "adult" things to be noted beyond this, but experience has shown that it's better to leave most of those details to people already moving somewhat parallel to our mad beacon. We risk boring everyone else to tears.

The thing about Secret Chiefs 3 that's probably most worthy of broader consideration is the fact that the sophistication of the compositional approach, which under normal circumstances would be considered extremely rarefied and "highbrow," has slipped beneath the radar to a surprisingly warm reception by the "masses." What passes these days for this term "masses" is debatable, but we find its rootless, sceneless, non-identity to be far and away the best place to remain "invisible." Especially for a music employing certain largely abandoned rigors of technique, and which therefore feels forced to concoct its productions in barely accessible mountaintop laboratories.

It should be pointed out that Secret Chiefs 3 is lacking in all post-Aristocracy funding, any academic support of any kind, and has no credibility in American and European avant garde circles (even less so in the "rock" circuit). Meanwhile, for ten years running, the aforementioned "masses" have been receiving copious doses of polytonality, tetrachordally exploded harmony, micro-tonal monophony, non-metric "swung" readings of meters like 19/16, and utterly anarchistic through-compositions from us. It's a wonder SC3 has any friends at all in the world, especially since we persist in open defiance of the kind of "wow… complicated" non-aesthetic of prog-rock gymnasticism that has somehow recently become acceptable. Probably the key to our spotty-but-permanent standing on this earth can be found in the one place where it matters: the music itself. And this is only right. Why we've gotten away with what we have is a matter of some debate, but for sure there has been little enough controversy to the average ear that the music has somehow gotten by on a basic and general musical "appeal." That's surprising, everything considered. We were actually once even proud of it.

That's because with self-sufficiency comes a certain brand of arrogance. For over ten years we've been building our fortress and answering to *no one*, which seems an enviable position to be in, to be sure. It's both a blessing and a curse, and will surely stay that way. In the meantime, we are not so blind as to overlook the brilliance of many of our peers and mentors. But we do confess to being sharply at pains lamenting the absence of any kind of a modern-day Adorno who could lucidly scrutinize the deeper dimensions of things musical. We've therefore decided that it's only healthy for us to litmus-test for good and bad musical omens in the reactions of four- and five-year-olds. As critics go, they seem to be the most informed. Those of our readers who ducked that barely veiled broadside are invited to take no heed of our ensuing polemics, as we, like they, are a good-humored lot. But it's fitting to give the gentle warning that, due to our seclusion, isolation, and bloodily earned self-sufficiency, we have acquired the habit of holding nothing back when dealing with others.

Into the Fire Threefold

Serious people always learn sooner or later that they only hurt their already-strained public image by focusing too much on what they are *actually trying to say*. So as a mercy to the reader we will limit the discussion to some ramifications of a central facet of our musical *weltanshaung*, something that might actually be beneficial to share with others. Then, after that, we will let our guard down and go haywire as a filament of the Electromagnetic Azoth comes ungrounded. But first this:

Culture is derived from Cosmology.

I can't seem to find a less pretentious sounding way of saying this, so I'll just blurt out that the music we make is rooted in Hermeticized Pythagorean cosmology.[1] Some people understandably get the impression that we have a fascination with Arabic culture. This isn't accurate. Definitely our cosmological framework has been inherited from Pythagoras via Suhrawardi[2] (the most lucid of any post-Neoplatonic sages), as well as the Ikhwan al-Safa,[3] while quite a few elements of the Pythago-Hermetic musicological/Philosophical tradition as they have been developed in the West also find their way in.[4] Nowhere in SC3 music is there an abiding fixation on any one culture, or even plurality of cultures, disconnected from the cosmological subject at hand. The heart that palpitates in distress over culture issues of the moment can rest assured that SC3's music sounds just as "foreign" to the average Arab as it does to the average American. We invite anyone to test this thesis and find it to be true. Another thing we encounter quite regularly is a certain positivistic/neo-liberal attitude from some well-meaning people who very much expect to find an ecumenical sentiment beneath our music, something that perhaps tries to resolve theological/cultural conflicts of the world with some kind of socio-musical "all are one" syncretic philosophy. They will certainly find no trace of that in SC3 either.

What they *will* find is that SC3 represents a simple, striving agency of a gnosis of Light, as something we know to be accessible to mankind with music playing a pivotal role. Through great diligence, inspiration, and effort, *this* aspect of what we try to do may in fact touch something that

1. For sure we mean the Pythagorean and Hermetic Mysteries according to their "monotheistic" interpretation. Not that we wouldn't happily admit that Pythagoras as understood by the pagan Iamblichus has been a major perk on our compass toward the *theurgic* possibilities of music. And the Pythagorean Plato of *Timeaus* and the *Myth of Er* and various musical allegories in the *Republic* (see the marriage allegory) are fundamentals. But the whole range of subsequent figures like al-Farabi, Fabre d'Olivet, 'Abd Al-Razzaq Lahiji, Marsilio Ficino, Da'ud Qaysari, Avicenna, and Shaykh Ahmad Ahsai tilt our scale inevitably towards the monotheistic understanding. By the way, it may be more accurate to say "Pythagoreanized Hermeticism," but who can be sure of these things?

2. Even with a cursory pecking through the endlessly rewarding works of Henry Corbin, one can't miss the cosmological, philosophical and Illuminist doctrines of Shihabuddin Yahya Suhrawardi speckled throughout. Suhrawardi's essential piece, *Hikmat al-Ishraq*, is a central work, very dear to us. His *Visionary Treatises* will seize the poetic imagination more immediately. *Hayakal al Nur* has also been central to our interpretations. John Walbridge's works on Suhrawardi, while good for technical and historical details, tend to refute the "better angels" of the Master, present in the way he is interpreted by his own school of Illuminism (surving to this day), as well as by Corbin, Nasr, and others close to the fire. So where topics outside of formal logic and history are concerned, we take Walbridge with less than a grain of salt. On a related note, we wish to thank our good friend Wahid Azal for his beautiful unpublished translations of Suhrawardi's prayer book, *Book of Hours.*

3. See in particular A. Shiloah, *"L'épître sur la musique des Ikhwan al-Safa,"* in *Revue des Etudes Islamiques* 1965 and 1967, also the lengthy section on the Ikhwan al-Safa in S.H. Nasr's indispensible *An Introduction to Islamic Cosmological Doctrines*, I.R. Netton's *Muslim Neoplatonists: an Introduction to the Thought of the Brethren of Purity*, Farhad Daftary's *The Ismailis*, and the section on the Ikhwan al-Safa in Joscelyn Godwin's *Music, Mysticism and Magic.* Rumor has it that a translation of the whole Rasa'il into English is being prepared in a secret dungeon at this time.

4. Most blatantly, the Sepher Yetzirah guides the final redaction of our schematic of "bands" and the distribution of motifs therein, esp. in Gra. version, which, after one gains some some maturity toward it, can be seen to accord profoundly with certain deeper elements in Tarot, esp. relevant in the P. F. Case version—though none of this is directly related to the elements of acoustic harmony under discussion. Other works—Kircher, Ficino, Fludd, others (brought up later)—are referred to for peripheral supporting material, although we consider some works of Guenon, Burkhardt, and Evola, especially the latter's *Hermetic Tradition*, to be every bit as useful for that, if not more so.

certain classes of musicians the world over may recognize that they hold in common. But that would be another discussion. We don't want to leave the impression that we arrived at our particular expression in some vacuum, some secret underground vault in America where surfboards and Templar treasure are stashed together in a great big neocolonial mirage. So here is a brief outline of the roots of our activity.

As indicated, we try to to tilt the best beacons of the Pythago-Hermetic musicological/Philosophical light of tradition toward our music, and it is undoubtedly the most recent expositor of great coherence, Suhrawardi (b. 1152), who has indicated a walkable path for the musician/philosopher of any clime or age that can lead to a workable life-pattern, with certain Pythagorean fundamentals being of central value in the creation of an *actual music*. In recent times, when thought of at all, these things tend to be just sitting in preservationist repositories, where they are revered but still considered arcane and musically inaccessible enough as mathematical problems to rot there along with all the other "obscure and outmoded" ideas of antiquity. Past that, the Harmony of the Spheres has been persistently subjected to a naïve popular consensus rendering it as little more than a primitive, inaccurate proto-solar-system model, and certainly this dismissal also hampers any understanding of its basic property as map of the microcosmic soul, with its correspondences to myriad aspects of the universe. Feeble-minded prejudices like this have been permanently overcome in recent works of great theoretical import, but have so far not been addressed much on a practical level, at least in a creative musical sense.[5]

Having skipped the entire post-Ghazalian chapter in the development of human thought and action, I believe we modern musicians have many essential and fundamental things to gain as to *method* from Suhrawardi in particular. By way of parallel and perhaps direct connection, there is certainly a fantastic and intimidating example of the infinite richness opened up by these processes, right here and now, in the total commitment required of the philosophical/musical/cosmological human being by Dastgah systems in Traditional Iranian music.[6] Consider Corbin: "Among all the mystical traditions we deal with in comparative religion,

5. The best being Alain Danielou's *Music and the Power of Sound: The Influence of Tuning and Interval on Consciousness*. Joscelyn Godwin's more readable and more western-oriented *Harmonies of Heaven and Earth* and *The Mystery of the Seven Vowels* are also excellent.

6. If the evidence of the ears is not enough, there is an accessible work in English called *Persian Music: A Study of Form and Content of Persian Avaz, Dastgah & Radif*, by University of Utah professor Lloyd Clifton Miller. While not flawless, at 515 pages, packed with good technical information and some very good overall contextualizations, it's by far the most thorough book in English on the subject, and should be much appreciated.

Persian mysticism stands out as having always tended towards a musical expression, and as finding its complete expression only in music."[7] Even as moderns simply seeking out some idealized concept of our own Quadrivium, Dastgah should encourage, as it proves by its very existence the persistence and solidity of everything from the nuts and bolts of the principles we're referring to, to their goal of the unfoldment of consciousness in Illuministic Theoria.

7. Henry Corbin, *The Musical Sense of Persian Mysticism*, p. 231 in *The Voyage and the Messenger: Iran and Philosophy*.

Again, we claim no direct traditional musical knowledge of any of the cultural expressions that are rooted into the Pythagorean formulas, but over many years we have deeply confronted many of the musical/philosophical problems and principles presented by Pythagorean cosmology and its musically relevant branches, and, thanks to Suhrawardi and a few others, have definitely begun to make our own musical sense of them. Expressions of this can be found in our music in a few different ways:

1) As organizing principles behind every expression and intent, placing even our essentially dim-witted surf-rock concepts of Western-tempered harmony in a certain "justification"; which extends also to the more contrapuntal filmic orchestral-scapes we've had the audacity to attempt.

2) In determining scales and rhythms used in the more "folkloric"-sounding end of our musical spectrum, compositions which, as natural as they sound (perhaps a welcome result of employing the principles under question!), are strictly bound by various tonal correspondences with the other traditional properties or attributes. A proprietary Neo-Pythaogorean system of tuning is adhered to rigorously. The instruments capable of accommodating the tonal specifics here employed include the saz, tar, violin, viola, esraj, sarangi (all players having adapted to the proprietary tonal system), casio AT-60 ("AT" for Arabic Tuning, which is actually 100% adjustable, unlike nearly all of the more "advanced" synthesizers), proprietarily intonationally modified bass and guitar, and an arsenal of other pitch-modifiable instruments. It is a great testament to the ability of the players involved[8] that they are able to adapt to the system and "own" this material. Simultaneously these fine folks are expected to find the natural "pocket" in what can initially strike some as dizzyingly bizarre meters.[9] The material under this umbrella is naturally the most fundamentally and organi-

8. Eyvind Kang, Timb Harris, Shahzad Ismaily, Elena Doroftei, Rich Doucette, Jai Young Kim.

9. Ches Smith, Danny Heifetz, William Winant, and Shahzad being real heroes to handle this madness as they have.

cally related to the Pythago-Hermetic presence—Dastgah it isn't, but it's not exactly baloney, either.

3) Last, in the dimension of the more challenging musical "esoterica" we occasionally indulge in, the cosmological principles under discussion actually go so far as to micromanage nearly every musical detail, often in an almost serial manner, but employed in an intuitive way. We don't feel that the creative moment is hampered by this kind of "serialism" because of the elasticity of the *fascism* required to maintain it. It's really not unlike the way a learned Magus would seriously approach the Tarot trumps. With great knowledge of the symbols and the mnemonic system inherent to that arcana, yet also with a clear enough mind to follow where the infinity of interlocking associations are *actually leading*, he would indeed *follow* and not lead. By a corollary of this process, we stumble upon musical items that are unmistakably-relevant-to-our-project again and again. It can't be argued that we unfold these things by any other means than a flatly "anarchistic" or "divinatory" method (informed at every turn by principles we've been discussing). Thus, their eventual incorporation into the whole is usually a matter for retrospective composition, all of which is done according to the broader organizing principles referred to in example 1.

Now, the "anarchy" we refer to is actually very consistent with our feeling for the strange and beautiful special effects released by equal temperament itself, which we consider on the whole to be a sort of very beautiful mirage. This is a necessary (and liberating) viewpoint. Many controversies have arisen over temperament. Since the entire range of musical experience falling under the umbrella of equal temperament is literally divorced from acoustic Reality, with pretty much all of Western music helplessly following suit, the tendency here is always going to be a despairing one, no matter whether one is on the offensive or defensive over the subject. But we still feel equal temperament has, despite convincing criticisms to the contrary,[10] a real possibility for validity as a "tonal" music. We believe this possibility lies in the direction of the conscious fashioning of musical "images" in composition, not unlike the way the painting of religious Icons or use of calligraphy in illuminated manuscripts is understood. We have been trying to take things in this direction (again inspired by Suhrawardi and Corbin), as opposed to trying to participate in musical Realities by haphazard guesswork and good intentions that have no

10. Not just convincing, actually. Inescapable. See Danielou, pp. 121–134, also 94–111. Should be required reading for all serious music students.

real hope for success. Certainly there is a danger in mistaking the production of these images for participation in musical Realities, and that would be pure error, and fertile ground for the spreading of more post-modern viruses (part of why we classify most of the music we do in the area of Western tonality under the alchemical icon of the Peacock). But they can certainly also be approached the same way Orthodoxies approach the use of Icons and Calligraphy: in this way it becomes incumbent upon us to orient ourselves correctly in relation to these images, and by extension to the Realities they represent, which is the whole point, in order that we may overcome the "idolatry" that is so likely *when a tonal system is divorced from acoustic Reality.*

Here we have too little time to go into the specifically musical aspect coming into being under a keen unfoldment of the Imaginal function, and how any subsequent entry into the world of the visionary Realities, Suhrawardi's *'alam al-Mithal*, Corbin's *Mundus Imaginalis*,[11] instantly reveals the apparitional nature of things below it, at the same time as re-epiphanizing them, or redeeming them, by finally allowing their participation in the chain of being to become active from gaining knowledge of their actual situative *place.*[12]

Now, we don't pretend to be making a Sacred music by any means, but we do find fit to mention that we embrace Western harmony fully according to the above understanding of its "place," particularly in order for it to cohere and *symbolize with* the previously discussed dimensions of our Work, and therefore, by extension, with the acoustic Realities themselves. Thus, in the micromanagement details of this third category of our method, we are not applying our principles very often to pitch and rhythm, but rather to the organization and distribution of motifs, the generation of arrangements and devices such as retrogrades, inversions, pivot-sequences, and certain aspects of articulation, etc. Fluidity in this

11. "...The authentication of prophetic visions and of perceptions of the suprasensible requires a third faculty of knowledge, lying between sense-perception and pure intellection of the intelligible world. This is the reason why such importance is accorded to imaginative consciousness and to imaginative perception as the organ of perception of a world which is peculiar to it, the *mundus imaginalis* ('alam al-mithal); and at the same time, in opposition to the general tendency of the philosophers, this organ is acknowledged to be a pure psycho-spiritual faculty, independent of the perishable physical organism." Henry Corbin, *History of Islamic Philosophy*, (Kegan Paul/Institute for Ismaili Studies: 1993), p. 56.

12. In light of this consider Iamblichus: "There is, also, an alliance in these sounds and melodies to the proper orders and powers of the several Gods, to the motions in the universe itself, and to the harmonious sounds which proceed from the motions. Conformably, therefore, to such like adaptions of melodies to the Gods, the Gods themselves become present. For there is not anything which intercepts; *so that whatever has but a casual similitude to, directly participates of, them.* A perfect possession, likewise, immediately takes place, and a plenitude of a more excellent essence and power. Not that the body and soul are in each other, and sympathize, and are copassive with the melodies; but because the inspiration of the Gods is not separated from the divine harmony, but is originally adapted and allied to it, on this account it is participated by it in appropriate measures." Section II, chapter nine of *The Mysteries*, Thomas Taylor translation (San Diego: Wizard's Bookshelf, 1997). A *lot* more could (and will) be said on this.

aspect is where study of some of the later, utterly brilliant gnostically minded (even some just techincally minded) musico-theoretical adaptors has been helpful to us. Names especially pertinent are Messiaen, Bach, Fabre d'Olivet, Ligeti, Slonimsky, Scelsi, Kircher, Part, Fludd, Debussy, and, recently, Zorn.

Finally, these three different "modes" of implementing the cosmological picture under consideration are orchestrated into a generic whole, by the splitting of SC3 into seven different "bands," assigned to developing the different harmonic (sometimes in the broadest sense) functions independently, or in certain collusions having to do with the movement of motifs between "bands," according to a grander geometrical schematic.[13] These things are quite exactingly executed, in fact, and it would definitely take a whole book to explain everything involved. What a bore that will be. But we'll probably have to do it eventually.

13. Barely touched upon in note 4.

In the meantime, please feel free to enjoy the following outburst. This is a Libretto and psychotic ejection from the Electromagnetic Azoth (one of the "bands," the one under the Peacock, in fact). It is an elaborate staging on the Theatron Animatronique of the lesser imagination, composed just for ARCANA. May the microbes of the marvelous now overtake the proceedings. I give you:

Nabataean Agriculture (in Five Short Acts), by *The Electromagnetic Azoth*

* * *

CONFESSIO:

> I used to hover in uncertainty. Approaching the indefinite in my ascension to the vague, my gut feel was that a pluralistic survey would convene at some point to approximate the Truth. It was a pathetic kind of idealism. Better than the Theosophical sort, but still … such a nausea. Such a cop-out to the pandemic virus of post-Enlightenment darkness, to wake up every day knowing you are just another carrier pigeon for the fleas of the Black Plague. Every direction feeble, each destiny all too familiar. Later on and by the mighty audacity of discipline, a hurricane named "Will" began to form in the toilet of my regrets. It was a standing bog filled with premature certainty. Yes, but a bog at least somewhat freed from the microbial determinism of the phages of desire. At first my arms were too short

for my hand to grasp the handle, and for a long time the suicidal gesture that sets the elements in motion remained unaccomplished. Like most natural disasters, however, the chaos of this hurricane turned out to be good for the crops—most of my personalities didn't even realize there was a drought before the deluge. It wasn't until everything was flushed out to sea, and the multiple faces were all congregated in the belly of the whale, that the possibility of their synchronous prostration was even imagined, much less revealed as the compulsory act of Tawhid. I can only confess these things now because I have abandoned the scuba gear needed for this kind of delirium. Those capable swimmers who scour the ocean for irrefutable debris are more qualified, I admit. May the peripheral fog that engulfs every form and identity show its mercy to mankind.

* * *

[Backstage preamble]

GG: "This bullet was boared, hollowed out—going once, twice… a reverb chamber to abandon your desires in. The hollow-life-points explode bigger on the other side. Goddamn is that ever a long reverb. And it's either a shotgun to the face or a Knock Knock joke. Ask Kurt…"

KURT: "Who's there?"

GG: "No, fucker, who's on first? … Right there, you're dead."

(Swigs from bottle of whiskey, spits it out, and leans forward into Kurt's face.)

GG: "No, really. What's on first? The Scumfuck or Nirvana?"

BON SCOTUS ERIUGENA: (sensing tension) "Hey hey … me and Courtney were planning a nice picnic by the pile of dead rockstar brains on third. Lotsa Crowleyheads out there in the left-field stands. (Picks up rifle.) For those about to cock [click] the cunt of this twelve-gauge into a twenty-two-letter birth trauma…we salute all such fan fuckers. [*BLAM*] Now scoop those brains up and throw 'em into the crowd. Bitches."

{Act 1}

* * *

[CURTAIN]

[Portrait artist is revising his work with painstaking precision as every new wrinkle forms on the face of his Eternal Subject.]

PORTRAIT ARTIST: "I will simply have to be forgiven if I haven't exactly been paying attention to what's been going on in the 'underground.'"

HIS ETERNAL SUBJECT: "Tell me about it. How is anyone in modern times supposed to service the Light unfolded in Theoria, and avoid being subsequently thrown to the lions of a sloppy, badly rendered, vague, and blatantly Genesis-derived-while-not-admitting-it pseudo-cosmology?"

(Turns sideways in a stiff profile.)

PORTRAIT ARTIST: (frustrated) "… I really do appreciate the empathy. But could you please stop moving around?"

PORTRAIT ARTIST: (interrupting) "Didn't Rabia carry a bucket to douse the fires of Hell in the one hand, and torch to burn Heaven in the other? And didn't Hafez say 'Stop Being So Religious'?"

HIS ETERNAL SUBJECT: "The prerequisite to 'Stop Being So Religious' *is to be too religious.*"

(Peering at artist in profile with one eye. He relaxes and shifts to a lounging position.)

"… But by all means, paint your little pictures, you innovative little occultist, you."

PORTRAIT ARTIST: (an angry silence) "... Music should be banned. Can you at least do something about that?"

MADAME POMPADEUS: "Oh no, Mister! You must let my shit stink all the way to the high heavens!"

HIS ETERNAL SUBJECT: "Whatever dagger may lurk under the clothing of you sheep, whatever vandalizing brush strokes emanate from the heart of you Judases of the Unseen, remember that the hand of God alone gave it power to act, even in error. So no."

MADAME POMPADEUS: (opening window) "Someone farted."

[An Easterly wind, spiced with Lavender and Cinnamon, blows in. Elephant-trunked Ganesha of the thresholds sounds horn on arriving East India Theosophical Line.]

FRANCIS BACON: "Ah *brilliant!* I see the Caravan to the Abyss of Enchantments has arrived! I'll be leaving you all forever now. Ta!"

HIS ETERNAL SUBJECT: (rolling eyes) "See you on the Lebensreform rebound, Swastika dick."

FRANCIS BACON: (to MADAME POMPADOUCE) "If Madame would like to join me beneath the duvet ..."

MADAME POMPADOUCE: (flustered) "Oh *really!* That's hardly appropriate. I'm barely even Indo-Aryan."

FRANCIS BACON: "No no, not at all, my dear! This is just yet another direction. A false, soft, pillowy dead end that you can fall into and hopefully go to sleep on. Nothing more."

MADAME POMPADOUCE: "Well, in *that* case ..."

[CURTAIN]

VOICE OF MAX MÜLLER: "Dear dear audience, endure, endure. As every formal revision chokes the thrashing serpent of intuition down into a baptismal basin filled only with the tongue's latest saliva, I promise to pull you up into a new world. Don't believe it when my heart feigns ambivalence towards these subjects. Actual content has always been scribbled there in the margins of piles and piles of well-researched books, not in these self-conscious ejaculations that have found their way into print. The irony-free truth naturally sidelines itself in hand-jotted exclamations, yellow-highlighted paragraphs, and eagerly underlined phrases. Its other, more fanatical acts of ventriloquism are well-enough known. Look, here one comes now …"

{Act 2}

* * *

[CURTAIN]

MAX MÜLLER (visible now, seeming prematurely bald): "Should we laugh or cry that its only our money that declares with any confidence 'In God We Trust'?"

GG: "Receding hairlines betray previously masked hairline fractures from a primordial concussion. The wisdom of the wind tosses and tussles the range of concepts under a darkening toupee. One must finally crack the Umm al-Kitab for a formal revision of the Archetypes."

MAX MÜLLER: (turning abruptly away from GG) "Yeah, but I think that whole 'Culture Is Derived from Cosmology' bit was pure Scheiße."

BRUCE LEE: "*Like a finger pointing to the moon …*" (points at moon).

(MAX MÜLLER stares at BRUCE LEE's finger.)

MAX MÜLLER: "Bruce, if the Corpus Hermeticum came in three waves, Pre-Diluvial, immediately post-Diluvial, and finally in its familiar form—"

BRUCE LEE: (smacks MAX MÜLLER on head) "*Don't concentrate on the finger!* Or you will miss all the heavenly glory ..."

(GG gets up, belligerent and violent.)

GG: "Horses gallop through puddles on the Left Hand Path, splashing through psychisms and obliterating all non-sequitors on the dead run to the post-abyss." (Sticks finger up to MAX MÜLLER's nose.) "Preconception holds a rancid stench up to the nose of all aspiring deities, and reads the reactionary face of all nostalgic referentials like the dial of a digital clock."

FRANCIS BACON: "Which reminds me: how exactly are we faring in this culture of the moment, boys?"

(GG puts on a wig sporting dangling, lice-infested dreadlocks.)

GG: "I live on the tip of each fragment of the iceberg of monoculture, and piss thereof into the wind ..."

(Drunkenly pisses; the others leave; stage darkens.)

GG: (Soliloquy) "Unencumbered by the illusory comfort of 'paradigm shifts' and crop circles, I will sink fast with my beloved iceberg when it melts. For I have carved the uncarved knowing full well that it remains ever uncarved."

[CURTAIN]

VOICE OF KURT: "Taking energy and flinging it around in the Horizontal always shares the same end: no matter how many multicolored Christmas balls the sorcerer or scientist hang from his filaments of discovery, they are all grounded in the superfluousness of the same circular movement… On this note, it becomes hard not to sympathize entirely with the existentialist castrati who inhabit the region of 'futility,' just south of the region of 'idealism.' But the door to *'alam al-mithal* 16 is always open, so… our sympathy for them should never run to Christic levels."

{Act 3}

* * *

[CURTAIN]

PORTRAIT ARTIST: "I see … so the image of the artist himself is being demoted, to paean and image-lackey servitor of an Abyss-seeking civilization. Well, it hardly seems appropriate to motivate anyone to that end."

HIS ETERNAL SUBJECT (now bearing the appearance of JIM MORRISON): "You're one to talk! You yourself are still seeking life-extension in the global neo-shamanic pharmacopeia. Hey, of course you are!—those rationalizing pyrotechnics of yours have since burned down the bridge to immortality; and the razor-thin asceticism that once sliced mercifully at your noble feet as you walked the path fell right down with it."

(MADAME POMPADEUX seems lost in thought.)

MADAME POMPADEUX: (abruptly) "I know! Let's go to the movies!"

[ABRUPT CURTAIN]

(Hijokaidan's *Windom* blasts for two minutes at ear-splitting volume.)

{Act 4}

*   *   *

[ABRUPT CURTAIN]

MAX MÜLLER: "Why would they have far less trouble contextualizing the Apocryphal visions of a Jacob Boehme, a Suhrawardi, or even a Pythagoras, in these places where the state of mind is blatantly 'intolerant,' 'medieval,' and ultra-orthodox (as we are told), than we do here in the supposedly all-inclusive parameters of our modern society? Are we perhaps, while claiming a universal suffrage, wearing a far more sinister brand of intolerance and ultra-orthodoxy on our arms like a badge of great pride ..."

BRUCE LEE: (rolling eyes) "Oh, what a bore to even bring this up ..."

MAX MÜLLER: "... that of pure materia ... lism."

KURT: (to BRUCE) "Anyone who would dispute this self-evident fact is even more of a bore, so to hell with you."

(BRUCE LEE pulls out a razor blade and quickly slits wrists, holding them up to Kurt's face.)

BRUCE LEE: (bleeding) "Drizzle Drizzle. It's raining criticism." (Pauses.) "And the limbo of pathological narcissism waits for us, ready to embrace even our most prominent adepti."

[Falls to the floor, laughing hysterically.]

BRUCE LEE: "Hey, look! I'm guilty of defining my guilt!"

MADAME POMPADEUS (looks down at BRUCE LEE, who is dying.)

[CURTAIN]

VOICE OF MADAME POMPADOUCE: "Most of the things your senses perceive come from the sound of Gabriel's wing ... you are one of the sounds of Gabriel's wing."[14]

14. Shihabuddin Yahya Suhrawardi, *The Sound of Gabriel's Wing*, trans. W.M. Thackston, from *The Philosophical Allegories and Mystical Treatises: A Parallel Persian-English Text* (Mazda Pub, 1999).

{Act 5}

[Soliloquy of Scotus]

* * *

[CURTAIN]

BON SCOTUS ERIUGENA: "There are no 'believers' who are afraid of anything but God."

[CURTAIN]

Fin

CHAPTER
28

TINNITUS: AN OCCUPATIONAL HAZARD

A Casualty on the Battlefield of Noise

J.G. THIRLWELL

TINNITUS is the perception of sound in the ears or head where no external source of sound is present.

The word derives from Latin, meaning "to tinkle or to ring like a bell." Hence tinnitus is often referred to as "ringing in the ears," although it can also take the form of hissing, roaring, whistling, chirping, or clicking. Tinnitus can be intermittent or constant. It can contain single or multiple tones, and its perceived volume can range from subtle to shattering.

(H) Ear Ring

My tinnitus is connected with my self-induced hearing damage. I incurred tinnitus by listening to a remix I was working on with headphones at painful levels for an hour or so. Exposure to loud noise can damage and even destroy the small hair cells, called cilia, in the cochlea of the ear. Once they are damaged, the cilia cannot be renewed or replaced. They are not self-healing. Despite the pain, I kept listening, because I was too high to care. I woke up the next day and my ears were ringing and it hasn't gone away since. That was in 1990. The tinnitus in my left ear is louder than the right. It makes me more precious of further damaging that ear. The sound is perhaps like water running from a faucet, not an old-fashioned faucet but like an aerated stream. It is a white noise hum in the upper-mid to high frequencies.

When performing live with a guitar/bass/drums/keys line-up version of Foetus in the 1990s, I seldom wore hearing protection on stage. I was singing, and I found wearing earplugs made it difficult to hear the vocals to pitch myself. We would monitor very loudly on stage as the drummer could never hear the other instruments, and everyone had to turn up around him. This onstage volume exacerbated my condition. My first album was prophetically entitled *DEAF.*

Resonance

Now when I work with string players I notice how incredibly protective acoustic players are of their hearing, and the slightest hint of feedback will cause winces and fingers to immediately go into their ears. Oh, that I had been so heedful.

As someone who has suffered hearing damage, I am terrified of worsening it and making the ringing louder. Now I always wear hearing protection when I am at concerts. I used to enjoy the pure power of volume rushing over me like an icy wind, blowing me backward and bathing me like the guy on those old Maxell commercials. Now I am cautious to the point of avoiding it, which is saddening. I can appreciate the power of, say, a Wolf Eyes show, but I would rather listen to the CD at home where I can attenuate the volume.

Hiss

As a result, I run the speakers in my studio quietly when I compose in my studio, as my ears can fatigue quickly. Sometimes I use small quiet sampled gestures that I modify and re-pitch. These sounds are recorded with room mikes, and the cumulative effect of the ambience of the rooms where the audio was recorded and tape hiss can build a compound roar that I often don't notice for some time over my tinnitus or the ambient noise in my studio, which is not enclosed. Eventually I have to roll off the hisses accumulated without destroying the timbral character of the composition.

I have learned how to differentiate my tinnitus from this type of hiss. My brain puts my tinnitus aside as I focus on the sounds. My hearing is more brittle, and the mid-range frequencies I often favor in my music can be difficult and fatiguing to listen to for any length of time. Music and sound creates a diverting focus, but it is transitory and temporal in nature—tinnitus is the gift that keeps on giving.

Hum

For a couple of years there was a plastics factory situated in the floor below my studio which had a piece of equipment which caused electrical/radio frequency interference through my mixing desk and monitors. It created buzzes and hums of various volumes, lengths, and pitches. This wasn't too much of an issue when I was programming with the computer or midi, but I couldn't record any audio without these buzzes also being recorded on the track. The factory operated from 8:30–5:00 with a break at 12:30–1:00 for lunch, so if I needed to record any audio during the day I waited for their lunchtime. Once I decided to record the hums on multiple tracks and see what composition would come about by chance, to create a hum symphony. I wanted to see how the chance buzzes would interrelate being built up over multiple tracks. But those particular hums evoked a resentment in me as I recognized them as the sounds that inhibited my work, and I couldn't get any pleasure out of using them as sound sources. It was too jarring. Those accidental frequencies were forever marred with their association of an interruption of my work. Their sound made me want to reach out for the volume knob and turn the monitors down as often one hugely loud buzz would pop thru the occasionally softer tide of hums. Mercifully, that factory has long since closed, so perhaps I could revisit that abandoned composition and capture that audio snapshot of the plastics factory with a distance. But really I have no desire to.

Mask

The tinnitus sufferer can use sound to mask or partially cover the tinnitus. Some masking tools can be white-noise generators, hard drives, fans, the sounds of roadways, an air purifier, air conditioning, or purring kittens. We seek an ambient electronic match for our condition. The hum of traffic over the Brooklyn Queens Expressway one hundred feet from my house undulates like waves on a distant beach. The roar of the D train over the Manhattan Bridge rattles a boxy report. The hard drive of my laptop hums at a very similar frequency to my tinnitus. These aid me as my white-noise generators, ambience creators, and blockers. Subtle washes and roars that surround me in my environment are my allies. I hear fluorescent lights buzzing in sympathy and in harmony with my head. When I am in my house, upstairs in my bedroom, I can still see the Brooklyn Queens Expressway, but it is behind a plexiglas window which attenuates and rolls off the high frequency of its white noise hum. When I am up there in my bed, the tinnitus is louder. Very loud and then louder as I lie and contemplate my day. The frequencies can envelope my skull like a glass brick. Its seeming eternity is depressing. Tinnitus is a constant which forms a carpet between empty space and sound-events and pushes itself to the foreground when the ambience recedes.

Toop

In his book *Haunted Weather*, David Toop states, "The randomness of white noise allows more possibilities of a very faint sound wave finding another wave with which it can resonate and so be reinforced."

I am destined to live with the frequencies in my ear that put me in terror of visits to the country side, as the quietness makes my tinnitus so much more audible. Although I have gotten used to it somewhat, I don't enjoy "listening" to my tinnitus in the same way that I listen to a nuanced piece of audio or environmental sound. If I'm listening to quiet chamber music, the tinnitus is very noticeable. When *4'33"* is performed, my tinnitus is the main soloist.

Rite

A colleague of mine, Jed Miner, said that he regarded tinnitus as a rite of passage, that inner-ear scarification was like the modern-day cliterectomy. Another colleague, Franz Pomassl, contends that the ear is a muscle that must be exercised, as if it could commit great feats of strength.

NY Noise

The sounds of New York City reach painful levels without asking. In New York City the screech of the brakes on the C train can reach tangible discomfort levels for me. The ambulance sirens, construction, and car horns create a deafening damaging symphony.

Recchion's Experience

Composer/sound artist Tom Recchion got tinnitus as a side effect of caregiver's syndrome, looking after a sick friend. It flares up when he is stressed out. At first a constant ringing, he would stretch his jaw or pop his eardrum to get rid of it. It had a doppler effect when he turned his head. It took him a while before he knew what was happening to him. It would switch back and forth between one ear and the other.

It was making him crazy because he couldn't escape it. It was really impossible to relax. It got so loud that he couldn't listen to music. He could "hear" music, but there was pitch and whining throughout everything he listened to, and the pleasure of listening was gone. Then the sound started to change quality from a constant piercing noise. At first Tom thought it was the high pitch of a nerve ending dying. (Some say the pinging high-pitched whining that often appears suddenly in one's ear and fade away is a cell dying, although Jacob Kirkegaard describes the phenomenon of otoacoustic emissions, whereby the cilia actually generate sound, which could account for this phenomenon.)

Then after a few weeks it changed quality and started to sputter like a loose connection. He could understand how this condition could drive some people mad. A squeaky undulating popping cracking sound. It became very difficult to concentrate, and he couldn't be in a quiet room and had to have a masking source. He would turn on a fan, or turn on a vibrator and leave it on the bed, under the pillow. After about four or five months his tinnitus suddenly stopped, although it has returned sporadically lately.

Now he finds he can't listen to high-frequency compositions. Tom says, "Volume had more allure, but loud doesn't interest me as much as it used to."

Silence

In the "absolute" silence of an anechoic chamber we focus on our circulatory system. John Cage contended there was no such thing as silence. The sound of our heart pumping, the pulse in our ears, the blood flowing through our veins, our breath, our tubercular lungs rattling, our bones creaking and shrinking from osteoporosis. Our hair and skin. Even cells make a measurable sound. Only outer space, where there is no air, is silent. But we aren't there to "hear" it. And what about that tree that falls in the woods? I am a captive "hearer" of my condition.

CHAPTER
29

CROSSOVER MELODIES: THE FORMULATION OF A COMPOSITIONAL METHODOLOGY AND A PERSONAL IDIOM

MATTHEW WELCH

My initial training, both instrumental and theoretical, was firmly rooted in the traditional techniques and musical language of the Scottish Highland bagpipe. As I learned the existing repertoire, I was quickly compelled to deepen my understanding of bagpipe music, and so at fifteen, an imaginative young sorcerer on the Gulf Coast of Florida, I began conjuring the magic of these archaic, far-off forms, composing new tunes in the traditional models I'd managed to access. When composing piobaireachd, the style that marks the most highly developed music form of piping, I tried expressly to be inventive, for this area of the repertoire was the most stylistically diverse, and its structural options allowed creativity in both composition and performance. As I increased and asserted my fluency in each of these aspects of the traditional music, I was simultaneously studying experimental music composition and writing chamber and electronic works. I found a home for my music in the world of the avant-garde in that I was experimenting and extending, albeit with identifiable utilization of bagpipe concepts or materials. There appears to be as much of an untapped potential in the utilization of bagpipes in non-traditional forms as there is in extensions and extrapolations of the traditional forms and devices.

This territory is largely unexplored, save a mere handful of innovators: Canada's Michael O'Neill, England's Paul Dunmall, New Zealand/New York's David Watson, and Scotland's Martyn Bennett all have done remarkable work with the bagpipe outside of its original context, all of them in unique directions. The late cult hero Rufus Harley was an early pioneer in using the bagpipe in jazz. These artists are more likely to find open ears in other listening communities, for many traditional players would criticize and reject their work. Perhaps the pressure to conform in contemporary bagpiping (now a breed of classical music and primarily competitive tradition outside of its martial and ritual contexts), combined with a lack of presentations of bagpipe music in a concert format, may have suppressed extensive formal and stylistic creativity. Individualism is sometimes allowed, though rarely encouraged explicitly in the approach to attaining a sound. It is likely that the Highland bagpipe's earlier possibility of extinction set forth a preservationist attitude as early as the latter half of the 18th century. The instrument has changed little in the ways other western wind instruments have developed since their inception into the orchestra; bagpipe makers have essentially been perfecting the same design for over three hundred years. Problems arise in integrating the pipes with modern western instruments. The tuning systems of western instruments and the pipes are different, not to mention the pipes have almost none of the dynamic and articulation techniques that have become commonplace in western ears. Despite the inertia of the bagpipe's hegemony, a proper cultural context, such as this current time period, given fractured diasporas and convenient global access, has helped cultivate mutations and forward-moving approaches to the bagpipe.

Another example of this global access was the opportunity to study Indonesian gamelan at both my undergraduate and graduate universities and travel to Indonesia to further those studies. Upon hearing the first stroke of a gong, I felt an instant affinity for gamelan, and began to perceive its uncanny connections to pipe music, though this has come to be more important to my recent musical directions. Sociologically significant, I suppose, traveling to Bali and composing and collaborating in Indonesia was not a ready option 100 years ago. A new generation of composers have been changed or challenged in some way by this increased cultural transparency; the bubble of strictly Western values and art forms has already burst. The taking up of gamelan some ten years ago has shaped ideas of instrumental relationships that bagpipe music didn't have, yet could yield theoretically and creatively, as expressed in my recent orchestral and chamber settings.

As a performer, I have tried to spread my interest between several forms of gamelan, though as a composer, I am particularly interested in the potential of gamelan ensembles with seven-tone pitch systems (gamelan saih pitu). The modern Gamelan Semara Dana (invented in the 1980s) is a hybrid species of Balinese gamelan formed from a merging of classical-era Semar Pegulingan Saih Pitu with the prevalent 20th-century Gamelan Gong Kebyar. I am particularly interested in these seven-tone pitch systems because of the flexibility and variety of colors that can be achieved through the use of interior five-tone subset modalities. The employment of various five-pitch subset modes taken from a parent seven-tone set is common to traditional practices stemming from the bamboo flute (suling) music that accompanies the ancient Gambuh drama. These differing modes, initially created by different fingerings on the suling, enhance the sense of character for roles portrayed in the Gambuh drama. For the most part, this multi-modal practice had come to pass due to more-dominant styles utilizing only one five-tone set or fewer pitches, yet in a recent resurgence both traditional and newer approaches toward subsets of seven-tone modal combinations and their effective juxtapositions (abundant modulation is a contemporary development in gamelan saih pitu) are being explored by current Balinese composers.

In my studies of bagpipe and Indonesian music I have always felt a sympathetic connection. Ensembles that best accommodate the melodic identities of bagpipe music based on my perception of compatibility are all of forms of gamelan rarer than Gong Kebyar, the nearly ubiquitous Balinese orchestra found today. These other forms utilize scales that can better approximate the bagpipe scale, yet maintain all of their own idiomatic timbres and textures, increasing the efficacy of a cross-cultural compositional directive. Great potential lies in this new yet rare type of seven-tone gamelan, Semara Dana. This ensemble can act as a "jack of all trades," referencing multiple other forms of gamelan in modern pieces by merely modulating between modes that are indicative of them, or by simply incorporating the repertoire of older forms. Semara Dana's quotational, post-modern quality enables it to characterize the various species and comment upon the development of gamelan in secular and ritualistic programs.

When last in Bali, I had the chance to experiment with a small group of musicians from the Balinese arts collective known as Cudamani, a very innovative group that specializes in playing Gamelan Semara Dana. I was able to compose for Cudamani the beginnings of a collection of pieces for Semara Dana drawing from bagpipe music and gamelan idioms, exploring the flexibility of seven-tone frameworks as described below. These Semara Dana pieces were used as my part in a multi-media collaboration with Ikue Mori. This collaboration is a modern spin on the Balinese Wayang Kulit, or shadow puppet theater. Ikue Mori has added image processing to her unique electronic sound manipulations to create a brilliant audio/visual performance animating characters from traditional Balinese paintings. Her extracts from the Kertha Gosa Kamasan (wayang style) paintings have an uncanny similarity to traditional Balinese puppets when animated through various software. Much in the manner of the dalang, or puppeteer and story teller, Mori's soundscapes often reflect the ambience and sound effects of a Balinese shadow play. Traditionally, the shadow play is always accompanied by live gamelan, and so I felt this material based on excerpts and arrangements of pibroch, the classical music of the bagpipe, mapped onto the pitch spectrum and idiomatic rhythmic, formal, and textural practices of the Balinese gamelan, would enhance Ikue Mori's project in progress. Consistent with Balinese approaches to the new Semara Dana, which can conjure with ease almost any style of Balinese gamelan heretofore, I tailored the music of the Scottish funeral into the modal procedures used to conjure up the Balinese Cremation gamelan ensemble (Anklung), as well as the shadow play's original ensemble (Gender Wayang) and a number of other Balinese styles (Kebyar, Jegog, Pegulingan). The result, I feel, is a thoroughly integrated style containing salient elements of both disparate traditions, appropriately genuflecting to the ritualistic purposes of both original musics. This intertwining yields a completely new music—a fictional world music, if you will. Some excerpts of these pieces are provided in Figures 2 and 3, below.

As I learned more about gamelan, I saw more clearly the plethora of compositional possibilities that could result from a coupling of these separate music traditions. In my meditations on these possibilities, I drew certain analogies between the mechanics, materials, and contexts of both traditions. The most pertinent commonalities are as follows.

Ritual

Both musics can be described as having (if not presently, then certainly historically) an ethnologically ritualistic purpose. The Highland bagpipe was used for purposes of battle, not only to frighten the brigade to be attacked, but to inspire the attacking brigade to fight fiercely. The bagpipes are also used to provide music for social occasions, dance formats, and funeral services. Balinese gamelans are primarily assigned to ritualistic functions, some ensemble types being specifically created for singular purposes, whether to provide an army with motivation and frighten opponents (the marching Gamelan Belaganjur), to provide music for cremation ceremonies (Gamelan Anklung), or to accompany elaborate dance-dramas.

Drone/Gong

Both musics are held up by a foundation of a sustaining, low presence. The low drone of the bagpipe cushions the shrill sound of the chanter (the double reed pipe on which the melodies are played) and lends character to the individual pitches of the chanter by their intervallic relationship to each other. The drone is also a fundamental to which the chanter is tuned, each instrument's minutely unique timbre affecting the approach toward chanter intonation. The larger gongs of a gamelan cover the lowest range of the gamelan, and, in their long sustain, create a foundation like a drone. The demarcations of cycle by the gongs create a prolonged sense of drone by reiteration of gong strokes, a drone by accumulation. The timbral character of the lowest gong shapes the gamelan maker's approach to the character and intonation of the remainder of instruments.

Cycles

Both musics are predominantly constructed with cycles or recurring metrical units.

Fused Timbres and Timbral Richness of Collections of Instruments

Both musics share a similar approach toward the overall timbre of a group of instruments. Both exhibit a dominance of self-similar instruments, e.g., many metallophones, many bagpipes. These timbres are extremely bright, rich, startling, and capable of being very loud. Often groups in each tradition prefer performing in open or outdoor spaces. Treatment to tessitura is similar in that softness of tone increases toward the lower ranges. Low gongs and bagpipe band bass drums are struck with large, padded mallets. Low metallophones are struck with padded mallets, and bagpipe drones are single reeded. Brighter and higher, high metallophones are struck with hard, wooden mallets, pipe band snare drums are struck with hard sticks, and bagpipe chanters are armed with bright, raucous double reeds. The collections of instrumentation play with forms of unison textures that when coupled to these timbral colors forms fused timbres, playing and sounding as one.

Alternative Tuning Systems—Just Intonation/Ombak

Part of the appeal of these disparate instrumental traditions is their unique tuning systems. Both systems gravitate toward intervals that fall outside of current western equal temperament. The chanter of the pipes approaches a tuning closer to a "just intonation." The individual pitches are tuned in relation to the sustained drone, and, when properly tuned, reflect a player's understanding of overtones and the natural harmonic series. Not only are the intervals in gamelan scales not western-tempered, but in Balinese gamelan, pairs of like instruments are provided with slight differences in tuning to create acoustical interference, or beating. This tremolo sound, called ombak in Bali, is highly controlled by gamelan tuners so that the entire ensemble will shimmer in unison.

Limited Pitch—Modality/Pentatonicism

In both musics, chromaticism is a completely foreign and unemployed concept. Most of the traditional repertoires of both idioms concentrate on smaller pitch sets or scales; furthermore, primarily those pentatonic. As discussed elsewhere, a reciprocal pitch mapping between Gamelan Semara Dana's expanded modal capability and the extant mixolydian scale of the pipes is possible. Bagpipe and Suling fingerings are mutually compatible, maintaining the same modal relationships.

Crossover Melodies—Limited Range and Large Range Representation

Aside from both traditions' use of limited pitch material, the range of the bagpipe and most gamelan instruments is fairly small, often that of one octave only. Characteristically, a melody with a larger range than that of a particular instrument will be crunched to fit the range of that instrument, substituting octave or consonant equivalents for pitches out of reach. This results in the transformation of conjunct passages to the disjunct. The illusion of a multi-octave or conjunct melody can be created by a composite effect between multiple instruments of narrow range in differing registers.

Variation—Sequential Versus Simultaneous

Both musics present idiomatic yet analogous forms of variation. In piobaireachd, the classical music of the bagpipe, a variation process is usually composed of a linear sequence of cycles of monophonic nature, all extensions upon a basic theme. This theme, which is usually an abstract and regular sequence of pitches never explicitly presented, is treated to many types of systematic ornamentations peculiar to the bagpipe. In Balinese and Javanese gamelans, a basic, perhaps abstracted, skeletal structure like the piobaireachd's theme (called pokok in Bali, and balungan in Java) is played by some of the instruments as a specific instrumental role. Other roles will entail other instrumentally idiomatic (likewise systematic) versions or negotiations of the basic melody, most often presented simultaneously and vertically in a paradoxically multifaceted yet self-similar heterophonic texture. A further analogy extends to the balance of core melodic material and a generous amount of ornamentation. Piobaireachd's voluminous ornamental vocabulary and process compare to the various strata of continuous figurations or ornamentation in gamelan practice, such as interlocking kotekan in Bali and cengkok in Java.

With these common principles in mind, I will now turn to the mechanics of my own compositions that weave these two worlds together.

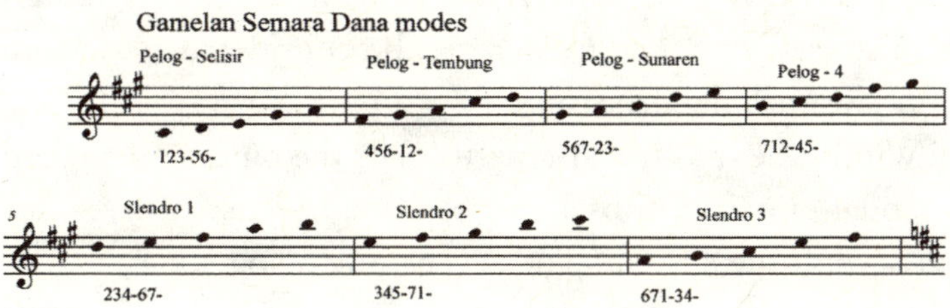

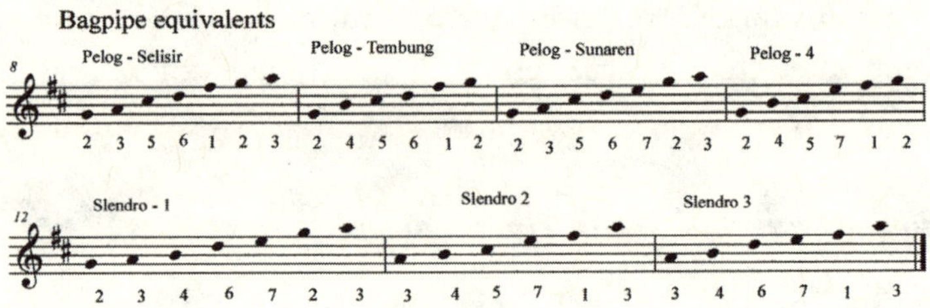

Figure 1.

Figure 1, above, is an explication of the various modal subsets available in gamelan Semara Dana. The seven pitch classes, in addition to the conventional western approximation in A major, are represented by the numbers one through seven (standing for the Balinese solfege ding, dong, deng, deung, dung, dang, and daing), a cypher notation common to various types of Southeast Asian musics. The first four modes are of the pelog variety, featuring conjunct steps varying from roughly a major third to a minor second. Stemming from the original Suling Gambuh fingerings, these are the primary modes used in larger forms of gamelan in Bali, such as Gong Kebyar, Semar Pegulingan, Selonding, and Gong Gede. The fourth pelog in the example is arguably called pelog baro, but there is little corroborating evidence, and the name baro has been assigned to other combinations.

The Slendro modes in Figure 1 show the possible Slendro approximations available in gamelan Semara Dana. The Slendro mode is characterized by more or less five equidistant steps to the octave, though more often exhibit conjunct steps of major seconds and thirds. Slendro is primarily used in forms of gamelan such as Gender Wayang and Anklung. Traditionally, Slendro is not viewed as a subset of seven-tone pelog, though innovative contemporary Balinese composers have found that these subsets in Semara Dana can be considered close approximations of traditional Slendro scales.

Within the traditional repertoire of the pipes, a very similar system of modal practice is observed regarding the use of five-tone modes within a seven-tone system. The seven-tone pelog scale is most closely represented in Western notation as the key of A major. When transposed down a fifth (D major, or A mixolydian), the result is synonymous with the written key and scale of the Highland bagpipe. As stated before, traditional bagpipe music tends to be pentatonic; it utilizes three pentatonic modes equivalent to Semara Dana's three possible Slendro scales. As with the discovery of possible Slendro modes within the pelog scale, the bagpipe scale can easily incorporate the four pelog scales as additional subsets of its diatonic scale. These equivalencies permit near-complete interchangeability of melodies from one culture to the next.

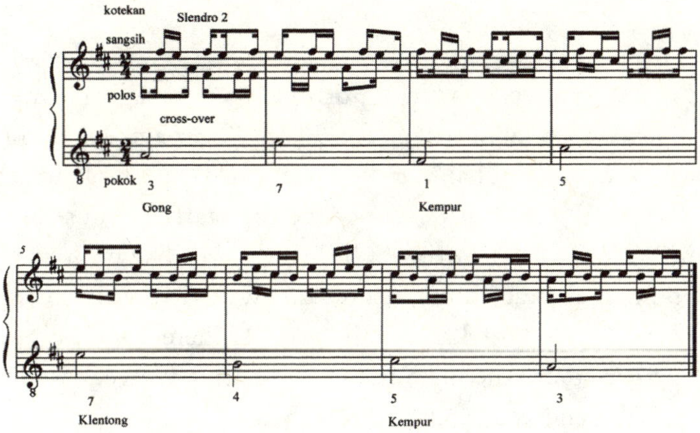

Figure 2.

Figure 2, above, contains a cycle from one of the Semara Dana pieces for the *Bhima Swarga* project. The sixteen-beat cycle is marked by the gong sequence: Gong, Kempur, Klentong, Kempur. These are various-sized hanging gongs, the largest and most significant being gong (gong ageng). This example is based loosely on a fragment from the piobaireachd *The Lament for the Harp Tree*. The modal relationship is maintained from the bagpipe's A pentatonic to Semara Dana's slendro 2. The pokok (dually notated by the half notes and numerical cypher notation) is a thematic abstraction of the contour of the original fragment, while the kotekan (16th-note line) is an elaboration on the contour of the original fragment. The two interlocking parts of a kotekan are named polos and sangsih, and are represented by diverging stem directions. These interlocking parts are played by separate players and separate instruments (played on metallophones called gangsa), the composite creating the full figuration. A crossover is employed at the beginning of the cycle to insinuate a conjunct figuration just above the gangsa's range.

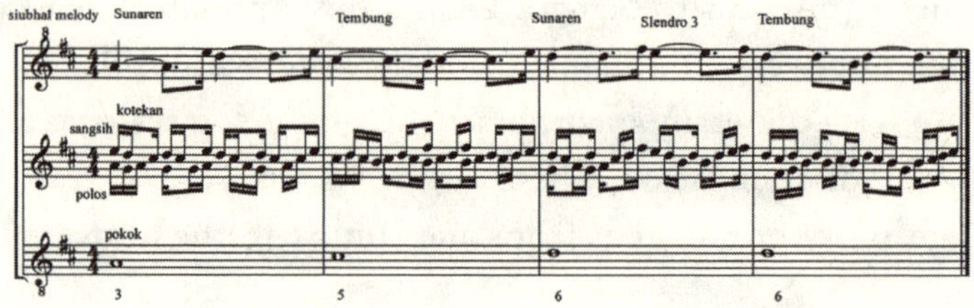

Figure 3.

Figure 3, above, contains a portion of a cycle again from my collection of Semara Dana pieces for the *Bhima Swarga* project. This material is based on the siubhal variation section of the piobaireachd *The Lament for the Viscount of Dundee*. The top staff contains the melody arrangement closest to the original bagpipe piece. The bottom line contains the pokok, abstracted one degree of rhythmic density further than that of Figure 2. The kotekan fills in constant heterophonic figuration, yet also further colors the melody by modulating between the Sunaren, Tembung, and Slendro 3 modes so readily available to Gamelan Semara Dana, creating a metaphorical effect of harmonic change.

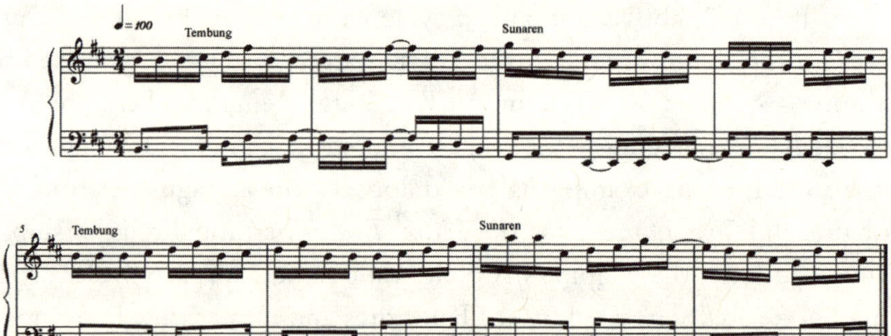

Figure 4.

Figure 4, above, contains a fragment of a composition, *Pak Gusti Aji*, for my ensemble Blarvuster. This displays a writing style equally referencing piping and gamelan musics. The top staff melody line imitates the Highland hornpipe and reel, yet also a composite kotekan figuration. The bottom staff bass line resembles a possible polos or sangsih component of a kotekan, yet also mirrors a syncopated melodic style of the trompong, a melodic leading instrument of the Gamelan Semar Pegulingan. The combination of the two creates a complicated heterophonic texture. This melody also creates a phrasing effect by modulating between the pelog modes Tembung and Sunaren.

Figure 5a.

Figure 5b.

Figures 5a and 5b are taken from another Blarvuster composition, *Bottoms Up*, a title referencing both drinking and crossover melodic effects. The instrumentation of Blarvuster takes into consideration the approach toward timbre and stratus. The bass guitar is plucked with the flesh of the finger and the tone is deep, but not bright. The electric guitar plays a simultaneous variation of the bass, and is timbrally set apart by its use of plectrum. The viola yet again plays a simultaneous variation in its stratus, timbrally unique in its use of the bow. Note the crossover melody at the entrance of the bagpipe at measure 73 of Figure 5b.

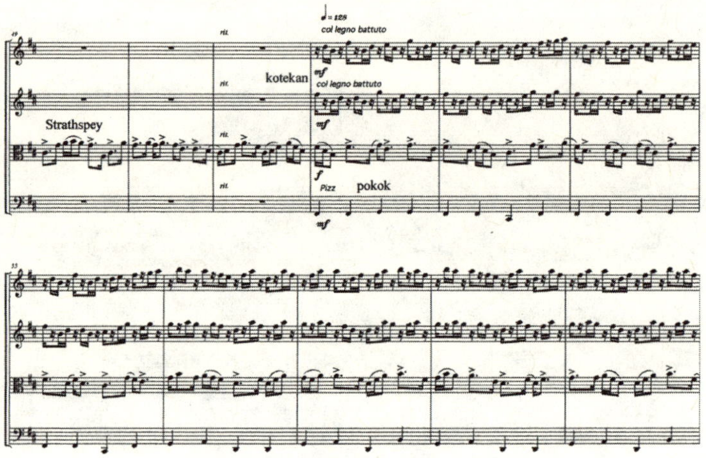

Figure 6.

Figure 6 is an excerpt from my string quartet, *Siubhal Turnlar*. The pokok is represented by a steady pizzicato in the cello. This pokok is primarily in the pelog selisir, yet incorporates pamero tones from the remaining two pitches of the full seven-tone pelog scale. The use of pamero tone is a characteristic of seven-tone gamelan practice, most commonly used to enhance the color of a melody by temporarily inserting outside pitches. The viola line is in the style of a Scottish Strathspey dance tune, distinguished by its dotted, jagged rhythms. As in the cello pokok, this viola Strathspey is in the selisir mode, including pamero tones. The two violins fill in a constant 16th-note figuration of the melody as a composite of two syncopated kotekan rhythms. The kotekan is played col legno battuto as a representation of the percussive aspect of gamelan playing.

Figure 7, below, is an excerpt from my violin and piano composition called *The House of Asterion*. The violin line presents a constant 16th-note melody in the manner of a Scottish reel or a kotekan composite. The melody is strictly diatonic and modulates frequently between pentatonic subsets as previously discussed. The piano part fragments the violin line into a complex form of kotekan, often substituting octave equivalents and accenting hemiolas and modulations with appropriate pentatonic clusters. This composition is an example of an extremely rigorous extension of the aforementioned rhythmic and tonal procedures.

Figure 7.

Producing multicultural work might only thrive in a context that mirrors it, such as New York City. Modern North American music embraces Asian methods, micro-tonality, just-intonation, steady rhythmic devices. Furthermore, a pulse-driven, tonal, or modal music can be expressed in a serious idiom. With the presence of both living gamelan and bagpipe communities in North America, one may be a regular constituent of both music cultures. Additionally, the achievements in form, materials, and systematic idiosyncrasies in American models of composition have been important to my understanding how to compose. This has allowed me to create this delicately balanced world of musical fiction.

CHAPTER
30

WHAT IS MUSIC?

YAMATAKA EYE

I don't know what music is. Just what is it really? Is it an exchange of energy? Is it a process to arrive at a thing called harmony? Or thinking in reverse, is there anything that is not music? A conversation of young lovers has a musical rhythm to it, as does their bickering.

A good cook can whip up natural ingredients with water and fire, often with split-second decisions … this requires time and timing—like music, it is an art that happens in time. These actions are often more like real music to me than music that is commercially packaged.

Some things are musical or contain an innate musicality…. Like the beautiful motion of planets revolving and orbiting around the sun. Just what is the origin of these natural phenomena—these repetitive motions that are so like music to me…. There must be a terminal somewhere, a station that is actually transmitting them…. And what we call "music" is downloaded directly from this home base, which is broadcasting it all beyond time and space.

Is musical phenomena equivalent to living phenomena, like an insect camouflaging itself, transforming itself into nature—into a leaf, for example. When you make music, it is your interpretation of nature…. And the more you try to create, the more it becomes nature, just like an insect. By making music, you are actually sending the sound back to its origin—back to the universe.

I think of myself as an organic life phenomenon, and try to listen to myself as music….

> A wolf howling at the moon is the singer.
> Thunder is the drummer.
> The crashing of waves is the guitarist.
> The tremors of an earthquake are the bassist.

If one wonders where to find a recording of music made by such an amazing band …

It's been right here with us all the time.

Translation: Ochiishi Augustmoon

ABOUT THE MUSICIANS

Christopher Adler is a composer, performer, and improviser living in San Diego, California. His compositions draw upon over a decade of research into the traditional musics of Thailand and Laos and a background in mathematics. He is internationally recognized as a foremost performer of new and traditional music for the *khaen*, a free-reed mouth organ from Laos and Northeast Thailand, and is the pianist and Composer-in-Residence with the ensemble NOISE. He received PhD and master's degrees in composition from Duke University and bachelor's degrees in music composition and in mathematics from the Massachusetts Institute of Technology. His teachers have been Scott Lindroth, Stephen Jaffe, Sidney Corbett, Evan Ziporyn, and, for studies of Thai classical music, Panya Roongruang. He is currently an Associate Professor at the University of San Diego. For more information, please see www.christopheradler.com.

Christopher Adler

Mick Barr

Borah Bergman

Mick Barr plays a lot of guitar. He has been playing since 1989 and has been playing the same guitar since 1992. He has released countless recordings on many formats over the years. He is from originally from CT, but has also lived in Washington, D.C., San Francisco, CA, and New York City.

Borah Bergman was born in New York City and gave up piano at thirteen, and resumed at twenty-four. He studied piano with Teddy Wilson and Daniel Hurd, and was a disciple of Lennie Tristano. He received his master's degree at New York University. Grants received: Ingram Merrill grant for composition and the New York State Meet the Composer. *Discover, Solo Piano* (1975) was his first recording. His second, *Bursts of Joy* (1976), received a four-star review in *Downbeat*, which stated that "Borah Bergman is to piano what Ornette Coleman or John Coltrane is to saxophone." In 1983 Borah began a long association with the Soul Note label, recording two solo albums in Italy (1983, 1984) and playing concerts elsewhere in Europe. In 1984 he worked with the Belgian composer Henri Pousseur, who arranged for Borah to teach seminars and workshops in jazz improvisation at the Royal Conservatories in Liege and Brussels. He gave a concert at the Pompidou Centre in Paris in 1985, and the following year played in six concerts in honor of Martin Luther King with an ensemble led by Archie Shepp and the violinist/composer Malcolm Goldstein, including Henry Threadgill, David Murray, Ray Anderson, Denardo Coleman, and Fred Hopkins. He toured Europe in 1987, performing at Donaueschingen and Berlin. He recorded his first two duo CDs with Thomas Chapin in 1992 and 2003. Other projects involved Roscoe Mitchell (1994, 2002), Oliver Lake (1999), drummers Andrew Cyrille (1992), Hamid Drake (1995), and Rashid Ali (1994), among others, with Anthony Braxton, Peter Brotzmann, Joe McPhee, Thomas Borgmann, Roy Campbell, Dennis Charles, Bobby Bradford, Pheeron Ak Laff, Jim Staley, Frode Gjerstad, Conny Bauer, Paul Hession, Lol Coxhill, etc. (1997 to 2004).

Lisa Bielawa often takes inspiration for her work from literary sources and close artistic collaborations. As Composer-in-Residence with the Boston Modern Orchestra Project under the auspices of the Music Alive program of Meet the Composer and the ASOL, she is creating new works for the orchestra and for soloists within the orchestra over three years, culminating in a recording of her orchestral music in 2009. She is currently at work on *Chance Encounter*, for soprano Susan Narucki and twelve instruments, for performance in public spaces, a multi-year project of Creative Capital. In 2007 the Tzadik label will release a CD of her music on the Composers Series. Recent works include *The Lay of the Love and Death*, for violinist Colin Jacobsen and baritone Jesse Blumberg, which premiered at Alice Tully Hall in March 2006; *Hurry*, for soprano and chamber ensemble, commissioned by Carnegie Hall and subsequently performed in the Seattle Symphony Made in America Festival in 2006, with the composer as soloist; and *The Right Weather*, commissioned by the American Composers Orchestra to celebrate the inaugural season of their Zankel Hall series. Lisa is also one of the Founders and Artistic Directors of the MATA Festival, which commissions and premieres work by young composers from all over the world.

Lisa Bielawa

Uri Caine

Uri Caine was born in Philadelphia and began studying piano with Bernard Peiffer. He played in bands led by Philly Joe Jones, Hank Mobley, Johnny Coles, Mickey Roker, Odean Pope, Jymmie Merritt, Bootsie Barnes, and Grover Washington. He attended the University of Pennsylvania and studied music composition with George Rochberg and George Crumb. Caine has received commissions from the Vienna Volksoper, the Seattle Chamber Players, Relache, the Beaux Arts Trio, the Basel Chamber Orchestra, and Concerto Koln. The Pennsylvania Ballet performed the *Goldberg Variations* in 2002, choreographed by Val Caniparoli. Caine was the Director of the Venice Biennale for Music in September 2003, where he also premiered his new work *The Othello Syndrome*. He has performed his version of the *Diabelli Variations* with orchestras including the Cleveland Orchestra, the Moscow Chamber Orchestra, the CBC Orchestra in Candada, and the Swedish Chamber Orchestra. In June of 2004 the JVC Jazz Festival featured his three *Bedrock*, *Mahler*, and *Goldberg* projects at the Village Vanguard. In 2006 he was named Composer-in-Residence for the Los Angeles Chamber Orchestra, and premiered his *Concerto for Two Pianos and Chamber Orchestra* with Jeffrey Kahane in May 2006.

Steve Coleman began playing music at age fourteen in Chicago. After being influenced by various recordings of Charlie Parker, Sonny Rollins, John Coltrane, and others, Steve then began listening to the spontaneous improvisations of Chicago premier saxophonists Von Freeman and Bunky Green. After moving to NYC in 1978, Steve joined the Thad Jones-Mel Lewis Big Band and subsequently played with the Sam Rivers Big Band, Cecil Taylor's Big Band, Doug Hammond, the Dave Holland Quintet, and Abbey Lincoln. Of those he came into contact with, it was mainly tenor saxophonist Von Freeman who primarily influenced Coleman as an improviser, saxophonist Sam Rivers who influenced Steve compositionally, and drummer Doug Hammond who was especially important in Steve's conceptual thinking. In 1980 Steve and trumpeter Graham Haynes started the group that eventually became Steve Coleman and Five Elements. Over the next five years this group would develop its sound in clubs in Harlem and Brooklyn. Their ideas were based on how to create music from one's experiences. Eventually these ideas were referred to as M-Base. However, unlike what most critics wrote, this concept was philosophical; Coleman did not call the music itself M-Base. In 1993 Coleman embarked on the first of many research trips, going to Ghana to study the relationship of language to music. This trip had a profound effect on Coleman's music and philosophy. However, the impact of the ideas that he was introduced to in Ghana would not be fully expressed in his work until late in 1994 after meeting the Kemetic philosopher Thomas Goodwin, whose influence on Steve's work was profound. Much of the activity from January 1996 on has been preserved in the form of a documentary produced by Eve-Marie Breglia entitled *Elements of One* (available at http://www.elementsofone.com/). The film is based on Steve's music and the theme of cultural transference.

Steve Coleman

Sylvie Courvoisier

Composer/pianist Sylvie Courvoisier was born and raised in Lausanne, Switzerland. She moved to Brooklyn, New York, in 1998, where she currently resides. She has played and/or recorded with John Zorn, Ikue Mori, Joey Baron, Mark Feldman, Tim Berne, Tony Oxley, Yusef Lateef, Dave Douglas, Joëlle Léandre, Herb Robertson, Butch Morris, Mark Dresser, Lotte Anker, Fred Frith, Ellery Eskelin, Michel Godard, and Mark Nauseef, among others. She has been commissioned to write music for concerts, radio, dance, and theater. Her works include *Concerto for electric guitar and chamber orchestra* (1999) and *Balbutiements*, for vocal quartet and soprano (1995–2000). Commissions include the Vidy Theater of Lausanne Switzerland, Pro Helvetia, and Germany's Donaueschingen Musiktage Festival. Sylvie is currently a member of Mephista, an improvising trio with Ikue Mori and Susie Ibarra; Abaton, a trio performing her compositions for piano, violin, and cello with Mark Feldman and Erik Friedlander; Lonelyville, her quintet exploring the connections between improvisation and contemporary composition with Ikue Mori, Mark Feldman, Vincent Courtois, and Gerald Cleaver; Herb Robertson Quintet with Tim Berne, Tom Rainey, and Mark Dresser; Vincent Courtois Trio, along with Ellery Eskelin. She also performs regularly in a duo with violinist Mark Feldman. Awards include Switzerland's

1996 Prix des jeunes créateurs and Zonta Club's 2000 Prix de la Création.

Trained in composition by Nadia Boulanger in Paris and Luciano Berio at Juilliard, NOAH CRESHEVSKY is the former director of the Center for Computer Music and Professor Emeritus at Brooklyn College of the City University of New York. His musical vocabulary consists largely of familiar bits of words, songs, and instrumental music which are edited but rarely subjected to electronic processing. The result is a music that obscures the boundaries of real and imaginary ensembles though the fusion of opposites: music and noise, comprehensible and incomprehensible vocal sources, human and superhuman vocal, and instrumental capacities. Creshevsky's most recent hyperrealist compositions explore the fragmentation and reconstruction of preexisting music in combination with original synthetic and acoustic materials. Moments suggest musical environments of indeterminate ethnicity—simultaneously western and nonwestern, ancient and modern, familiar and unfamiliar.

When he is not being a public servant, Melbourne resident CHRIS DENCH is a composer. His militantly (un-Post)modernist works include *Agnî—Prometheus—Lucifer*, *beyond status geometry*, *funk*, *asymptotic freedom*, *ik(s)land[s]*, *light-strung sigils*, *Permutation City*, *'e/meth*, and *the sadness of detail*. He is a CD addict, and harbors delusions of profitability.

Noah Creshevsky

Chris Dench

Dave Douglas

Trevor Dunn

DAVE DOUGLAS is a composer and trumpeter living in New York. Mr. Douglas began recording his music in the early 1990s, and his discography includes recordings on the RCA Victor, Hat Art, Soul Note, New World, Arabesque, Songlines, and Winter & Winter labels. He now operates his own Internet-based label, Greenleaf Music. Since 2003 Mr. Douglas has served as artistic director of the Banff International Workshop in Jazz and Creative Music, collaborating in performances and master classes with Bill Frisell, John Abercrombie, George Lewis, Jason Moran, Han Bennink, Mark Turner, Louis Sclavis, and many others. Since 2002 Mr. Douglas has served as Founder and Director of the annual Festival of New Trumpet Music, an original music festival based in New York and dedicated to presenting the broadest possible spectrum of new music being made by and for trumpeters. A 2005 Guggenheim Fellow, for the past decade Mr. Douglas has repeatedly been named trumpeter, composer, and jazz artist of the year by such organizations as the New York Jazz Awards, *Downbeat*, and the Italian Jazz Society. He has twice been nominated for Grammy awards. Dave Douglas continues to perform with his own ensembles. He also composes new music for small chamber ensembles. For more information, please see http://www.greenleafmusic.com.

TREVOR DUNN was born in 1968 behind the Redwood Curtain traversing a fine line between hippies and rednecks. His first instrument was the clarinet, and he began to focus on the electric bass at age thirteen. Four years later he cofounded the avant-rock band Mr. Bungle. In 1990 he received a BA in music from Humboldt State, where he performed Koussevitsky's *Concerto for Double Bass* with the HSO. In 2001 he was commissioned by the Elaine Kaufman Cultural Center to write a solo bass piece for Jon Deak. Mr. Deak performed *Depaysemant* for prepared contrabass later that year at

Merkin Hall, Lincoln Center. Currently Dunn lives in Brooklyn, NY, and can be heard on over sixty recordings. Recent bands include Fantômas, John Zorn's Electric Masada, Moonchild, Curtis Hasslebring's New Mellow Edwards, a duet with harpist Shelley Burgon, and occasional appearances with David Krakauer, Marc Ribot, G. Calvin Weston, Raz Mesinai, Rob Price, and/or Andrew D'Angelo. For more information, please see www.trevordunn.net and www.myspace.com/convulsivebeauty.

JASON ECKARDT played guitar in rock and jazz bands until, upon first hearing the music of Webern, he immediately devoted himself to composition. Since then, his music has been influenced by his interests in perceptual complexity, performance virtuosity, and self-organizing processes in the natural world. He lives in New York.

Jason Eckardt

Jewlia Eisenberg

Annie Gosfield

JEWLIA EISENBERG is a composer, extended-technique vocalist, lay cantor, and founder of the diaspora girl group Charming Hostess. Her work explores the intersection of text and the sounding body, pushing for translation strategies between verbal and nonverbal languages. CDs include *Sarajevo Blues*, which sets Bosnian resistance poetry, and *Trilectic,* a look at the political-erotic world of Walter Benjamin. Jewlia is now at work on *The Bowls Project*, a large-scale installation based on magic and sex in Babylonian Jewish amulets. She has been an Artist-in-Residence at MIT and the University of Denver; she has studied with Bukharan sozanda Muna Nissimova, Fred Frith, and Daniel Boyarin. Jewlia has collaborated with the anarcho-lit magazine *Fantom Slobode*, choreographer Jo Kreiter, and filmmaker Lynn Sachs. In addition to Charming Hostess, Jewlia also sings with Red Pocket, Dropkin, and Graham Connah's Sour Note Seven. Commissioned work includes *Harmonices Mundi* (Sloan/EST), an opera about Kepler's mother, and *Red Rosa* (Puffin/SF Goethe Institut), a song cycle based on the letters of Rosa Luxemburg. Hobbies include class war, knitting, and smashing SUV windshields. Raised in a Black and Jewish commune in East New York Brooklyn, she now calls Oakland home. File under: Nerdy-Sexy-Commie-Girlie.

ANNIE GOSFIELD divides her time between performing on piano and sampler with her own ensemble and composing for others. She uses traditional notation, improvisation, and extended techniques to create a sound world that eliminates the boundaries between music and noise, while emphasizing the unique qualities of each performer. Her music often explores the inherent beauty of nonmusical sounds, and is inspired by diverse sources, such as machines, destroyed pianos, warped 78 records, and detuned radios. Active as a composer, performer, and improviser, Gosfield's music has been performed at festivals internationally, including Warsaw Autumn, the Venice Bienalle, the Santa Fe Chamber Music Festival, Festival Musique Actuelle, Wien Modern, Company Week, and the Festival of Radical Jewish Culture. In addition to writing chamber music, she has composed a site-specific work for a factory in Germany, created a video for an imaginary orchestra of destroyed instruments, and collaborated on installations with guitarist Roger Kleier and artist Manuel Ocampo. Gosfield held the Milhaud Chair in composition at Mills College in Oakland, California, and was Composer-in-Residence at California Institute of the Arts. Her music is featured on three CDs on the Tzadik label. The most recent release, *Lost Signals and Drifting Satellites*, features work scored for solo violin accompanied by satellite transmissions. For more information, please see www.anniegosfield.com.

Milford Graves was born in Jamaica, New York, and started playing drums at three years old. Studies in African and Afro-Caribbean music/drumming began at eight years old. Milford started studying jazz in his early teens. In 1965, he studied North Indian Music/tabla drumming with the renowned Doctor Wasantha Singh, an Indian/Buddhist musician-guru. He attended City College of New York, New York Community College, Eastern School for Physicians Aides (NY), and the Occidental Institute of Chinese Studies (Canada). He is listed in *Who's Who in America*, *Groves Encyclopedia of Music*, *Encyclopedia of Jazz*, as well as many interviews, articles, and featured stories in various international publications (newspapers, magazines, journals, and books). During the past forty-two years Milford has performed in many music events, and given countless lecture-demonstration/workshops on medicine (herbology, acupuncture, nutrition, etc.) and body-movement/martial arts on an international level, including the 1983 International Conference on World Medicine at the Waldorf Hotel in New York. From 1971–73, he developed and conducted a clinical laboratory for a private animal hospital in New York. On July 1, 1993, a special forty-five-minute documentary video, titled *Legend Drummer Milford Graves*, was televised throughout Japan on NHK-Television at a time called the Golden Hour. He is presently director of the International Center for Medicinal and Scientific Studies, co-director of the Institute of Percussive Studies, co-director of the George Washington Carver Botanical Garden in Jamaica, NY, and has been Professor of Music/Holistic Medicine at Bennington College in Vermont since 1973.

Milford Graves

Carla Kihlstedt

Lukas Ligeti

Violinist, vocalist, and composer, Carla Kihlstedt is a founding member of the groups 2 Foot Yard, Tin Hat, and Sleepytime Gorilla Museum. A collaborator by nature, she has had the opportunity to work with many wonderful musicians, including Fred Frith, Tom Waits, Erik Friedlander, Satoko Fujii, Lisa Bielawa, Ben Goldberg, Zeena Parkins, and the Rova Saxophone Quartet. She has written scores for choreographers/directors Jo Kreiter of Flyaway Productions and Shinichi Iova-Koga of inkBoat. She has been an Artist-in-Residence at both the Headlands Center for the Arts and the Civitella Ranieri Center and was a recipient of the Bang on a Can People's Commissioning Fund award. Her most recent project is a staged song cycle called *These Necessary Monsters*, developed with poet Rafael Oses and theater director Paul Bargetto and based loosely on *The Book of Imaginary Beings*, by Jorge Luis Borges.

Lukas Ligeti is interested in new forms of ensemble interplay, polymetric and polytempo structures, and the creative use of influences from music traditions of various parts of the world, as well as of technology. Born in Vienna, Austria, he studied composition and drums at the Vienna Music University, then spent two years (1994–96) at the Center for Computer Research in Music and Acoustics at Stanford University, and has lived in New York City since 1998. He has received composition commissions from Ensemble Modern, Bang on a Can, the Kronos Quartet, Colin Currie and Hakan Hardenberger, the Vienna Festwochen, the American Composers Forum, etc. As an improviser on drum set he has played with Raoul Björkenheim, Benoît Delbecq, James Ilgenfritz, Henry Kaiser, Gary Lucas, Michael Manring, Eyal Maoz, Jim O'Rourke, Pyrolator, John Tchicai, John Zorn, and many others, and he performs solo on electronic percussion. He frequently collaborates with musicians from nonwestern cultures. In 1994, he cofounded the experimental ensemble Beta Foly, based in Abidjan, Côte d'Ivoire; currently, he co-leads the electronica band Burkina Electric, from Ouagadougou, Burkina Faso. In 2006, he was Composer-in-Residence at the University of the Witwatersrand in Johannesburg, South Africa. For more information, please see http://www.lukasligeti.com.

José Maceda was one of the most highly respected composers of contemporary concert music in Asia, his unique compositions blending Western and Asian musical traditions in a highly original manner. Elements such as drone, distribution of labor, separation of musical functions, relative pitch values, and timbre levels are ideas leading to a new theory of music. The humanistic values of communal agricultural work in East and Southeast Asia were an important influence on his compositional methods. José Maceda was born in Manila in 1917. Between the 1930s and 1950s he led a career as a concert pianist studying in Paris with Alfred Cortot (1937–41) and with E. Robert Schmitz in San Francisco (1946–49). He studied musicology-ethnomusicology at Columbia University, the University of Chicago, Indiana University, and UCLA, where he received a PhD in 1963. He subsequently joined the faculty at the University of the Philippines in Quezon City, where he established an important archive that now contains more than 2,500 hours of field recordings of over fifty Philippine linguistic groups. His research on music in the Philippines and Southeast Asia produced articles on time; scales; gongs and bamboos in Southeast Asia; machines, drone, and populations in Asia; Aristotelian logic in Tang Court Music; and bipolarity, four counts, and the fifth interval in the court musics of Asia. He continued composing and writing at his home in Quezon City, Philippines, until his death in 2004 at age eighty-seven.

José Maceda

Ernesto Martínez

Ernesto Martínez (b. 1953, Mexico City) studied composition at the National School of Music, U.N.A.M. In 1986 he formed a composition/performance technique called Micro-Ritmia, which proved to be a powerful tool for developing new music textures. He began working with the Mexican pianist and composer Eduardo Gonzàlez in 1994, and after a year of rehearsing they began performing concerts and master classes in various cities of Mexico, Cuba, and the United States. The first Micro-Ritmia CD was released in 1997.

LAWRENCE D. "BUTCH" MORRIS is recognized internationally as the principal theorist and practitioner in the evolution of Conduction®, and a leading innovator in the confluence of jazz, new music, improvisation, and contemporary classical music. Mr. Morris's work redefines the roles of composer, conductor, arranger, and performer, and bridges the gap between the composer, interpreter, and improviser. Since 1974, his career has been distinguished by unique and outstanding international contributions to television, film, theater, dance, radio, interdisciplinary collaborations, concerts, and recordings. He has been Composer-in-Residence, Conductor-in-Residence, or Visiting Lecturer in over thirty institutions and is represented on 126 recordings either as composer, conductor, cornetist, arranger, or producer. Employing more than 5,000 musicians in twenty-three countries and sixty-three cities, resulting in twenty-two CDs over a twenty-year period, Conduction has amply demonstrated its capacity for cultural diplomacy by uniting communities and serving as a powerful example of a new social logic based on collective interpretation and personal interaction. Fellowships include the Music OMI Fellow (Omi, New York, 2006 and 1997); Atlantic Center for the Arts (New Smyrna Beach, Florida 2006); Civitella Ranieri Fellow (Umbertide, Italy, 2001); DAAD Fellow (Berlin, Germany, 1995–96). Honors include the 2006 Alpert Award in the Arts, Ambassador of Music Award (2003 Lunar New Year Festival Committee, New York), and "Boris Vian Award" (1980, for "Europe-America Big Band," France).

Butch Morris

Jim O'Rourke

Evan Parker

JIM O'ROURKE works with music, film, and whatever he can get a handle on. Since 1986 he has worked in a variety of areas seemingly disparate, but all interrelated. He has scored films for Werner Herzog, Shinji Aoyama, Olivier Assayass, and others. He has been a member of the bands Sonic Youth, Red Crayola, amongst others, and has worked with and produced records for a range of artists from Tony Conrad and John Fahey to Wilco and Beth Orton. His own music has encompassed improvised and composed and places in-between.

EVAN PARKER was born in Bristol, England, on April 5, 1944. He began playing saxophone at the age of fourteen. Following his never-completed studies in botany at Birmingham University, he moved back to London, where in late 1966 he began playing with the Spontaneous Music Ensemble (SME) with John Stevens. Early in 1968 he left the SME and started to work regularly with Derek Bailey, at first in duo and then with the Music Improvisation Company, which lasted until 1971. He founded Incus records with Bailey in 1970 and subsequently passed full ownership to him in 1986. He has formed a number of important long-term associations, including the trio with Paul Lytton and Barry Guy, Kenny Wheeler, Peter Broetzmann, Irene Schweizer, Peter Kowald, Alexander von Schlippenbach and Paul Lovens, Ned Rothenberg and George Lewis. During the forty years of his musical life, Parker has collaborated with distinguished musicians from a wide range of musical directions but almost always with the emphasis on open improvisation. Collaborations with Sainkho Namtchylak, Anthony Braxton, Paul Bley, Cecil Taylor, Charlie Watts, Scott Walker, John Tilbury, Richard Barrett and Paul Obermayer,

Spring Heel Jack, Gavin Bryars, Michael Nyman, David Toop, AMM, and Django Bates attest to an insatiable curiosity and unshakable belief in the improviser's method. In 1990 he began work with his ElectroAcoustic Ensemble, seeking to develop music using the new computer-based instrumentalists in interaction with acoustic players. Parker is the creator of a radical new solo saxophone language that has influenced several generations of musicians. Extended techniques of articulation and circular breathing create complex, overlapping, repetitive soundscapes in an instantly recognizable personal language. In 2001 Evan Parker started his own record label, psi, to document, in his words, "the art of the individual."

Zeena Parkins, multi-instrumentalist, composer, improviser, sound artist, well-known as a pioneer of the electric harp, has also extended the language of acoustic harp with the inventive use of unusual preparations, playing techniques, and layers of digital and analog processing. She describes her harp as a "sound machine of limitless capacity." Zeena's unique vision seeks to both meld and highlight opposites and extends to her work for her compositions. She has composed and recorded an extensive body of solos and chamber works within which she has blurred boundaries between improvised and composed, acoustic and electric, digital and analog, and processed and concrete sounds. She achieves this engagement of contrasts by using instrument blending and morphing, the recombination of cut-up sounds to form odd and breathtaking soundscapes, and scoring and formal constructions derived from extra-musical sources. Zeena Parkins has also dedicated her career to collaborative process. She has received numerous commissions to compose music for film, video, and theater, and has created over forty scores for dance works. In this context Zeena has been inspired to explore unpredictable orchestrations and ambitious sonic presentations, including a quadraphonic bubble-wrap score for Jennifer Lacey and a sixty-speaker installation for a solo work by the choreographer; live mixes/assemblages for Neil Greenberg; live scores performed with Jennifer Monson; a score for string quartet with live quadraphonic processing for Emmanuelle Vo-Dinh; a live multi-channel score for John Jasperse; and a twenty-five-speaker installation for DD Dorvillier. Other collaborators include Björk, Matmos, John Zorn, Nels Cline, Ikue Mori, Fred Frith, Thurston Moore, Elliott Sharp, filmmaker Cynthia Madansky, and visual artists Daria Martin and Mandy McIntosh. Awards include the Prix Ars Electronica Honorary Mention, Bessie for the score to Jennifer Monson's *Sender*, Foundation for Contemporary Arts award, NYSCA commission, Rockefeller MAP, Mary Flagler Cary commissions, and a Civitella Ranieri Foundation fellowship.

Zeena Parkins

Maja Ratkje

Maja Solveig Kjelstrup Ratkje is a composer and performer. She has composed a large number of pieces for small and big ensembles, acoustic or electronic, for theater, film, installations, dance, and literature, from noise infernos or tutti orchestra to quiet improv or acoustic solos. Known from groups such as SPUNK, Fe-mail, Agrare, and the collaboration with musicians like POING, Jaap Blonk, Jazkamer, Klangforum Wien, she has toured and released her music covering most continents. She has been called the "enfant terrible" of the Norwegian avant-garde, but she states that provocation is not an issue in her music, even though she has stirred a large number of besserwissers by experimenting with such clichés as the opera or the classical concerto form. She has received awards for her work such as UNESCO's Rostrum prize, second prize from the Russolo foundation, and a Distinction award at Prix Ars Electronica. In 2001 she was the first composer to receive the Arne Nordheim prize. Voice is her main instrument, but she has a general interest for all possible and impossible sounds. For more information, please see www.ratkje.com.

Marina Rosenfeld is a New York–based composer, artist, and turntablist. Since the mid-90s, her work has explored the social and situational contexts of music-making, digital/analogue culture, and experimental or open forms in a variety of formats, including photography and video (*fragment opera).* As a turntablist, she's developed her distinctive sound by playing exclusively her own custom acetate records, or "dub plates," which are imprinted with original, fragmentary sounds she mixes and manipulates live. She's also noted for a series of large-scale performance works developed in situ, often featuring non- or amateur musicians with whom she develops custom performance strategies (*The Sheer Frost Orchestra, Emotional Orchestra*). Recent works (*White Lines*) have explored the expansion of graphical notation into digital animation. Rosenfeld performs frequently in the U.S. and Europe, and has performed with many contemporary artists, including the Merce Cunningham Company, Sonic Youth, Christian Marclay, and Laurie Anderson. Rosenfeld's work has been presented in a wide variety of contexts, including by the Whitney Museum of American Art (Biennial 2002, *Bitstreams*), the Tate Modern Museum, the British School at Rome, the London Musicians Collective, the Kitchen, and festivals, including Donaueschingen, Ars Electronica, Maerz Musik, Mutek, Wein Modern, Vancouver New Music, and Taktlos Bern. She studied at Harvard and California Institute of the Arts, and currently teaches in the electronic music department at Bard College.

Marina Rosenfeld

Ned Rothenberg

Ned Rothenberg composes and performs on saxophones, clarinets, flute, and shakuhachi. He has been internationally acclaimed for both his solo and ensemble music, presented for the past twenty-five years in North and South America, Europe and Asia. He leads the trio Sync, with Jerome Harris, guitars, and Samir Chatterjee, tabla, and is active in the cooperative groups RUB, New Winds, and The Fell Clutch. A strong underlying element of his instrumental voice is the extension of the woodwind language to incorporate polyphony and accurate microtonal organization. He does this through the manipulation of multiphonics, circular breathing, and overtone control, not only using his horns in their standard melodic role but also as rhythmic and harmonic engines in both solo and ensemble contexts. Collaborators include Sainkho Namchylak, Paul Dresher, John Zorn, Marc Ribot, Yuji Takahashi, and Evan Parker. For more information, please see http://www.nedrothenberg.com.

Born in 1969, TREY SPRUANCE grew up in Eureka, CA, listening to Devo and getting stuffed into garbage cans by rednecks. He studied music voraciously, using Ligeti scores as a kind of magical armor against the seductions of the Abyss. Spruance and bandmates from Mr. Bungle moved to San Francisco in 1990 to record an album. Once in SF, he was exposed to a very diverse and somewhat inscrutable underground music scene, which was kind enough to embrace him as a participant. Through the 90s he led a double life in this hidden world on the one hand, and in Mr. Bungle touring and recording exploits on the other (never the twain shall meet), all the while privately immersing himself in a world of Muslim Neoplatonic "Peripatetic," Ishraqi, Ismaili, and "ghulat" Philosophy and gnosis. The Secret Chiefs 3 was born in this third dimension, now reaching adolescence in its twelfth year.

Trey Spruance

J.G. Thirlwell

Matthew Welch

J.G. THIRLWELL is a composer/producer/performer based in Brooklyn. He was born in Melbourne, Australia, where he studied art at Melbourne State College for two years before moving to London in 1978. After working with the experimental group Nurse With Wound, J.G. started making his own records in 1980, initially releasing them under his own label, Self Immolation. He was inspired by the post-punk explosion of creativity in the UK, which engendered the accessibility of DIY, and the writings of John Cage and systems music, among other things. He then relocated to NYC in 1983, where he still lives in Brooklyn, between travels. J.G.'s catalog is extensive, under many pseudonyms, including Foetus, Steroid Maximus, Manorexia, Baby Zizanie, Wiseblood, and others. If there is a common thread to his varied musical styles it is a dramatic intensity and an evocative, cinematic quality. He considers the studio his main instrument. His oeuvre stretches the gamut from cathartic noise-rock to abstract electronics, orchestrations, big band and sound sculpture, serial music and imaginary soundtracks, sometimes all in the same piece. In recent years, with works for Kronos Quartet and Bang on a Can, and in his occasional eighteen-piece ensemble, he has been increasingly interested in electronically and sample-generated music being rescored for traditional instrumentation, played both conventionally and not. J.G. is also a member of the "freq_out" collective, who creates on-site sound and light installations with Carl Michael Von Hausswolf. Additionally, he has made some site-specific laptop performances and collaborations, and has been scoring *The Venture Brothers* show on Adult Swim/ Cartoon Network. For more information, please see www.foetus.org.

MATTHEW WELCH (b. 1976) holds two university degrees in Experimental Music Composition, a BFA from Simon Fraser University (1999), and an MA from Wesleyan University (2001), studying with noted composers such as Barry Truax, Rodney Sharman, Alvin Lucier, and Anthony Braxton. The eclectic breadth of his interests in Scottish bagpipe music, Balinese gamelan, minimalism, improvisation, and rock converge in compositional amalgams ranging from traditional-like bagpipe tunes to electronic pieces, improvisation strategies, and fully notated works for solo instruments, chamber ensembles, orchestra, and nonwestern instruments.

YAMATAKA EYE. Mid 1970s: home recordings. Beginning of the 1980s: begins noise performances driving a bulldozer with hAnAtArAsh. Mid 1980s: starts Boredoms. 1990: performs with Naked City and begins Puzzle Punks with Shinro Otake. 2000: begins to DJ and performs on turntable with three drum sets in V∞redoms. Art activity includes several art exhibitions, monographs, and cover design for Beck's CD *Midnight Vulture*.

Yamataka Eye

John Zorn

Drawing on his experience in a variety of genres, including jazz, rock, hardcore punk, classical, klezmer, film, cartoon, popular, and improvised music, JOHN ZORN has created an influential body of work that defies academic categories. A native of New York City, he has been a central figure in the downtown scene since 1975, incorporating a wide range of musicians in various compositional formats. He learned alchemical synthesis from Harry Smith, structural ontology with Richard Foreman, how to make art out of garbage with Jack Smith, cathartic expression at Sluggs, and hermetic intuition from Joseph Cornell. Early inspirations include American innovators Ives, Varèse, Cage, Carter, and Partch, the European tradition of Berg, Stravinsky, Ligeti, and Kagel, soundtrack composers Herrmann, Morricone, and Stalling, as well as avant-garde theater, film, art, and literature.

RECOMMENDED LISTENING

Christopher Adler
Epilogue for a Dark Day Tzadik
Rubble 2 Accretions/Circumvention
Christopher Adler, khaen Artship
Mineralia pfMENTUM
Transcontinental 9 Winds

Mick Barr
OV Ipecac
Iorxhscimtor Tolotta
Asristir Veildrioxe TMU
2nd 18/O4 Norildivoth Crallos Lomrixth Urthiln Threeoneg
Ocrilim TMU
Uppragn Srilimia Ixioor Ocrilim Nollfithes Mrithixyl Peterbilt
Anoint I+Ear
Octis: Iohargh Wended Tzadik

Borah Bergman
The Human Factor Soul Note
The Fire Tale Soul Note
Reflections on Ornette Coleman and The Stone House Soul Note
Exhilaration Soul Note
A New Organization Soul Note
The River of Sounds Boxholder
The Italian Concert Soul Note
Meditations Tzadik
Toronto '97 Boxholder
Acts of Love Mutable Music

Lisa Bielawa
A Handful of World Tzadik
Roam BMOP

Uri Caine
Moloch Tzadik
Uri Caine Ensemble plays Mozart Winter&Winter
Shelf-Life Winter&Winter
Dark Flame Winter&Winter
The Diabelli Variations Winter&Winter
The Goldberg Variations Winter&Winter
Solitaire Winter&Winter
Bedrock Winter&Winter
Urlicht/Primal Light Winter&Winter
Live at the Village Vanguard Winter&Winter

Steve Coleman
Genesis BMG
The Opening of The Way BMG
The Sonic Language of Myth BMG
The Ascension To Light BMG
Resistance Is Futile Label Bleu
Alternate Dimension Series I Label Bleu
On The Rising Of The 64 Paths Label Bleu
Lucidarium Label Bleu
Weaving Symbolics Label Bleu
Elements of One Label Bleu

Sylvie Courvoisier
Lonelyville Intakt
Malphas Tzadik
Abaton ECM
Masada Recital Tzadik
Entomological Reflections Tzadik
Deux Pianos Intakt
Y2K Enja
Music for Violin and Piano Avant
Music for Barrel Organ, Piano, Tuba, Bass and Percussion Enja
Signs and Epigrams Tzadik

Noah Creshevsky
Circuit Opus One
Broadcast Opus One
Sonata Opus One
Celebration Opus One
Drummer Opus One
Man & Superman Centaur
Auxesis Centaur
Who Centaur
Hyperrealism Mutable Music
The Tape Music of Noah Creshevsky, 1971–1992 EM

Chris Dench
Music for Flute 1981–91 Etcetera
tracts NMC
Ik(s)land[s] NMC

Dave Douglas
The Full Book, Dave Douglas Quintet Live at the Jazz Standard Greenleaf Music
Meaning and Mystery Greenleaf Music
Keystone Greenleaf Music
Mountain Passages Greenleaf Music
Strange Liberation Bluebird/RCA
Freak In Bluebird/RCA
The Infinite Bluebird/RCA
Charms of the Night Sky Winter & Winter
Soul on Soul—Celebrating Mary Lou Williams RCA Victor
Constellations Hat Art

Trevor Dunn
California Warner Brothers
In These Great Times Tzadik
Fantômas Ipecac
Houdini Live Ipecac
Filmworks XIII Tzadik
At the Mountains of Madness Tzadik
Six Litanies for Heliogabalus Tzadik
Sister Phantom Owl Fish Ipecac
Debutantes & Centipedes Challenge
Baltimore Skirl

Jason Eckardt
Out of Chaos Mode
So Long, Thanks Capstone
Multiplicities Metier
Ritual Protocol Kleos
American Spiritual CRI

Jewlia Eisenberg
Dropkin ShakeMeDown
Punch Recommended
Sarajevo Blues Tzadik
Thick Tzadik
Trilectic Tzadik
Eat Vaccination

Annie Gosfield
Lost Signals and Drifting Satellites Tzadik
Flying Sparks and Heavy Machinery Tzadik
Burnt Ivory and Loose Wires Tzadik
The Extreme Guitar Project Mode
Swine Live! Caprice
Bang on a Can Classic Cantaloupe
Cobra Tzadik
Deep Night, Deep Autumn Starkland
Klangenbang Rift

Milford Graves

Milford Graves Percussion Ensemble ESP
Nommo SRP
Dialogue of the Drums IPS
Babi IPS
Real Deal DIW
Grand Unification Tzadik
Stories Tzadik
Milford Graves/John Zorn Duo Tzadik

Carla Kihlstedt

The Sad Machinery of Spring Hannibal/Rykodisk
Book of Silk Ropeadope
The Rodeo Eroded Ropeadope
Helium Angel/EMI
The Compass, Log and Lead Intakt
Two Foot Yard Tzadik
In Glorious Times The End
Of Natural History Mimicry
Traineater Anti-
Carla Kihlstedt and Satoko Fujii Henceforth

Lukas Ligeti

Burkina Electric: Paspanga AtaTak/Seydoni
The Williamsburg Sonatas Wallace
Mystery System Tzadik
Shadowglow TUM
Heavy Meta Ecstatic Yod
Immersion Starkland
Lukas Ligeti & Beta Foly Intuition Music
Hybrid Beat Cuneiform

José Maceda

José Maceda ALM
Dissemination Fontec
Distemperament Fontec
Music for 5 pianos ACM
Soundstreams AUIT/Tunugan Foundation
Gongs and Bamboos Tzadik
Strata Tzadik

Ernesto Martínez

Micro-Ritmia Lejos del Paraíso
Mutaciónes Tzadik

Butch Morris

NUBLU Orchestra Conducted by Butch Morris nublu
Holy Sea Splasc(h)
Tit for Tat For 4 Ears
Berlin Skyscraper FMP
Burning Cloud FMP
Testament: A Conduction Collection New World
Dust to Dust New World
Homeing Sound Aspects
Current Trends in Racism in Modern America Sound Aspects
In Touch But Out of Reach Kharma

Jim O'Rourke

Insignificance Drag City
In Bern HatArt
Born Again in the U.S.A. Drag City
Terminal Pharmacy Tzadik
Outside the Dream Syndicate Alive Table of the Elements
Mimidokodesuka Polystar
Tomorrow Knows Where You Live Victo
Sonic Nurse Geffen
Comfort of Strangers EMI
Womblife Table of the Elements

Evan Parker

The Topography of the Lungs psi
Saxophone Solos Chronoscope
At the Unity Theatre psi

From Saxophone & Trombone psi
The Snake Decides psi
Process & Reality FMP
At the Vortex Emanem
Lines Burnt in Light psi
The Eleventh Hour ECM
Time Lapse Tzadik

Zeena Parkins

Persuasion Tzadik
Phantom Orchard Mego
Money Shot casestudy
Devotion Table of the Elements
Pan-Acousticon Tzadik
Mouth=Maul=Betrayer Tzadik
Isabelle Avant
No Way Back Atavistic
Nightmare Alley Table of the Elements
Something Out There RecRec Germany

Maja Ratkje

Adventura Anatomica Semishigure
Blixter Toad Asphodel
Ballads Dekorder
Voluptuous Vultures PsychForm
En aldeles forferdelig sykdom Rune Grammofon
MAJAAP Kontrans
Music for Loving Bottrop-Boy
Syklubb fra Hælvete important
Voice Rune Grammofon
Den øverste toppen på en blåmalt flaggstang Rune Grammofon

Marina Rosenfeld

joy of fear Softl
The Sheer Frost Orchestra—drop, hop, drone, slide, scratch & A for anything Charhizma
theforestthegardenthesea—music from fragment opera Charhizma

Ned Rothenberg

Intervals Animul
Port of Entry Intuition
Harbinger Animul
Inner Diaspora Tzadik
Ghost Stories Tzadik
The Lumina Recordings Tzadik
Are You Be Animul
The Fell Clutch Animul
Power Lines New World
Opposites Attract New World

Trey Spruance

Book of Horizons Mimicry
Book M Mimicry
California Warner Brothers
Second Grand Constitution and Bylaws Mimicry
Eyes of Flesh, Eyes of Flame (live) Mimicry
First Grand Constitution and Bylaws Mimicry
Disco Volante Warner Brothers
Faxed Head 7" Stomache Ache
Elegy Tzadik
Mr. Bungle Warner Brothers

J.G. Thirlwell

HOLE Self Immolation/Some Bizzare
THAW Self Immolation/Some Bizzare
GASH Sony/Columbia
LOVE Ectopic Ents/Birdman
DAMP Ectopic Ents
DIRTDISH K422
Gondwanaland Ectopic Ents/Big Cat
Ectopia Ectopic Ents/Ipecac
Volvox Turbo Ectopic Ents
Radiolarian Ooze Ectopic Ents

Matthew Welch

10 [solo bagpipe] Compositions 2000
Parallactic
Composition No. 247 Leo
Ceol Nua Leo
Hag at the Churn Newsonic
Dream Tigers Tzadik

Yamataka Eye

Unlimited Freakout or die
Wow2 Avant
Super roots WEA
Super roots #5 WEA
Super roots #6 WEA
Super æ WEA
Vision creation newsun WEA
Super roots #9 WEA
Chocolate syhthesizer WEA
Pipeline Ginza Art Space catalog

John Zorn

IAO Tzadik
At the Mountains of Madness Tzadik
Madness, Love and Mysticism Tzadik
Magick Tzadik
Rituals Tzadik
Mysterium Tzadik
FilmWorks Compilation Tzadik
Moonchild Tzadik
Astronome Tzadik
Six Litanies for Heliogabalus Tzadik